BBC Women Reporting the World

Colleen Murrell

BBC Women Reporting the World

Conversations with Foreign Correspondents

Colleen Murrell
School of Communications
Dublin City University
Dublin, Ireland

ISBN 978-3-031-85197-1   ISBN 978-3-031-85198-8   (eBook)
https://doi.org/10.1007/978-3-031-85198-8

© The Editor(s) (if applicable) and The Author(s), under exclusive license to Springer Nature Switzerland AG 2025

This work is subject to copyright. All rights are solely and exclusively licensed by the Publisher, whether the whole or part of the material is concerned, specifically the rights of translation, reprinting, reuse of illustrations, recitation, broadcasting, reproduction on microfilms or in any other physical way, and transmission or information storage and retrieval, electronic adaptation, computer software, or by similar or dissimilar methodology now known or hereafter developed.

The use of general descriptive names, registered names, trademarks, service marks, etc. in this publication does not imply, even in the absence of a specific statement, that such names are exempt from the relevant protective laws and regulations and therefore free for general use.

The publisher, the authors and the editors are safe to assume that the advice and information in this book are believed to be true and accurate at the date of publication. Neither the publisher nor the authors or the editors give a warranty, expressed or implied, with respect to the material contained herein or for any errors or omissions that may have been made. The publisher remains neutral with regard to jurisdictional claims in published maps and institutional affiliations.

Cover design Cover photos (l-r): Lyse Doucet BBC with Afghan mujahideen leader Jalaluddin Haqqani in 1991. She had to "dress like a man" to travel to the frontline with his forces; Kate Adie with Prime Minister John Major in Saudi Arabia during the first Gulf War, 1991; Caroline Wyatt and camerawoman Julie Ritson in Helmand Province, Afghanistan, 2011; Elizabeth Blunt's Senegal press card, 1988. All reproduced with permission of the owners.

This Palgrave Macmillan imprint is published by the registered company Springer Nature Switzerland AG
The registered company address is: Gewerbestrasse 11, 6330 Cham, Switzerland

If disposing of this product, please recycle the paper.

Preface: The Monstrous Regiment

The seeds of my interest in this group of women foreign correspondents probably began on an overnight shift at BBC TV Centre back in the 1990s when I had great difficulty turning a radio stringer's track and rushes into an edited TV package. There was a paucity of usable pictures—virtually no "general views" (GVs) or framing shots for the interviews. The next day I asked a manager what training this radio reporter had had for television, only to be told "probably none". This person added, (referencing the term used in a sixteenth-century polemic by John Knox) that the woman in question was "one of the 'monstrous regiment of women' who traverse the armpits of the world in sensible walking shoes". Instantly my interest was piqued. While during my time at ITN and the BBC I had been on multiple foreign assignments to Lebanon, Syria, Jordan, Israel, Kuwait, France, Greece, Cyprus and the US et cetera, I was personally not attracted to living in conflict-ridden places for any length of time. I loved working as a news editor and I enjoyed my social life and was looking to settle down. But I was fascinated to know what attracted these women to some of the most inhospitable, and female-unfriendly places on the planet.

Today such women are trained and adept at multimedia journalism, publishing and broadcasting daily stories for online, radio and television. During Covid-19, when an earmarked grant was shifted to pandemic research, I thought about this topic and began researching. I had originally thought that the book might get published in time for the BBC centenary however, this quickly proved hopelessly optimistic when the BBC Written Archives and the British Library shut down for long periods, and teaching and the annual Reuters Digital News Report Ireland commanded my time. It also proved hard during Covid to interview these correspondents in the passing moments that they visited London.

This book begins with a chapter explaining the background to the BBC's employment practices and its changing relationship with its women reporters over the years. It explores recent research into the pioneers who took on important roles behind the scenes but also questions why it took the BBC so long to allow talented women to get behind the microphones and in front of the cameras. The previous literature it examines is most closely related to BBC employment practices, rather than to the wider literature of foreign correspondents working for companies other than the BBC. Obviously there is a growing list of books related to women reporters (in particular Americans) since World War II and beyond.

The book then moves on to profile ten women who have broken down the barriers to contribute successfully to the BBC's international coverage. I would have liked to have ranged wider and included more interviews with women correspondents, but at the time I picked out my ten women to profile, it was just not possible to travel too far during Covid. I was particularly sorry to miss out on interviewing Ofeibea Quist-Arcton, who blazed a career as a black journalist and was appointed to the role of BBC West Africa Correspondent in 1990. She went on to have a very successful career as a broadcaster for a number of international organisations but was unwell at the time I was conducting my interviews.

The women whom I selected represent for me a range of the different obstacles that stood in the way of female ambition depending on when they started their careers and the different pathways they selected within the BBC. What these women have in common is drive, ambition, bravery, an ability to learn languages, and specialist knowledge of particular regions and their politics. They have opened up new career paths for young women who do not want to be hemmed in by conventional attitudes regarding what work befits a woman today. These women have put their careers at the forefront of their lives and along the way many have lost relationships to the job: only three have children. They have seen tremendous events unfold and have put their lives in harm's way many times. Eight of the ten initial interviews were conducted in person during different stages of Covid lockdowns. Orla Guerin was interviewed online from her home in Istanbul and Diana Goodman, who lives in New Zealand, was unwell and preferred to do the interview by email correspondence. In January 2022 I managed to interview Shaimaa Khalil while visiting my daughters in Sydney for the first time after two years of lockdown. I have since stayed in touch with these women, catching up periodically to check on their news.

In the interests of full disclosure when I was a journalist I worked mostly in foreign newsgathering. I started out with a Master's degree in International Journalism from City, University of London. But just as Liz Blunt explains in her chapter, I mostly hid this fact—particularly in my first roles at ITN. Many of my bosses at the time were middle-aged men who had climbed the greasy pole "the proper way" from teaboy to manager; it was preferable as an ambitious woman to keep silent on some parts of your skillset. Young women today will not be able to fathom this, but so many of the examples and anecdotes found within this book are ones that I have experienced myself. At various times I took different pathways to these selected women—for example when I was offered and turned down a foreign bureau chief role. In the end I reached some of my own goals—becoming AP's youngest ever news editor (according to AP's then president Lou Boccardi), and taking on many different foreign newsgathering roles at the BBC, working mostly as a foreign duty editor. When I moved to Australia and after having children, I worked as a journalist and presenter for ABC's *Radio Australia* service to the Pacific and for SBS's *World News* programme and bulletins. Personally I found it hard to square the hours required with limited childcare options and so made the move into academia. I completed a PhD (2011) at the

University of Melbourne on the role of fixers in international news gathering, and have since climbed another greasy pole—from lecturer to full professor of journalism. These days I mostly research international news coverage, global news agencies, public service broadcasting, and digital media. I am also the chair of the editorial board of *The Conversation UK* and write regularly for that publication. I am hoping that today's young women will be able to combine their careers more easily with parenting, should they so choose, and that work-life balance will be improved for those with a journalism vocation.

Dublin, Ireland   Colleen Murrell

Acknowledgements

This book is dedicated to my husband Cameron, my sister Helen and my two smart, sassy and talented daughters Cassandra and Xanthe. They are my constant source of pride, delight and joy.

I would also like to thank the correspondents who gave me their time despite their busy lives. Their bravery and intelligence is always an inspiration.

Thank you to the publishers, in particular Richard Woolley, the good folk at the BBC Archives in Caversham and the British Library in London for finding ways to open here and there during Covid lockdowns.

My friend and former colleague at the BBC, Dr. Vivien Marsh, has done a tremendous job of copy-editing the draft and checking for inaccuracies; any that remain are down to me. And finally, thank you to DCU for giving me a semester off which helped bed down the book.

September 2024   Colleen Murrell

Contents

The BBC's Employment of Women Correspondents Through the Years — 1

Kate Adie, CBE, Former BBC Chief News Correspondent Currently freelance presenter of 'From our Own Correspondent' on BBC World Service & Radio 4 — 17

Diana Goodman Correspondent in Bonn, East Berlin and Moscow (1986–2000) — 43

Elizabeth Blunt, MBE, West Africa Correspondent 1986–1990, India TV producer 1993–1994 & Ethiopia Stringer, 2007–2009 — 67

Lyse Doucet, CM, OBE, Chief International Correspondent Previously worked as a correspondent in Ivory Coast, Pakistan, Afghanistan, Jordan and Israel — 87

Orla Guerin Senior International Correspondent based in Istanbul. Orla has worked as a BBC correspondent previously based in Los Angeles, Rome, Jerusalem, Johannesburg and Islamabad ... 109

Carrie Gracie WS China Reporter, NCA China reporter, China Correspondent and China Editor ... 131

Sara Beck Bureau Chief in Moscow, Jerusalem and Singapore, Head of the Russian Service and BBC Monitoring ... 151

Caroline Wyatt Presenter on Radio 4 PM. Formerly Berlin, Moscow, Paris, Defence and Religious Affairs Correspondent ... 169

Sarah Rainsford Eastern Europe Correspondent, previously a correspondent in Moscow (twice), Istanbul, Madrid and Havana ... 189

Shaimaa Khalil Tokyo Correspondent (Previously Islamabad and Sydney Correspondent) ... 207

Appendix	223
Glossary	225
BBC Journalists & Presenters	229
Index	233

List of Figures

Fig. 1	BBC poster showing its correspondents posted across the globe (1987)	10
Fig. 1	Kate Adie speaking in Salisbury's Guildhall in 2024	34
Fig. 1	Diana Goodman pictured in front of a tank in Romania (1989)	52
Fig. 1	Liz Blunt and Diana Goodman, the first two women foreign correspondents, photographed outside the BBC in London (1986)	70
Fig. 1	Lyse Doucet dressed as a man in order to travel to the frontline in Afghanistan to meet Mujahideen Commander Jalaluddin Haqqani, pictured on the left (1991)	93
Fig. 1	Orla Guerin pictured in Eastern Ukraine (2022)	126
Fig. 1	Carrie Gracie standing in front of the Forbidden City in Beijing, during Prince William's visit (2015)	141
Fig. 1	Sara Beck pictured at the Reuters Institute at Oxford University (2022)	165
Fig. 1	Caroline Wyatt and camerawoman Julie Ritson pictured in front of armoured vehicles in Helmand Province, Afghanistan (2011)	180
Fig. 1	Sarah Rainsford in London in 2022	200

Fig. 1 Shaimaa Khalil reporting from the Tokyo streets (2024)   218

The BBC's Employment of Women Correspondents Through the Years

On 24 February 2022 when Russia invaded Ukraine, I was so transfixed by a BBC bulletin that I took a screenshot of three women in different capital cities discussing the day's extraordinary events with presenter Clive Myrie in Kyiv. The three women were Europe Editor Katya Adler, North America Editor Sarah Smith and then Political Editor Laura Kuenssberg. Also in Eastern Ukraine that day were Eastern Europe Correspondent Sarah Rainsford and Senior International Correspondent Orla Guerin, and in Kyiv there was Chief International Correspondent Lyse Doucet. Whereas over the past few decades, I have become accustomed to seeing solitary women foreign correspondents reporting from a hotspot, this time there were women aplenty and I felt that with this conflict something had finally changed for front-of-camera BBC women. This is why I am starting this book with an examination of how the BBC has employed women journalists over the years. In terms of them being either in front of the camera or behind the microphone, it has been a long and challenging journey for women to reach the level of equality with men that they have today.

The BBC was born more than one hundred years ago in 1922, when the government of the time brought together six wireless manufacturers to create the British Broadcasting Company.[1] Ten years later in 1932 the BBC began shortwave broadcasts overseas which heralded the start of what became the BBC World Service. John Reith, later Lord Reith, was recruited as the first General Manager of the BBC, despite declaring "I know nothing whatsoever about broadcasting".[2] In 1928, six years after the dawn of the BBC, women aged over 21 won the right to vote and the BBC proceeded to employ women, in particular graduates, as women had recently been allowed to earn university degrees. Hilda Matheson stood out as head of Talks, creating the first news service and becoming the most senior woman in the company. According to David Hendy,[3] under Matheson's leadership, "Talks rapidly became the most exciting part of the BBC in which to work" as the staff rounded up the great and good of the era to get them behind the microphone. Among the female contributors at the time were newly successful women MPs plus two writers from the Bloomsbury set, Virginia Woolf and Vita Sackville-West. As Hendy notes, although most women were to be found as "secretaries, typists, clerks, [and] caterers" there were the odd few who rose through the ranks to higher office, including Mary Somerville who was in charge of the Schools programmes. The BBC was, in comparison to other companies of the time, a great place for women to work. According to Hendy, "Although women occupied a disproportionate number of the lower-ranked posts, men and women on the same grade usually received the same wage".

Kate Murphy writes of this time that, "The BBC of the 1920s and 1930s was uncommon in its treatment of women".[4] She points out that three women became directors—Hilda Matheson at Talks (1927–1932), Mary Somerville in School Broadcasting (1931–1947) and Isa Benzie at the Foreign Department (1933–1938). She lists the many different roles women held across the organisation from the press office to the drama department, and notes that the BBC grew from employing four people

---

[1] Robert Seater, *Broadcasting Britain: 100 Years of the BBC* (London: DK, 2022), 10.
[2] Seater, *Broadcasting Britain: 100 Years of the BBC*.
[3] David Hendy, *The BBC: A People's History* (London: Profile Books, 2022), 51.
[4] Kate Murphy, "New and Important Careers: How Women Excelled at the BBC, 1923–1938", *Media International Australia* 161, no. 1 (August 25, 2016): 19, https://doi.org/10.1177/132 9878X166649.

in 1922 to employing more than 4,000 by the outbreak of World War II, with one third of those employees being women. Virginia Madsen, writing about this era at the BBC, compares it to the early days of broadcasting at the ABC in Australia, noting that, "in addition to offering women leadership roles, the BBC generally gave women broader employment opportunities than the ABC".[5] The first General Manager of the BBC John Reith sent a memo in 1926 to his station managers across the country, which read:

> "The class of women we are now employing (or should be employing) is such that they should rank on the same footing as men assistants [...] They should be as eligible as men for promotion. There is no reason why a woman should not be a Station Director, though, of course, I realize it would be extraordinarily difficult to find one suitable".[6]

However, after the start-up phase, the BBC changed its attitude towards the employment of women to be more in keeping with other large employers, such as the Post Office, teaching and the civil service. While it had been pioneering in offering Mary Somerville maternity leave in 1928, four years later it introduced a "marriage bar", a piece of legislation in place across other UK workplaces which forced women who married to then resign from their jobs. Different reasons were put forward by Murphy (2014)[7] for this change—including male unemployment levels during the Depression and conformity to society's expectations. In terms of how this marriage bar operated, it seems that while all women were equal, some were more equal than others. Murphy notes (Ibid) the BBC introduced its own distinct "Marriage Tribunal" in 1933, to decide who qualified as "exceptional" and was therefore worth retaining:

---

[5] Virginia Madsen, "Innovation, Women's Work and the Documentary Impulse: Pioneering Moments and Stalled Opportunities in Public Service Broadcasting in Australia and Britain", *Media International Australia* 162, no. 1 (November 24, 2016): 19–32, https://doi.org/Volume 1https://doi.org/10.1177/1329878X16678933.

[6] John Reith, "Reith Memo to Regional Station Managers", April 30, 1926, BBC Written Archives Centre.

[7] Murphy, K. (2014) 'A marriage bar of convenience? The BBC and married women's work 1923–1939'. Twentieth Century British History, 25(4).

Women who put forward a case for retention were judged on five criteria including loyalty, efficiency, and indispensability along with career-mindedness and an ability to balance married life with office work.[8]

In practice, the outcome favoured the more "highly placed" women who had financial means to employ domestic help to offset their so-called "marriage burden". According to Murphy (Ibid) many senior BBC managers pondered if one outcome of the marriage bar was to enforce celibacy on women employees possibly leading to an outcome of an "embittered, because compulsory, spinster". (Ibid, 109) The marriage bar was temporarily lifted during World War II, but on the proviso that it would be reinstated after the end of the war. In the end the decision to reintroduce it was finally dropped in 1944.

During these early decades, there were women in broadcasting roles at the BBC as actors, and talks presenters in areas such as education. As Virginia Madsen[9] notes (2017), citing an article in *The Listener*, "The BBC was the traditional home of clever lady graduates and Oxbridge bluestockings". However women were largely confined to what were seen as suitable areas—such as education and feature-type programming. According to Anna Karpf, "Belief in the unsuitability of women's voices for announcing began in the early days of radio, in both the US and Britain".[10] In the US in 1927, John Steinberg had even stated, "The speech characteristics of women, when changed to electrical impulses, do not blend with the electrical characteristics of our present-day radio equipment".[11] In the BBC there was a widespread feeling that news was too serious for women to take on *in front* of the microphone.[12]

---

[8] Kate Murphy, "A Marriage Bar of Convenience? The BBC and Married Women's Work 1923–39", *Twentieth Century British History* 25 (November 14, 2014): 533–61, https://doi.org/10.1093/tcbh/hwu002.

[9] Madsen, "Innovation, Women's Work and the Documentary Impulse: Pioneering Moments and Stalled Opportunities in Public Service Broadcasting in Australia and Britain".

[10] Anne Karpf, *The Human Voice* (London: Bloomsbury Publishing, 2006), 268.

[11] John Steinberg cited in Anne McKay 'Speaking Up: Voice Amplification and Women's Struggle for Public Expression' in Chris Kramarae, ed., *Technology and Women's Voices: Keeping in Touch* (London: Routledge, 1988), 203.

[12] Karpf, *The Human Voice*.

In the memoirs of Lionel Fielden (who worked under Hilda Matheson on "Week in Westminster") he noted, as quoted by Charlotte Higgins, "women were, (and are) almost never good broadcasters. I don't know why this should be, but it is a fact".[13] Women were also deemed not to be able to achieve "the impersonal touch".[14] In yet another excuse not to use women they were also cited as "lacking in mic personality".[15] Asa Briggs in his history of the BBC, quotes Alvar Lidell, a popular announcer, who when asked in 1943 if he might be replaced by a woman, replied that this would not happen as "she might have to read bad news".[16]

Audrey Russell (1906–1989) was one such purveyor of bad news when she became the first woman reporter at the BBC. During WWII, this determined Anglo-Irish woman was working as a "firewoman" in the Auxiliary Fire Service,[17] close to the BBC offices. One day she was talent spotted in 1941, while giving an interview to two BBC reporters. She was then interviewed multiple times and became quite well known. Her career took off when she was offered a secondment to the Air Ministry "to do six five-minute BBC talks on the work of the WAAF",[18] a job with the BBC "Overseas Service". Soon after, in 1942, she was offered "a war-time appointment as an observer" in the Overseas Service and began to report on the Blitz. In an interview in 1977 she said,

> There was no prejudice against women at the time. I was a pair of hands and I think they were glad I was there in spite of the blunders I made. I just learnt on the job. I took on assignments as if I was a taxi on the rank.[19]

---

[13] Charlotte Higgins, *This New Noise: The Extraordinary Birth and Troubled Life of the BBC* (London: Guardian Books, 2015), 29.
[14] Karpf, *The Human Voice*, 270.
[15] Karpf, 272.
[16] Asa Briggs, *The BBC: The First Fifty Years* (Oxford University Press, 1985), 214.
[17] Audrey Russell interviewed by Sue McGregor 1972 cited in Martha Kearney, "Martha Kearney on the BBC War Correspondent Audrey Russell", History of the BBC, n.d., https://www.bbc.com/historyofthebbc/100-voices/pioneering-women/journalism/.
[18] Audrey Russell, *A Certain Voice* (Bolton: Ross Anderson Publications, 1984), 37.
[19] Audrey Russell, *Interview with Audrey Russell* (British Library, London, 1977), BBC Oral History Collection.

When you listen to the radio recordings of Audrey Russell during this period,[20] her calm manner and clipped tones betray her earlier training as an actor. However her overall delivery was still warm and she was clearly able to persuade many people to open up to her, even though they were often traumatised after their houses and streets had been bombed. Audrey also spent a great deal of time in and around the port of Dover, covering the shelling of the area and transmitting her material back to London. She recorded stories for later broadcast on the secret building of the prefabricated Mulberry harbours and the arrival of the first convoy of British soldiers to return from France, following the D-Day operation. For Audrey there were many firsts, including becoming the Corporation's first accredited woman war correspondent. Among the stories she covered was one on the first British women to take part in a war as combatants overseas. For this story she was sent to Belgium with the Auxiliary Territorial Service. She went on to cover war stories across Belgium and the Netherlands, staying mostly in British army barracks or army-converted hostels. Here she would find herself often the only woman in these outposts, but for company she had other foreign correspondents, including the BBC's Frank Gillard, Howard Marshall and Wynford Vaughan Thomas, and Australian ABC's Chester Wilmot.

At one point the BBC in London urged her to go to Antwerp, which was in British hands but under "heavy attack of flying bombs in a desperate attempt to put the port of Antwerp out of action".[21] She went happily, despite Frank Gillard protesting he thought that "it was just too tough" for her. After her successful reporting trip, someone in London noticed she was not being paid fairly, and so she investigated "and a series of letters arrived advising her that her salary had been raised".[22] She noted, "I was still being paid less than the men, in fact most of my career I have been paid less than the men, but on this occasion I know they were shamed into doing something".[23]

---

[20] A collection of Audrey Russell's recordings are housed at the British Library in London.
[21] Russell, *A Certain Voice*, 59.
[22] Kearney, "Martha Kearney on the BBC War Correspondent Audrey Russell".
[23] Russell, *Interview with Audrey Russell*.

After the war Audrey continued to report from across the UK and also from Norway, Holland, France and Germany. She desperately wanted to be a live commentator for major events but encountered resistance from her fellow journalists, in particular from Richard Dimbleby. In her autobiography she recounts that he was scornful, saying "Audrey, do give up this idea. There will never be a successful woman commentator. Why? They haven't got the stamina".[24] Audrey went on to prove them all wrong. Soon she was commentating on British and European royal weddings, funerals, coronations and state visits abroad, including alongside Richard Dimbleby and Frank Gillard. She also continued reporting news for many years, but did discover again that she had been paid less than her fellow reporters and commentators.

> I was very angry when on one occasion I discovered on a royal tour that one commentator, a very great friend of mine, was being paid £25 a week more than me and we were both doing exactly the same job, exactly the same weary miles and in fact I think my output was larger than his. I resented that and I complained and well, I was very severely ticked off, but that didn't bother me.[25]

While some women in the early years and during WWII had been promoted to important positions behind the scenes, after the war, as in many workplaces, women's career paths appeared to be stymied.[26] There were no more women staff reporting from abroad. Meanwhile in the 1970s a number of important changes were happening in society—feminism and the women's movement were campaigning and educating women about their rights, and in workplaces women were busy signalling they wanted changes to hiring and promotion policies. In 1970 the UK's Equal Pay Act was introduced and five years later the Sex Discrimination Act. Inside the BBC managers were being asked why there weren't more women in management, and they launched a number of

---

[24] Russell, *A Certain Voice*, 66.
[25] Russell, *Interview with Audrey Russell*.
[26] Suzanne Franks, "Attitudes to Women In the BBC In the 1970s—Not so Much a Glass Ceiling as One of Reinforced Concrete", *Westminster Papers in Communication and Culture* 8, no. 3 (2017): 123–42, https://doi.org/10.16997/wpcc.136.

inquiries into related matters over the coming years. Jean Seaton[27] noted that in 1970 the report "Women and Top Jobs"[28] warned that "The number of really senior women will fall sharply, [as those] remarkable women first employed during the war retired". Seaton added, "Women were often in jobs without departmental responsibility, and those who succeeded remained single, treating the job as a vocation". Seaton goes on to list countless programmes that women created and directed, without ever being given proper titles within the organisation. She noted[29] that Grace Wyndham Goldie, who had helped create BBC 2 among many other creative endeavours, had been told by Charles Curran, the director-general, that "No woman will ever be appointed above the level of assistant controller".

Discrimination was particularly bad in the area of news reporting and presenting. According to Seaton,[30] the 1973 report on "Limitations to the Recruitment and Advancement of Women in the BBC" found a litany of supposed problems that would ensue if News employed women in more prominent positions. In the radio news department there were then six women out of a staff of 120, and no female reporters. In the report women were variously accused of being no good for "hard news"; potentially being incapable of reporting unhappy news; they tended to sound too posh; they would distract audiences if on television; and men would face a burden of having to protect them in dangerous places such as Northern Ireland and the Middle East; that is when men weren't having problems with taking instructions from women. According to Seaton the report revealed how women couldn't win—if they smiled, they wouldn't be taken seriously but if they didn't then audiences wouldn't like it. "'Announcing represents the supreme authority of the Corporation', so needed 'a man's voice which is suited to all occasions'". Among the many trite and hostile reasons given by the head of

---

[27] Jean Seaton, *"Pinkoes and Traitors": The BBC and the Nation, 1974–1987* (London: Profile Books, 2015), 211.

[28] Michael P. Fogarty et al., *Women in Top Jobs: Four Studies in Achievement* (London: Routledge, 1971), https://doi.org/10.4324/9781315276533.

[29] Seaton, *"Pinkoes and Traitors": The BBC and the Nation, 1974–1987*, 211.

[30] "Limitations to the Recruitment and Advancement of Women in the BBC, Report to the Board of Management" (BBC, 1973).

radio news for not recruiting women reporters was this: "Those who are dedicated… are not really women with valuable instincts but become like men". Further reports in the 1970s appeared to largely confirm the views revealed in the first report.

However, there were a few signs that things were gradually changing. In 1970 Anne Nightingale became the first presenter on BBC Radio 1; in 1972 Hylda Bamber became the first woman newsreader on Radio 4 (although she was axed after six months) and Angela Rippon became the first TV news reader in 1975. In an interview with Suzanne Franks, Meryl O'Keefe, who became a presenter on World Service News in 1975, remarked that previously it had generally been assumed "there was an undisputed truth that women's voices would not carry on short wave; that they lacked authority—so the news would therefore be weakened in impact on the listener".[31] Sue MacGregor joined the presenting team on Radio 4's Today programme in 1984. The press debated whether or not she was up to the job. Years later she found out that she was being paid less than the male presenters.[32]

According to Suzanne Franks, "It could be argued that the expectations of the 1960s only arrived in legislation by the mid-1970s, and only arrived in the workplace reality for women in the BBC by the late 1980s".[33] The Sims Report[34] called "Women in BBC Management" was published in 1984 and this report (which included surveys and interviews with senior women) recommended the setting up of an equal opportunities officer, women-only management courses and more career advice for women. These internal and external policy documents of the 1970s and 1980s reveal the context to this study. This is the era when some of the interviewees in this book were embarking on their careers and trying to get on camera or behind a microphone. The role

---

[31] "Limitations to the Recruitment and Advancement of Women in the BBC, Report to the Board of Management".
[32] Paul Donovan, *All Our Todays: Forty Years of the Today Programme* (London: Arrow Books, 1997).
[33] Franks, "Attitudes to Women In the BBC In the 1970s—Not so Much a Glass Ceiling as One of Reinforced Concrete".
[34] Monica Sims, "Women in BBC Management", 1984, BBC Written Archives Centre.

of women was changing in society—in universities and in other workplaces—but was it changing fast enough for the would-be reporters and correspondents?

Due to the passing of the legislation described above and the advice of many reviews, the BBC was forced to improve the job prospects of women by the 1980s (Fig. 1). At this time there was one pathway at the BBC World Service which did enable women to work in international news abroad, which was to become a freelancer or "stringer" or, under a scheme set up by a news editor at Bush House, a "super-stringer". Former BBC manager, Ian Richardson, explained to me that these roles were interviewed in the normal way via a BBC "board" (job panel) but the difference was the contract. A super-stringer would have a fixed salary—at the time of roughly £10,000 per year—to complete an agreed amount of reporting for World Service radio, and anything that the person did on top of this resulted in extra payments. They were also able to work part-time for other outlets such as *The Guardian, The Times* or *The Daily*

Fig. 1 BBC poster showing its correspondents posted across the globe (1987)

Telegraph or other broadcasters based for example in the US, Canada, Australia or New Zealand.

However, the first woman who rose to prominence as a staff reporter on a normal salary was **Kate Adie** (See Chapter 2). She reached the BBC national newsroom in 1980 and proceeded to occupy a highly visible role on television. One could argue that perhaps her very success masked the lack of available opportunities for women reporters more generally. From a base in London, Kate was what was known in the business at the time as a "fireman"—a correspondent who would travel to scenes of drama and disaster to report back to the British public. With a background in regional radio and television she had both feet firmly planted in the domestic, national "reporters' room" and her main loyalty was to the One, Six and Nine O'clock TV news bulletins. Kate was enjoying the kind of exciting career that women who came before her could only dream about. But her pathway to this job had meant fighting battles with a lot of sexist assumptions by managers and co-workers in order to prove she was every bit as worthy as her male colleagues. According to Kate, she was regularly sent abroad on stories from her earliest days of arriving in the national newsroom, much to the envy of women reporters from the commercial broadcaster ITN at the time.

As many posters of the era show (p. TBC) the national ("domestic") and World Service newsrooms did not employ any women staff foreign correspondents in bureaux based abroad. Under some concerted pressure to do so, it trumpeted two new appointments in 1986 of **Diana Goodman** (see Chapter 3) and **Liz Blunt** (see Chapter 4). Diana had come up through the national and regional radio side of the BBC since arriving in the UK from New Zealand, and she became the first woman foreign correspondent and was sent to Bonn, the capital of West Germany. Some two weeks later, Liz Blunt, who entered the BBC through the World Service, became the West Africa Correspondent, based in Abidjan in Ivory Coast. Diana went on to have an extremely successful run as a foreign correspondent for fourteen years—from Bonn she moved on to Berlin and from there to Moscow. She interviewed many of the world's most important leaders of the time and witnessed the fall of the Eastern European communist states. She had to fight assumptions about both her background ("as a colonial") and her gender, being a woman whom colleagues frequently underestimated. For Liz the challenge at the outset had been in securing a job in "News" when her background was more in "Talks". Liz was awarded an MBE for her groundbreaking reporting work (and subsequent charity work) in Liberia. She spent much of her career working in "behind the scenes" roles as a producer and programme editor in the World Service radio and TV newsrooms, and retained her particular interest in African news. Towards the end of her BBC career she returned to Africa to work as a reporter in Ethiopia.

Lyse Doucet (see Chapter 5) was another "wild colonial girl" this time hailing from Canada and with what was often deemed an unacceptable New Brunswick accent. At the start of her work with the BBC, Lyse freelanced from Ivory Coast and she got her first job working alongside Liz Blunt's predecessor Alexander Thomson. Lyse's determination to work in Africa and the Middle East meant that she was often viewed as an outsider at the start of her career as she hadn't come up through the normal internal BBC pathways. She struggled for a while to get more secure employment and her accent remained a barrier to her attaining some posts. After decades of being based in West Africa, Afghanistan, Pakistan, Jordan, and Israel, she now calls London home, from where she continues to roam the globe as the BBC's Chief International Correspondent. She travels often to Afghanistan and Libya and in the past year has divided her time between the conflicts in Ukraine, Israel/Gaza and most recently Iran.

Orla Guerin (see Chapter 6) earned her journalism stripes with Ireland's public service broadcaster, RTÉ. Already a seasoned correspondent in Eastern Europe when she applied for her first BBC post as a "domestic news reporter", she was almost immediately sent back to the Balkans to report and has remained abroad for her entire career. Orla's postings have included Los Angeles, Eastern Europe (with a base in Italy), Israel, South Africa, Pakistan, Egypt and now Turkey. From Istanbul today she covers a similarly wide patch as Lyse Doucet, which can mean anywhere from Libya to Venezuela and for long periods over the past two years Ukraine, Israel and Lebanon.

Carrie Gracie (see Chapter 7) joined the BBC via a graduate intake position in production. She had spent the year before her arrival teaching

English in China. A passion was born and she went on to settle in the World Service while at the same time pursuing her studies in Mandarin. As Carrie's expertise in China grew, she eventually worked as a reporter, correspondent, and editor in Beijing and as a presenter in both radio and television. Her trust was shattered however when the BBC published the salaries of its top earners and she discovered that she was being paid much less than a male colleague in a similar position in the US. Her fight to secure equal pay for equal work is explored in this chapter.

Sara Beck (Chapter 8) studied French and Russian at university and first joined the BBC through the Russian Service on the programmes side. She worked as a producer and editor with a focus on arts and literature. She was sent to Moscow as a bureau producer, discovering that she preferred this role to reporting. From there, her career took off when she was appointed as a hub bureau chief based in Moscow. This was a senior role that took in the newsgathering of not just Russia, but adjoining countries. This role led to a similar posting based in Israel, followed by Singapore. Once back in London Sara took on increasingly important managerial roles and her career is quite different from the other women who pursued the reporting pathway. Since leaving the BBC she has worked in management consulting roles outside the Corporation.

Caroline Wyatt (Chapter 9) was a graduate trainee having studied for a postgraduate degree in magazine journalism at City, University of London. Another reporter with a skillset in writing and languages, she went on to cover post-Cold War stories in Germany and Russia. She was then a correspondent in France and covered the Second Gulf War as an embedded correspondent in 2003. Later in her career she became the first female BBC Defence Correspondent and after that she took on Religious Affairs. In 2024 Caroline works as a presenter across a number of different news and current affairs programmes.

For **Sarah Rainsford** (Chapter 10) her career also all began with Russia. After studying the subject at university, she came into the BBC via the World Service and in particular the language services. Starting out as a producer, and working in Moscow for Caroline Wyatt and for Orla Guerin, Sarah moved from producing to reporting. Among the stories she covered were the Dubrovka Theatre siege (2002) and the Beslan School siege (2004). After her first Moscow posting she became a correspondent in Turkey, Spain and Cuba, before returning to Russia in 2014. Sarah was then based in Moscow until she was thrown out of the country by the Russian government after being declared "a security risk". Sarah is now the Eastern Europe Correspondent, covering in particular the ongoing conflict in Ukraine.

Shaimaa Khalil (See Chapter 11) started life in the Egyptian port city of Alexandria, moving to the US and then to Qatar as a teenager, and launching her career in the latter on an English-speaking radio station. She entered World Service radio via an internship which turned into a producer role, and received a significant career lift while working in Cairo during the Arab Spring. Shaimaa has fought hard to move into current affairs programme presenting and also into a correspondent role. She is currently a correspondent based in Tokyo. Previously she was the correspondent in Islamabad and in Sydney.

For the scholars among my readers, I used a form of open-ended qualitative interviewing based on revealing what Pierre Bourdieu termed the social and cultural capital that affects people's positions and their "habitus" within the field of journalism. I wanted to know what embedded capital they had which enabled them to succeed within the field of foreign reporting in the 1970s, 1980s and onwards. All correspondents were asked about their childhoods, their study, their start in the field of journalism and their opportunities and challenges along their journeys.

Obviously over the course of long interviews, questions and discussion became more closely related to an individual's personal experience. The interviewees were all contacted for updates through to 2024 and their ongoing work has been analysed.

The women profiled here have climbed the BBC ladder to prestigious roles and insisted on developing fulfilling careers, but throughout they continued to have to deal with unfairness related to equal pay for equal work. The field is not levelled by any means but roles are now available to women that weren't there at the start of my career at the tail end of the 1980s. The BBC began its life as a groundbreaking employer of women. Along the way women got sidelined and excluded from promotions and viable career pathways. Now that the Corporation has been forced to admit to its unequal pay issues, perhaps it is on a path to being a much better prospect for young women reporters of the future. Perhaps also it won't be too long before there might even be a female director-general of the corporation.

This book now hands over to the correspondents who are profiled in each of the following ten chapters. You will find that there are common themes that crop up concerning the challenges they faced and overcame in terms of being taken seriously and paid equally. There are sacrifices that a travelling job demands and the repercussions are felt in terms of relationships with partners and family. There are many examples and anecdotes which demonstrate how some male colleagues didn't accept or want this new competition that women were offering, however, in the common vernacular #NotAllMen. Younger correspondents appear not to dwell as much on these issues, so we can see improvement. But mostly what shines through in the following chapters is the passion for the job—what one can still understand as the "vocation of journalism", to be a witness to history and to tell the stories of people which might otherwise go unreported. All are united about the importance of "being there" and of reporting as a reliable witness in this era of misinformation and disinformation. Back in 2010 a former head of BBC Newsgathering Richard Sambrook devoted a study to asking "Are Foreign Correspondents Redundant?"[35] I hope this book demonstrates that they still play a vital role, in combination with local producers, reporters and fixers, in covering world news for a national and international audience.

References

Briggs, Asa. *The BBC: The First Fifty Years*. Oxford University Press, 1985.
Donovan, Paul. *All Our Todays: Forty Years of the Today Programme*. London: Arrow Books, 1997.
Fogarty, Michael P., A. J. Allen, Isobel Allen, and Patricia Walters. *Women in Top Jobs: Four Studies in Achievement*. London: Routledge, 1971. https://doi.org/10.4324/9781315276533.

---

[35] Richard Sambrook, *Are Foreign Correspondents Redundant? The Changing Face of International News* (Oxford: Reuters Institute for the Study of Journalism, 2010).

Franks, Suzanne. "Attitudes to Women In the BBC In the 1970s—Not so Much a Glass Ceiling as One of Reinforced Concrete." *Westminster Papers in Communication and Culture* 8, no. 3 (n.d.): 123–42. https://doi.org/10.16997/wpcc.136.

Hendy, David. *The BBC: A People's History*. London: Profile Books, 2022.

Higgins, Charlotte. *This New Noise: The Extraordinary Birth and Troubled Life of the BBC*. London: Guardian Books, 2015.

Karpf, Anne. *The Human Voice*. London: Bloomsbury Publishing, 2006.

Kearney, Martha. "Martha Kearney on the BBC War Correspondent Audrey Russell." History of the BBC, n.d. https://www.bbc.com/historyofthebbc/100-voices/pioneering-women/journalism/.

Kramarae, Chris, ed. *Technology and Women's Voices: Keeping in Touch*. London: Routledge, 1988.

"Limitations to the Recruitment and Advancement of Women in the BBC, Report to the Board of Management." BBC, 1973.

Madsen, Virginia. "Innovation, Women's Work and the Documentary Impulse: Pioneering Moments and Stalled Opportunities in Public Service Broadcasting in Australia and Britain." *Media International Australia* 162, no. 1 (November 24, 2016): 19–32. https://doi.org/10.1177/1329878X16678933.

Murphy, Kate. "A Marriage Bar of Convenience? The BBC and Married Women's Work 1923–39." *Twentieth Century British History* 25 (November 14, 2014): 533–61. https://doi.org/10.1093/tcbh/hwu002.

Murphy, Kate. "New and Important Careers: How Women Excelled at the BBC, 1923–1938." *Media International Australia* 161, no. 1 (August 25, 2016). https://doi.org/10.1177/1329878X166649.

Reith, John. "Reith Memo to Regional Station Managers," April 30, 1926. BBC Written Archives Centre.

Russell, Audrey. *A Certain Voice*. Bolton: Ross Anderson Publications, 1984.

Russell, Audrey. *Interview with Audrey Russell*. British Library, London, 1977. BBC Oral History Collection.

Sambrook, Richard. *Are Foreign Correspondents Redundant? The Changing Face of International News*. Oxford: Reuters Institute for the Study of Journalism, 2010.

Seater, Robert. *Broadcasting Britain: 100 Years of the BBC*. London: DK, 2022.

Seaton, Jean. *"Pinkoes and Traitors": The BBC and the Nation, 1974-1987*. London: Profile Books, 2015.

Sims, Monica. "Women in BBC Management," 1984. BBC Written Archives Centre.

Kate Adie, CBE, Former BBC Chief News Correspondent
Currently freelance presenter of 'From our Own Correspondent' on BBC World Service & Radio 4

"And I never quite got over that: tearing off to the airport. Getting the last seats on the plane, ending up in a place where you went 'ah'".

In the 1980s Kate Adie made young women like me think that anything was possible. She strode the globe, alighting in zones of conflict and tragedy just long enough to conduct the pertinent interviews and give you a sense of the horror on the ground, before hightailing it to the next hotspot. She gave a high energy performance of perseverance, courage and authority. In the 1980s and 1990s, while working as the BBC's Chief News Correspondent, she seemed to prove that success for women in journalism could be achieved by simple hard work and determination.

Today Kate lives in a picture-postcard village in deepest Dorset in a renovated cottage with a river running through the garden. She remains a bundle of high energy and woe betide you should you mention retirement, because she is still very much in the journalism game. She is welcoming, courteous, and organised. Her home is beautifully decorated and extremely tidy, despite a recent canine arrival. She has a studio upstairs in the attic from where she records the links for her weekly programme *From Our Own Correspondent* which airs on Sundays. She is also the Chancellor of Bournemouth University and plays an active role mentoring students in its journalism course. This Deputy Lieutenant of Dorset is on numerous committees and charity boards, and she appears to know personally every colonel and major hidden in the surrounding hills.

A few of her many awards are on display in her house. She has two statuettes from BAFTA, one for reporting on China in 1989 and a BAFTA fellowship awarded in 2018. Another is the Golden Nymph from the Monte Carlo Festival of Television (1990) for her reporting on Tiananmen Square. But most of her awards adorn the walls of her lavatory—including her OBE (1993), CBE (2018), and assorted honorary doctorates and fellowships. There are also photos from her newsgathering days—some of her alongside news teams in the field, several of tanks, and copies of the articles written about her travails with Conservative Party Chairman Norman Tebbit regarding her reporting of the US bombing of Tripoli in 1986.

Kate didn't grow up dreaming of a journalism career. Her family had a small screen TV which she says she found "fascinating", and she read the newspapers. But that was as far as it went:

> I never thought of working for a newspaper. I never thought of being a reporter. A reporter was one of the slightly scruffy lads who worked for the *Sunderland Echo*, and they seemed to do rather humdrum articles about the shipyards and shipping and coal mining and people who lost their purses on the tram.

Kate had a happy, middle-class life with her adoptive parents in Sunderland, where her father was a pharmacist. At her private school she was mostly interested in playing tennis and taking part in drama productions. She has rosy memories of her last school summer holidays taking part in the National Youth Theatre course in London, where she was "absolutely entranced". She didn't expect to go to university; she insisted this was seen as a "bluestocking" option, and that wasn't her.

She recounted that amongst her school peers there was "no great ambition" and the possibilities mentioned were nursing, teaching or some sort of "posh secretarial academy".

Kate admitted that her A-level results were a bit of a disappointment; nonetheless her headmistress insisted she enrol at university, made some calls, and got her into the University of Newcastle, where she read Scandinavian Studies and German. This was the start of her adventures abroad, under the mentorship of an ex-BBC World Service broadcaster and polymath Professor Duncan Mennie. At one point he found she hadn't accumulated the number of necessary hours spent in Germany, so he said, "Go to London and get on the train to Ostend and from there get a train to Berlin. A girl like you should be able to do that". When Kate arrived at the Freie Universität in West Berlin in the mid-sixties, it was in the full swing of student protests. She scarcely knew what the different protests were about but joined a sit-in one day which morphed into a riot and resulted in her arrest and an overnight stay in a police station.

> So I learned something about being incarcerated. I also learned that there was nobody you could contact. And also, when people get arrested in other countries, how frightening it can be - different laws, different attitudes to the people arrested. And that is truly frightening, truly frightening. And you don't seem to have recourse to all the things they said you would if you're arrested. Always made me wary when I was a reporter as well. What they can do. Yeah, the powerlessness of being arrested.

On another occasion she crossed Checkpoint Charlie into the East. On the way back she caught a train through the semi-sealed corridor linking East Germany to the West. En route the passengers, who had permission to leave, were mistreated by the authorities who boarded the train and called on East Germans to leave the carriage and stand with their hands in the air. Everybody was screaming with fear and a couple thrust a baby into Kate's arms, hoping it would be safer there if they were arrested. Kate, clutching her British passport, held on to the baby for dear life. After a while the "Ossies" were allowed back onto the train. Kate recalled that after the train moved off, "they were in such a state.

I'd never seen human beings like that. I'd seen films of the war, but I think this was the first time I'd experienced absolute bullying by men with guns". When they reached the West, and a border guard hopped on board to welcome them, the couple retrieved the baby and inside the baby blanket was all their jewellery and money for their journey.

> It was extraordinary. I had gone through all of this. I was a complete outsider, and I felt as if I was an alien who dropped in on a drama [...] And I was full of the idea that people should know this was going on. I think that's the seed that was planted.

Kate's studies also took her to the Arctic Circle in Sweden. There she learned how to be resourceful in unfamiliar surroundings. She recalled it being the coldest winter in 40 years, and she became completely immersed in the local culture as she was the only British person for 300 miles up in the north: "I even became the honorary Vice-Consul, because I was the only Brit there. It was so adventurous and such fun". At the end of her studies, she had no idea what she was going to do next, unlike the many male engineering students in her year. She went along to a graduate talk by a man from the BBC, who answered her question about graduate applications with, "Well, we tend to take Oxbridge. And we tend to take men". Thereafter she took and passed the civil service exams, but her heart wasn't in it. Back home in Sunderland in 1967, she saw a newspaper advert for a programme assistant at the soon to be established BBC Radio Durham. In a programme about the BBC archives broadcast in 2015, the presenter, John Wilson, pulled out her application form and revealed she had written that she didn't have much experience but did have judo and drama skills.[1]

She told me she was amazed they took her on as it was an all-male newsroom. "And it was two blokes; women were not going to go in there. And you know, we were peripheral. I read news on air, and I went out with a radio car because I learned how to work it, and they needed extra people". Pretty soon she was operating as a studio manager, producing programmes, and serving the local community. "We did everything. We

---

[1] "Kate Adie", *Meeting Myself Coming Back* (BBC, November 21, 2015), BBC Sounds, https://www.bbc.co.uk/sounds/play/b06ppm2m.

nailed down the carpets, we mended the copying machine. We dealt with all kinds of crises". Along the way, she attended an eight-week training session in London where she was taught about "the principles of the BBC, and a lot of practical stuff".

This course was set up for the eight new local radio stations, of which Radio Durham was one. She was shown how to operate a Uher tape recorder and was sent out to learn to interview people. She claimed that her first forays into interviewing were particularly hopeless, but back in Durham she improved in leaps and bounds. Looking back she was thankful for all the opportunities it afforded her: "I mean I drove the radio car, I twiddled with bits of equipment, I mended bits of equipment. I sorted out the gramophone library". In short succession she ran the local *Thought for the Day* programme and a farming programme. The way Kate recalls her early career, it is as if it had a haphazard quality, but my suspicion is that she had a determination to make things happen at every stage. Anybody who has taken part in editorial meetings (or faculty meetings) will understand this scenario:

> [The boss] said we ought to do a farming programme and there was dead silence. Nobody wanted any more work. And then he said, 'Well, who knows anything about agriculture?' and we all stared at the ceiling. And then he said, 'Who likes animals?' I said, 'I do' and so, I became the BBC farming producer. I mean, I just tried anything. Tried everything. You learn so much. You learnt how to interview. You learnt how people weren't often very comfortable being interviewed. You learnt how to put people at their ease. And we were talking most of the time not about well-known people in the news. We were talking about everyday people or housewives. We were talking to working men about their lives. We were talking to people who join societies keen on pigeon fancying and athletics - all sorts. You learn to turn your hand to everything and anything - that was local radio. I think it was the best training you could have, that training.

On one particularly memorable evening in 1968 she was sent out to cover the escape from jail of a notorious armed robber called John McVicar. She filed her story, only realising later that she had bumped into him in a narrow street. She said:

I haven't got a 'nose for journalism'. I just sort of knew that I hadn't got this automatic business of knowing 'oh that's a story and that is'. […] I didn't feel like the guys in the newsroom. Because also I didn't feel for the sort of stories they wanted. They were always looking for things which I thought were quite a lot of sexist stuff.

She moved from Radio Durham to Radio Bristol and was promoted to a producer job. She was given "a woman's programme" but changed it to a magazine programme arguing with her "horrified station manager" that it was for "anybody with a brain, and that includes all women". She recalls that despite "quite a feminist streak coming by then in the 1970s" she was still not part of the newsroom and hadn't received any specific training in that area. She was interested in longer form programme making and documentaries, which she enjoyed as it allowed people to speak and explain their lives at length. Many of her programmes were about local homelessness, rough sleeping and disability issues. She laughed when she recalled that she even covered sport and interviewed sports people, "which was always difficult because I didn't have much to say really. Everything was there in local radio—it was a smorgasbord ". During her time there she brought in 20 freelance contributors who were housewives, students and people with part-time jobs. They were paid one pound for interviews and stories. Among them was Diana Moran (later famous as the keep fit "green goddess"). She said, "These women had all of these talents, all of this extraordinary ability. And you taught them the rudiments of interviewing, of editing, and presenting. And a lot of them went on into broadcasting. But local radio gave them the opportunity". Kate has never regretted spending most of her 20s in local radio. She felt she had been able to learn and make mistakes there, and confessed she had made a few.

A more "kindly boss" recommended her for a TV job in her late 20s and she moved to Plymouth. She said, "It was a very blokey thing. And women weren't really tolerated. The news editor was a misogynist. And so were a lot of people". She didn't stay long and applied for a local reporter job in BBC South in Southampton. After a while, BBC South opened a branch office in Brighton, and she moved on. "And I really felt like a fish out of water. I also found the approach of regional television weird—folksy, a bit patronising, not at all newsy". She lasted a year before getting fired for covering a gangland double murder instead of the embroidery competition she had been assigned. After receiving a neighbour's tip off, she called her crew: "We got amazing pictures. I mean, it was rather grisly. There was a body hanging over the fire escape, you know the railings, extraordinary!" BBC South didn't run the story, but when an Australian news organiser from the BBC in London called and heard about it, he sent a car to take her and her pictures to a nearby local station and the story led that evening's bulletin. By Monday she had a job as a reporter in the London BBC TV newsroom.

She had already done some weekend reporting shifts at BBC TV Centre when she landed this new job. She followed two reporters inside and recognised one as a "big cheese from Vietnam. And I was the only woman". She was used to this scenario as everywhere she went in professional circles from the judiciary down to the local magistrates' courts there were only ever one or two women.

> With the exception of a few women, the world was still, in the 1970s, run by men. So, you expected it, and it was misogynistic as well. And you stated your case, you stood your ground. But you knew at times you were going to be pushed and you would have to push back. But you could only do a set amount. There was no sense of being pioneering […] All I knew was I had to do the job and do it well.

She spent the next decade covering everything from floods, royal tours, and union strikes to the Troubles in Belfast. She enjoyed the challenge of covering Northern Ireland in the "completely mad newsroom". She worked around the clock and learned a lot about conflict reporting. She was also sent to continental Europe, travelling to the Netherlands to cover the outbreak of polio in an extreme Protestant sect and doing multiple stories in Italy, "I became a sort of Italy Correspondent". She reminisced that she never knew in the morning where she would end up. She'd see something brewing and before she knew it, she was on a plane. "It was extraordinary. A huge variety of stuff. We did shift work, but really once you're on a story, you expected to see it through. There was no real pattern you could adhere to". She loved working with her new colleagues in the national newsroom because "there were people at all levels to help you and the crews were so knowledgeable". They all had experience "in riots and wars. They were sensible. They knew their stuff. Very, very tough".

Although she made some very positive remarks about crews to me which echoed what she wrote in her autobiography (2002), she also described some very sexist camera operators with whom she worked on the road, including one man who called her to his hotel room pretending to have a news update who then opened the door "stark naked and leering".[2] She didn't complain as she thought it would upend her career. It was the 1970s and women in competitive jobs often didn't want to rock the boat. She reasoned:

> "I had no rules to go by. Any fuss would rebound, and anyway, these were days when women were breaking new ground everywhere, grabbing opportunities, being given such wonderful chances—why wreck them? It would only have been seen as 'not able to hack it'."[3]

Instead with "careful planning" she learned how to avoid certain teams. She was very thankful for producers she worked with who would help her and correct her when needed. The editors would also help, saying, "You do know that this happened 10 years ago like this, so make a reference to it". She enjoyed the stimulation of her new work environment and the camaraderie on the road.

> And then you saw the programme, absolutely being flung together with very little time to go, absolutely right up to the minute. And it had to go out without mistakes. And it was an enormously professional operation. But everybody was there pulling together. And that was phenomenal: it was a huge engine. And it worked immensely well. Of course, there were rows, there used to be stand up rows - occasionally there were fights. It was a very, very blokey newsroom. There were a few women typists, one or two junior producers. There had been other women, but women

---

[2] Kate Adie, *The Kindness of Strangers: The Autobiography* (London: Headline, 2002), 109.
[3] Adie, 109.

tended to come on attachment and not stay, there were two or three I remember. But then we were never more than a couple of us, two or three of us.

She has fond memories of the "news organisers", the people who chose and dispatched reporters. She said of the four men doing the job at the time, none of them were sexist. She mentioned the late Chris Cramer, who went on to become head of newsgathering, as being particularly supportive.

> None of them said, 'Oh, we won't send a woman' or even thought that. They just said, 'Off you go'. And that's the interesting thing. I talked frequently to ITN reporters I saw on home stories asking why they stayed on home stories, because none of them were sent abroad. There were three women. And they were all very good for a long period that I was reporting alongside them in London. And they'd say, 'how do I do it?' I said, 'Well, I don't. I just get sent'. They didn't. ITN was much more sexist. Yeah, very much so and they were good reporters.

She singled out Carol Barnes and Joan Thirkettle, alongside others who came later. She acknowledged that they got paid more at ITN but said that she didn't care because she was enjoying the work and in particular the travel.

> And I never quite got over that: tearing off to the airport. Getting the last seats on the plane, ending up in a place where you went 'ah'. And it suddenly smelt warm and dusty and different or tropical or somewhere in the Middle East and you're going, 'Wow'.

Although there weren't the instant deadlines of today, there were much more significant obstacles at a time when there were no mobile or satellite phones, social media or online journalism. Once you were "on the road", there was no being in touch, until you made it later to a phone in a TV station.

> You were hoping there wasn't going to be a delay et cetera, and you had the Nine O'clock News coming up and you knew the minimum time it

would take technically to get stuff together. How you thrashed around, and you know by seven o'clock you were managing to get it together, et cetera. You know, get on the ground, go to the story. There was no going to hotels or anything, right? Go to the story, get the stuff, get the piece to camera, write the script on the way back to the television station, edit at the TV station, having argued your way in, got an editor who could do things et cetera, and on it went absolutely. It was seat of the pants stuff.

Kate had a high profile among the public, and the press were also very interested in her. This was particularly because one story, early in her time in London, had made her famous—the storming of the Iranian embassy there in May 1980. Again, Kate described her role in this reporting coup as a happenstance, a "sliding doors" moment that might not have ended with her in the right place at the right time. I would argue that she proved her resourcefulness and capitalised on the opportunity the situation afforded her to do live reporting from the scene.

She recounts how she had been one of the hundreds of reporters down at the Iranian embassy in central London, working shifts during the siege. Six armed anti-government activists had taken hostages at the embassy. Among them were two men from the BBC, Sim Harris and the aforementioned Chris Cramer, who were applying for visas to visit Tehran. Kate had been reporting on the siege from the start. On day six, she was told she was doing the night shift, from 8pm to 8am, "because I was the junior reporter". The dayside reporter on this public holiday rang the organiser and asked if Kate could come in a bit early as "nothing was happening" and he wanted to go to a dinner party. An embarrassed news editor then called her saying the reporter would probably leave a few minutes early and could she pop over there early, at say 7.50pm. Luckily Kate went down at 6.20pm. There she found the reporter had left his post. The SAS stormed the building within the hour:

> [We] got the lot and went live. It was the first time ever there was a television news break unannounced, into what turned out to be the snooker final, with millions watching on BBC One. And I commentated for 38 minutes. I was lying on the ground with a microphone but going live and saying to myself, stick to what you can see. Do not speculate. […] It's a

huge temptation, which of course, is more common now because people are told to talk for longer periods than they have facts for. So, you say it's possibly this or it's likely that. I didn't do that. I kept to what I could see. […] I didn't appear at all. I was just a voice. I was laying on the ground. I was flat on the ground because we had heard explosions. And we were all - every hack there was on the floor because we were Belfast creatures. We'd had stuff coming over us, we knew what bomb explosions were. I'd seen stuff explode.

All Kate had was a microphone linked to an outside broadcast van. Usually there were just a few deadlines a day, and reporters scarcely ever went live. However, when the SAS stormed the building a female continuity director in Television Centre decided to break into the World Snooker Championship on BBC One.[4] This resulted in a sitting target of millions of viewers who were watching a final between Alex Higgins and Cliff Thorburn. From the archives you can hear Kate is calm and in control as she crouches behind a car door. The background noise is chaotic, full of explosions, gunshots and dogs barking but Kate continued to speak over the bangs:

> "A few minutes ago, there was a massive explosion from the back of the embassy at about 7-24pm. A pall of smoke rose from the roof. There were shots fired, and about 30 seconds, 45 seconds later, a second explosion. We can't see much from here. We've all been told to get down. Shots are still being fired. There's gunfire going on. A number of policemen obviously moved in towards the front of the building. There was a lot of automatic firing. There's still smoke at the front of the embassy, and I think there has been some action at the back of the embassy. A minute ago on the second floor, there was a signal with a white handkerchief being waved."[5]

This being the BBC at that time there were no "herograms". She told me that the next day, "I think I headed off to do a pools' winner". As a

---

[4] Kate Adie, "Kate Adie on the Terrifying Moment That Changed News Reporting Forever", *The Telegraph*, May 3, 2020, https://www.telegraph.co.uk/women/life/kate-adie-terrifying-moment-changed-news-reporting-forever/.
[5] "Kate Adie".

general reporter, and for a while even a royal reporter, Kate roved around the UK and Europe chasing features, disasters, dramas and unfolding events. She was not so much a specialist correspondent as a speedy cab off the rank. She spent a lot of time in Brussels, gathering updates on the European Economic Community, which Britain had joined in 1973. When the Falklands War with Argentina started in 1982, Kate was ill and therefore wasn't in the running to become part of the embedded team on the ships sent to South Georgia and the Falklands. Instead, Brian Hanrahan went for the BBC. Kate ended up doing a lot of Falklands-related stories in the UK and in Europe, Ecuador, and in Punta Arenas in Chile. The BBC plan had been to launch her from Chile to the Falklands, but in the end this didn't happen. She said:

> I'm subsequently enormously glad, I couldn't have done it. I was too junior. And also, with regards to the misogynist lot on the ship, because I know two of the senior Fleet Street reporters would have made sure that I wouldn't have ever got ashore. I know that. I heard things later about that, you know the sort of talk. So, in a way, I didn't have that much experience of working with the military. So, I ended up having the most fabulous trip to South America.

In 1984 Kate was interviewed for an article in Company Magazine,[6] in which she said she was longing for women in television to be taken more seriously.

> There's an old-fashioned, prejudicial, tabloid view that there are no women on television, only 'girls'. How many telly boys are there?"

A few years later, in April 1986, Kate made the headlines again when she ended up in a row with the British government over her coverage of the US bombing of Tripoli and Benghazi. The Conservative Party Chairman Norman Tebbit made a complaint "that the BBC's reporting portrayed the raids, for which the Americans were granted use of British

---

[6] Jenny Danks, "How to Be a Watched Woman", *Company Magazine*, November 1984.

air bases, as bullying".[7] Sir Norman compiled a dossier on the BBC's bulletins (Ibid) claiming the coverage was "riddled with inaccuracy, innuendo and imbalance". The BBC responded with a firm rebuttal of all charges. This is what Kate remembers:

> We witnessed from our hotel balcony, and then went to the places where the bombs fell, where people were still digging in the rubble, got the evidence, sent it back that night.

Kate said people from the Ministry of Defence later told her that the small group of Conservative MPs around Prime Minister Margaret Thatcher hadn't believed that pictures of the bombing would come out. "They thought Libya was some small, backward place. Their ignorance". They also assumed that the American bombing would be successful. She believes Sir Norman targeted her because he was facing disbelief from his Tory colleagues who hadn't been let in on the secret US agreement. Kate was adamant that the charges against her were political:

> ... because one of those politicians, to try and save his name, attacked me and said, 'Oh, this was made up and you were taken to these places'. Except he seemed to have not done his homework and hadn't realised that one of the people we interviewed was the French ambassador, who said 'My embassy has been bombed'. [...] If you didn't actually believe that - you have a problem. Ludicrous, really, that people when they're cornered, and they've got things wrong, do that.

She was very thankful the BBC stood by her, saying the people at the top were brilliant in their responses:

> The man who really did it was Michael Grade [then Controller, BBC1] and I owe him, but very much. Absolutely. Just knowing what we had done took time. He was head of BBC One, he took charge of things. Made sure we'd got it right. And then said right, right, and went out and made statements and went on the attack. Quite rightly so. Brilliant man.

---

[7] "The Libyan Bombing - 1986", History of the BBC, accessed February 17, 2023, https://www.bbc.com/historyofthebbc/research/editorial-independence/libyan-bombing.

When I asked Kate what she thought was the biggest story of her career, the one with the most impact, she was clear that it was her reporting on the Tiananmen protests in Beijing in 1989.

> The Tiananmen special, because it's still resonating 30 years after it. I got the evidence of what the Chinese authorities did to their own people, which was sending soldiers who slaughtered them. And what we know 30 years on is there were far more killed than was estimated then. The estimates now go up to 10,000. It happened all over the city, but there was no one there to report it all over the city. And the suppression afterwards was phenomenal, and it just continued. So that's the story that really matters. It shows why you do news, why you get to it, why you get the evidence. And you go the extra mile, which we did that night.

Kate was sent to Beijing (then Peking) due to one of the bureau's reporters being off sick and another needing to return home. She admitted she was not in any way an expert on China, but the student protests in the capital had been a feature of international news bulletins for some weeks, and everybody was wondering how much longer the Chinese authorities would allow them to continue, particularly in the capital's Tiananmen Square. The day before the crackdown Kate's TV piece showed the students still in control, and troops around the square being demoralised and having lost face.

On 3rd June 1989, Kate took a call around midnight from one of the producers who said they had been phoned by one of the bureau's "helpers", a sympathetic Chinese professor who lived on the edge of the city. He said there was fighting in his street and soldiers in trucks were appearing. Kate got hold of her crew and headed for Tiananmen Square. At the start they got stuck down a side road, and then they saw trucks going past, but they didn't know what was happening. Then, she said, "People around me fell on the ground. And they were dead. People, in particular students, dashed to help them". She and the crew delivered one injured woman to a clinic where Kate counted dozens of bodies. They had bullet holes from high powered army rifles. The army trucks were "shooting to kill". All in all, she and the crew spent five hours filming in the streets, and also in the Square. There were bullets raining down and "terrible, terrible things going on". They saw more bodies being carried out and found that the main slaughter did not happen in the Square but in the surrounding streets. When they noticed a formation of soldiers who were kneeling down and preparing to "possibly fire repeating volleys" they decided to split up to increase their chances of getting the cassettes back to the hotel. Kate took one and set off across the Square:

> And as I was starting, the shooting really started and there were people running in all directions. It was terrifying. And someone crashed straight into me. I fell over, went my length, tore all the skin off my forearm on the gravel. And he fell on top of me. And he was dead because a bullet had hit him. And as I lay on the ground, I saw something very odd, I saw little red ticks. And they were bullets hitting the ground. And I got up and I just ran.

Kate headed to the Beijing Hotel where she found the gates chained shut, forcing her to climb over an eight-foot-high wall. When she got near the hotel entrance, a Swiss couple shouted a warning to her, but she still ran into the police as she entered.

> And one of them came towards me and I just attacked him. They went right over. Oh absolutely, by that time I was out of my mind with rage and determination and the other two [were in my way]. I went all over, one got a kick, another one I hit with furniture. I was lucky they never pulled their guns. And I went for the stairs, and I remember going up those stairs to this day.

Kate joined her colleagues Julian O'Halloran, John Simpson and four producers who were in the office. Kate arrived just in time for the late bulletin that Saturday night in the UK. After the presenter Michael Buerk summarised events over stills of the aftermath of the shooting, he threw to Kate on the phone and introduced her as "Our correspondent Kate Adie reports from the bloody streets of Peking". Here is some of what she reported:

> "In the main road east of the Square people are gathered in total waiting defiance of the line of soldiers 300 yards away. The troops have fired on

them unremittingly. I've seen scores of people injured and several killed. In a hospital I visited earlier there have been over 150 casualties in the first hour and a half. Fires are burning in many of the roads. Army trucks set alight, and there is gunfire from over a wide area. As I came away from the Square a short while ago there was a huge volley of shots; hundreds of people fled in panic."[8]

Against the clock Kate edited some TV stories, before making copies of the video cassettes. She was worried that the BBC wouldn't be able to get more material out and so she sent the copies with "helpers" who concealed them inside their clothing. The helpers then took off to the airport heading for multiple destinations, including Singapore, Japan and Malaysia. The first cassette to land was in Japan, where the person.

> … stood on a table in arrivals, with this cassette and a sign saying 'BBC' and asking, 'Can anyone help?' We told them to say 'NHK', which was our partner [station], and to head to the TV station, and the Japanese just came forward and whisked them off. It was brilliant. I mean so fast just literally within seconds. 'We know what this is'. And they whisked them off to NHK. And NHK was alerted, and they were waiting, and it went straight out.

Kate's main TV story from that night, with two pieces to camera filmed in the Square, can still be accessed on YouTube[9] where, as of 2024 it had been watched 3.9 million times since 2014. It shows some of the most astonishing moments of TV journalism in terms of the sheer scale of the shooting, the panic among the crowd and the horror of the chaotic hospital corridors overflowing with wounded people on trolleys. This piece underlines the importance of an eye-witness account of history that cannot be gainsaid. In the following days, the crackdown continued and there was more trouble with the authorities on the streets. The other TV networks arrived in force, and Tiananmen Square was cordoned off. One of Kate's colleagues, "the lovely Brian Barron" was held at gunpoint,

---

[8] *BBC Late News (3rd June 1989)* (London, 1989).

[9] "Chinese Troops Fire on Protesters in Tiananmen Square", *BBC News* (BBC, June 4, 1989), https://www.youtube.com/watch?v=kMKvxJ-Js3A.

"kneeling with a gun to his head in the main street coming from the Square. I mean terrible".

For Kate the ripples from her Tiananmen coverage continue down the years. She is shocked at how, even today, the denials from Beijing continue. A couple of years before our interview she had given a talk at the School of Oriental and African Studies (SOAS) in London, and there were dissenting student voices shouting "You're a liar! This never happened. You made it up". She had been warned by university authorities that this might happen, but she was still surprised. "And I showed them the footage and they were still going "No, it can't be. It's fake, fake". And I said, "How can I fake all these Chinese faces? How can I fake the background in Tiananmen Square?"".

Other stories for which Kate is particularly remembered were the Gulf War of 1991 and the years of fighting during the break-up of the former Yugoslavia plus the coup in Romania. In her book "Into Danger: Risking Your Life for Work" Kate argued that journalists find "common cause" with the military, "The hours are rubbish, the conditions in the field are one degree above slum-dwelling and the pay is average".[10] However, she believes that this common cause deviates because the military's mission is "to bring order" whereas the journalist's mission is to "witness this process and spread the information back home". When she was embedded in the first Gulf War (1990–1991) she said it was the first time she had lived alongside the army. She had covered wars, but as a journalist, she had kept her distance from the army. This time, she said, there was no disagreement between the BBC and the military because,

> We had an understanding with them about how any editorial controls were done. And that was done by me and a colonel on the back of an envelope. And we did not have any major arguments with the Army about what you can and can't say at all. We knew exactly what we were going to say and said it (Fig. 1).

In another of her books, Kate wrote that the initial scramble for embedded places was cut-throat among the written and the broadcasting

---

[10] Kate Adie, *Into Danger: Risking Your Life for Work* (London: Hodder & Stoughton, 2009), 10.

Fig. 1 Kate Adie speaking in Salisbury's Guildhall in 2024

media, "Those of us in TV blackened each other's reputations, then ganged up to disqualify stations which couldn't produce a cameraman bearing bodily scars acquired during wars in Beirut and Afghanistan".[11] In Saudi Arabia the British army spent months trying to get the journalists battle-fit and sent them on live fire practices that were "terrifying". Her group of journalists, who were eventually given the OK to "go forward" into battle, slept in huge tents. Between them they set up their 12-person tent, but that first night it fell down on top of them, "I mean we journalists hadn't a clue". As a reporter, she was the only woman attached to a British combat unit. In this war there were no female soldiers in British combat units.

---

[11] Kate Adie, *Corsets To Camouflage: Women and War* (London: Coronet Books, 2003), 254.

Thirteen years later as Lindsey Hilsum, Channel 4 News's International Editor was setting out to cover the Second Gulf War, she thought of herself as heading to Iraq "while the shadow of Kate Adie hangs long over those of us who happen to be female and report for TV".[12] She noted that Kate was still "the only woman war correspondent most British people [had] ever heard of". Over the years she would often hear "bitchy" stories about Kate, mostly from male TV reporters, "A lot of it is jealousy because she managed to communicate to the public better than the rest of us. With her clipped sentences, precise voice, and detached air, she got the story across, and people remembered both who she was and what was said."

In between the two wars in the Gulf, Kate was constantly on our screens covering the Balkan Wars after the break-up of the former Yugoslavia in the 1990s. Here she found a very different conflict experience to that in the Gulf, "careering around" in BBC armoured cars through villages and hamlets fraught with danger, and hiding out with local people whenever there were no hotels nearby. There were few safe places.

> "And foreigners like us were fair game—culpable propagandists who refused to understand and sympathise with the 'right cause'; we were therefore ranged in the shooting-gallery, with the word PRESS on our vehicles marking the target."[13]

Being bold and forthright and on our screens daily, Kate sometimes attracted the kind of ire from viewers that we have got used to reading in this social media age. Back then, angry people had to make more effort to complain. They would have to phone or write in to the BBC or the papers. She had skirmishes with different government departments. After her clash with the Conservative government over the bombing of Libya, she incurred the wrath of the Labour government led by Tony Blair when it complained she had given away secret information about his imminent visit to Oman, against security advice. Richard Sambrook,

---

[12] Lindsey Hilsum, "In the Shadow of Kate Adie", *The Guardian*, February 3, 2003, https://www.theguardian.com/media/2003/feb/03/broadcasting.Iraqandthemedia.
[13] Adie, *The Kindness of Strangers: The Autobiography*, 294.

the BBC's head of news, denied that this was her fault and said, "the mistake was down to BBC editors".[14] In the end Kate sued *The Sun* for the report that blamed her. She was awarded undisclosed libel damages and legal costs.[15]

In 2003 Kate quit the BBC at the age of 58 just as the Corporation was gearing up to cover the second ground war in Iraq. She told me that in the run up she had been in dispute with American officials about how they were going to control access to information in this war. *Guardian* reporter Claire Cozens wrote at the time that Kate believed she had been sidelined by the BBC in favour of younger and "less difficult" reporters.[16] Matt Born of *The Telegraph* reported that the BBC insisted that Kate had "not been forced out" but that the decision for her to leave was "mutual" and she would continue to work for the BBC in a freelance role.[17] There was further speculation in the press that her departure may have been down to her public complaints about the Corporation. Two years earlier at the Cheltenham Literary Festival she claimed that news agendas were becoming more glamorous and sensationalised, and she bemoaned the "trivialisation of news".[18] She described herself as "a terribly old-fashioned old trout" and accused the BBC of wanting "people with cute faces and cute bottoms and nothing else in between". When talking to me about the demands of her job, Kate stressed that foreign reporting was a physically demanding job, in particular when reporting on conflicts or natural disasters. She said reporters should have no privileges as the locals were having hell and everything had been taken from them.

---

[14] Matt Wells and Patrick Wintour, "Adie Fury as Error Follows Error in BBC Row", *The Guardian*, October 11, 2001, sec. Politics, https://www.theguardian.com/politics/2001/oct/11/uk.media.

[15] Press Association, "Adie Wins Libel Case against Sun", *The Guardian*, July 24, 2003, https://www.theguardian.com/media/2003/jul/24/bbc.politics.

[16] Claire Cozens, "Flak Jacket and Pearls", *The Guardian*, January 29, 2003, https://www.theguardian.com/media/2003/jan/29/broadcasting.bbc1.

[17] Matt Born, "Kate Adie Quits BBC's Front Line", *The Telegraph*, January 30, 2003, https://www.telegraph.co.uk/news/uknews/1420495/Kate-Adie-quits-BBCs-front-line.html.

[18] Matt Wells, "Adie Retreats from BBC Front Line", *The Guardian*, January 30, 2003, sec. Media, https://www.theguardian.com/media/2003/jan/30/broadcasting.uknews.

And you are a visitor, a bird of passage. And so, you've got to grit your teeth and put up with conditions that they're putting up with and not complain [...] And people can be very aggressive, unpleasant. People are often very stressed. They take it out on you, and why not? You're the foreigner poking your nose in. And you've got to be ready for that.

Kate has pragmatic responses to my questions regarding what she thinks of today's news formats compared to those in the past. She is less fond of the 24-hour news channels which rely more on "live stuff and also on repetitions". She concedes that younger people will be looking at their phones for updates and that it is the older generation for whom sitting down for a half hour programme is a news habit. She thinks plenty of choice is a good thing:

[Some] like snacks, some people like meals, some people like to graze, some like heavy food, some like that. It's a bit like food in a way. At least the choice should be there. And there should be (as with food), there should be a spine in the whole sort of skeleton of food which is nutritious, and which does you good and keeps you healthy. And the same with information and news. There should be stuff which is honest, which is true, and which informs you properly and openly.

She applauds the BBC for still going for the audience who want "a half hour compendium of information" and believes there is still an audience for that as it has impact, "and it's watched by a lot of people in power—that matters". With regards to the BBC's problems with equal pay for women that have come to light in recent years she is happy to put some of the blame onto a previous Director-General, John Birt. She said she had to argue a couple of times about her pay, demanding a pay rise when she became chief news correspondent. She argued that being on agreed "pay grades" previously meant everything used to be transparent. When John Birt arrived on the scene that all changed:

And the system got completely crumpled, because he too wanted to double his salary as the boss. And so, the system, which had been open and very democratic, was suddenly personalised with personal bonuses and things, all of that coming in from business. And it caused immense disruption. [...] The world of business, which is basically male, has got into most institutions in this country where people have to 'manage' rather than people being producers or people being experienced in the subject. And with that comes, who gets the biggest salary? It's got into not just the BBC, it's in the NHS - managers who earn more than doctors.

In the last couple of years a number of other cases of possible discrimination have come to light,[19] when women have found out they were being paid less than men or were passed over for continuing contracts for presenting jobs. Kate is angry:

Kate: I know it's awful, the unfairness of it. I mean, the sneakiness of it. We used to be a very public business, John Birt ruined that, ruined it. Absolutely, yeah. And a lot of other things in news. But the pay was one of them. Led by him.
Me: Which was, I presume, to do with secrecy, because some people were deemed to be '*more popular?*'
Kate: Of course—favourites. There were all sorts of instances of people with relationships.
Me: Do you think it's being sorted now?
Kate: I wouldn't know. I'm not part of it. What I read in the past two years tells me not entirely.

Kate is happy to see that in terms of promotion, women are doing better these days both inside the BBC and outside—although "not as many as you would still think is right or is fair". She concedes there are many more women CEOs of organisations, or women who are in charge of public services and more women in parliament, and that more are wanted:

More sensible ministers. Women take more care. I actually think - most of them. They do. I've met some very impressive women who have been in Parliament and it's tough. Again, it's a boys' club run in a kind of minor public-school atmosphere. You know, and the women have to be

---

[19] Charlie Moloney, "BBC Presenter Martine Croxall Returns to Screen after Bringing Tribunal Claim", *The Guardian*, May 26, 2024, https://www.theguardian.com/media/article/2024/may/26/bbc-presenter-martine-croxall-returns-to-screen-after-bringing-tribunal-claim.

very tough to make it and they're wonderful. So, women generally have done better [even if] there are steps backwards.

Since leaving her BBC staff position more than 20 years ago, Kate has written five books and continues to make one-off documentaries, including one in which she revisited Tiananmen Square. Her books include an autobiography, and others chart the history of men and women in the military doing extraordinarily brave jobs. Kate's 2005 book "Nobody's Child: The Lives of Abandoned Children" reflects her interests in her own and other people's adoptions. After the Gulf War she tracked down her birth mother Babe Dunnett and her three half-siblings. She was able to have 20 years of a relationship with her mother before her death, which she treasured. One brother, Alastair, a retired schoolteacher, lives next door to her in her Dorset village and he and his wife spend a lot of time involved with Kate and the local community in their retirement. Late on, she finally tracked down her birth father's family to Ireland after a public campaign in Irish newspapers to find him. Sadly, she was too late as he had died some years earlier. But she now has a growing relationship with her Irish half-brother from her father's marriage and is in close touch with the wider family she has now discovered. She is delighted with these new links and shows me photographs of her Irish ancestors. Later I met this brother, and he told me how shocked but thrilled he was to discover a new sister.

Kate still oversees the weekend edition of BBC Radio's *From Our Own Correspondent*, recording her links and interviews in her studio upstairs at the cottage. In 2019 she started a ten-year role as chancellor of Bournemouth University, and she is Honorary Professor of Journalism at Sunderland University. These days she tells students that the biggest safety aid to foreign reporting isn't a flak jacket but good manners, "It saves quite a lot of lives. Don't antagonise. You have no right to. Good manners, and people might just help you or at least not attack you".

References

Adie, Kate. *Corsets To Camouflage: Women and War*. London: Coronet Books, 2003.
Adie, Kate. *Into Danger: Risking Your Life for Work*. London: Hodder & Stoughton, 2009.
Adie, Kate. "Kate Adie on the Terrifying Moment That Changed News Reporting Forever." *The Telegraph*, May 3, 2020. https://www.telegraph.co.uk/women/life/kate-adie-terrifying-moment-changed-news-reporting-forever/.
Adie, Kate. *The Kindness of Strangers: The Autobiography*. London: Headline, 2002.
BBC Late News (3rd June 1989). London, 1989.
Born, Matt. "Kate Adie Quits BBC's Front Line." *The Telegraph*, January 30, 2003. https://www.telegraph.co.uk/news/uknews/1420495/Kate-Adie-quits-BBCs-front-line.html.
"Chinese Troops Fire on Protesters in Tiananmen Square." *BBC News*. BBC, June 4, 1989. https:/ /www.youtube.com/watch?v=kMKvxJ-Js3A.
Cozens, Claire. "Flak Jacket and Pearls." *The Guardian*, January 29, 2003. https://www.theguardian.com/media/2003/jan/29/broadcasting.bbc1.
Danks, Jenny. "How to Be a Watched Woman." *Company Magazine*, November 1984.
Hilsum, Lindsey. "In the Shadow of Kate Adie." *The Guardian*, February 3, 2003. https://www.theguardian.com/media/2003/feb/03/broadcasting.Iraqandthemedia.
History of the BBC. "The Libyan Bombing - 1986." Accessed February 17, 2023. https://www.bbc.com/historyofthebbc/research/editorial-independence/libyan-bombing.
"Kate Adie." *Meeting Myself Coming Back*. BBC, November 21, 2015. BBC Sounds. https://www.bbc.co.uk/sounds/play/b06ppm2m.
Moloney, Charlie. "BBC Presenter Martine Croxall Returns to Screen after Bringing Tribunal Claim." *The Guardian*, May 26, 2024. https://www.theguardian.com/media/article/2024/may/26/bbc-presenter-martine-croxall-returns-to-screen-after-bringing-tribunal-claim.
Press Association. "Adie Wins Libel Case against Sun." *The Guardian*, July 24, 2003. https://www.theguardian.com/media/2003/jul/24/bbc.politics.

Wells, Matt. "Adie Retreats from BBC Front Line." *The Guardian*, January 30, 2003, sec. Media. https://www.theguardian.com/media/2003/jan/30/broadcasting.uknews.

Wells, Matt, and Patrick Wintour. "Adie Fury as Error Follows Error in BBC Row." *The Guardian*, October 11, 2001, sec. Politics. https://www.theguardian.com/politics/2001/oct/11/uk.media.

Diana Goodman
Correspondent in Bonn, East Berlin and Moscow (1986–2000)

"What an amazing gift: to be tasked with informing and educating the public about what was going on in the world while working with extraordinarily talented colleagues".

Diana Goodman decided early on that she wanted to be a journalist and she wanted to travel: neither of these options seemed particularly likely in provincial Gisborne in the 1950s. According to Diana the New Zealand where she grew up was "a prosperous, relatively egalitarian society, reliant on the export of wool and lamb" but she found it boring and stultifying and longed to escape. She thought that perhaps this led to her being "annoyingly disruptive" at school, "talking constantly, challenging the rules and what the teachers had to say". In one of her school reports a teacher had written just four words: "Scold's bridle. Ducking stool?".

But at home Diana was encouraged to have opinions "and reading—including newspapers—was considered an essential pastime in our house". As the youngest of five siblings, it took some years to achieve equality in the family in terms of pronouncing her opinions, as "he who talks loudest holds the floor". She was educated at Lytton High School in

Gisborne and then she boarded at Samuel Marsden Collegiate School in the capital, Wellington. Most people didn't travel internationally in those days, and overseas magazines took three months to arrive, but the local radio broadcast BBC programmes which fed her imagination. The radio also delivered one of her favourite programmes from the USA called "Night Beat", in which the reporter, Randy "Lucky" Stone, covered the overnights for *The Chicago Star*. She found the whole world of the newsroom fascinating and each episode ended with the word "Copyboy!" as Randy filed his story. She thinks she may also have been intrigued by the world of journalism due to her uncle, a renowned physicist, dying in a famous Australian murder mystery:

> The news came through on New Year's Day when my grandfather was staying with us in Gisborne and he had to be driven immediately to Auckland to get a flight to Sydney to be with the family. We children were warned that we must not breathe a word to anyone in case journalists found out about our connection and came knocking. I was both worried and intrigued at the idea of journalists holding so much power. And I thought that would be a very interesting job to have.

Diana's father Harry was a civil engineer and her mother Helen was a domestic science graduate. Diana was acutely aware of the restrictions placed on her mother's career at the time. Her mother came from an academic family and had wanted to study medicine. However, there wasn't enough money to allow her to spend years at university like her brothers, both of whom went on to become Rhodes Scholars and "had to come first". Her mother was teaching domestic science when she met her husband and would have gone back to teach after her first child "but education boards had the right to dismiss married women". Later her mother would return to university to gain more qualifications and she became a mathematics teacher. "My mother always stressed the necessity of having a fulfilling career and I sometimes got the impression growing up that she considered it more important than having children". In later years, however, she said that children were life's greatest reward. Both parents had an old-fashioned sense of civic duty and were on the committees of many different community groups and public bodies. Her mother was a Justice of the Peace, and both parents were members of the city council into their late 70s. Diana said their values were foundational to her own work.

Diana was sure that she wanted to study journalism, and she enrolled in a one-year course at the Wellington Polytechnic School of Journalism. There she learned the basics of the profession, writing and touch-typing and "loved the maxim that journalism was the first rough draft of history". She worked on the student newspaper, and had recently dug out some old copies for a reunion speech. "Our principal concerns seemed to have been fighting for the right to smoke during all lectures and to have more cigarette machines on the campus".

Diana's first job in the media was with the Cook Islands Broadcasting and Newspaper Corporation. Her father's career took the family to Rarotonga where he was overseeing the building of the first international airport. Here she continued to dream of living abroad:

> One of my tasks was to transcribe the world news that came crackling over the shortwave radio from the BBC in London. It seemed like some kind of magic. I remember sitting at my desk in a low-slung building on this tropical island in the middle of the Pacific, looking out at the palm trees and being riveted by the sound of correspondents reporting from around the world. I wonder whether that was when I set my sights on the BBC and perhaps on eventually becoming a foreign correspondent.

After she graduated she undertook a cadetship at the broadsheet newspaper *The Dominion* in Wellington. Here, she says, she spent many nights listening to the police radio, "Shades of Randy Stone!" She didn't think there was any difference between the stories men and women were asked to cover, but did notice that women "were not promoted beyond a certain point—even those who had been there for 20 or 30 years. The paper's first female editor was not appointed until 2009". According to Diana, there was bothersome low-level sexual harassment but the female staff learned early on to cope with it. After the newspaper, she tried her hand at radio, working for the New Zealand Broadcasting Corporation in the city of Napier. Here she got a chance to do some TV reporting but she "mostly wrote news stories and dashed about with a tape recorder, sharpening my radio skills". Ironically, she notes, the senior producer wrote in her annual appraisal that he "wasn't sure I'd ever have the right voice for radio". She was very glad to prove him wrong.

In 1975, at the age of 23 Diana moved to England "to start my real life—that was how I thought of it. Leaving New Zealand had been a question of when, not if". She travelled by ship because it was cheaper than flying and sailed via an exotic list of ports including Suva, Papeete, Acapulco, Balboa, Curaçao, Lisbon, Naples and Genoa. Travelling to Britain to get some OE (overseas experience) was a rite of passage for many Australians and New Zealanders and she was following in the footsteps of other young creatives such as the writer Clive James and public intellectual Germaine Greer.

In the UK she did temporary office work while writing to every radio station she could find. Eventually, she landed her first job at Radio Trent in Nottingham.

> It was a great start, but also a rather steep learning curve. I had to get to grips with a new job and at the same time get rapidly clued up on British politics, culture, and the law as it related to journalism. I loved every minute of it.

There she met her first husband, who was also a journalist at the station. Along the way she worked at Radio Tees in the North East and at BBC Radio Manchester, while her husband was news editor at Piccadilly Radio. She was working as a producer when she got an attachment to the network radio reporting pool in London. This was the BBC domestic radio service, and not the World Service, whose reporters and correspondents at the time were separately funded. The attachment then morphed into a permanent position. The only woman she knew of who had been there before her was Julia Somerville who had moved from general reporter to Industrial Affairs Correspondent. Diana was thrilled:

> Walking into the huge radio newsroom at Broadcasting House for the first time felt a bit like venturing onto hallowed ground. The bulletin editors sat in the middle of the open plan room with sub editors, the home and foreign news editors, typists (all stories were dictated then) and

the local radio desk fanned out around them. Overall, the newsroom was welcoming, but in the news pool down the corridor, where we reporters waited to be dispatched on stories, it was rather a different matter. I was the only woman in a team of more than 20 men and a number made it pretty clear they thought women weren't up to the job. That's not to say that they were overly chummy with each other—every other reporter was competition, after all. But they seemed to believe that women were not physically or emotionally strong enough to tackle tough assignments.

Diana was also refreshingly frank when discussing these issues in a lengthy interview on a 2016 Radio New Zealand programme celebrating her career.[1] When asked if the men in the reporters' pool were supportive, she said:

They were not. No, no, the men I mean. The management was supportive and they had appointed me so they were supportive, but I was one woman and it was about 26 men. They were very, very defensive. I suppose it was the days of feminism and men had become aware that they were going to have a whole lot more competition. And from their point of view, that's what I was, but they also were very chauvinistic.

She was determined to hold the line and not lose focus. She wanted to be a foreign correspondent, as she told me:

I can see that my male colleagues were increasingly aware that the world was changing, and they were soon going to have to compete with women for jobs. There'd be double the number of competitors in a field they'd previously had to themselves. And since many of the pool reporters wanted to become foreign correspondents, where there were a limited number of positions, they found that a daunting prospect. I buckled down to prove myself.

Diana did not experience problems with the class system that can be so pervasive in the UK, as she was a New Zealander and therefore her background was hard to pin down. Asking her which school or university she

---

[1] "Breaking Glass Ceilings at the BBC", *Sunday Morning* (Radio New Zealand, May 29, 2016), https://www.rnz.co.nz/audio/player?audio_id=201802485.

went to neither opened nor shut doors as "no one knows whether your family owns a huge sheep station or whether you come from the wrong side of the tracks". She recalled the former chairman of ITN, Sir David Nicholas, telling her that "he liked reporters from New Zealand and the Midlands because they were resourceful and—perhaps most importantly—had the right degree of disrespect for authority. There may be something in that".

Diana thought her colleagues' antagonism worsened when she secured a seven-week reporting assignment covering the visit by the Prince and Princess of Wales to Australia and New Zealand. The travelling was relentless and it was a hot and challenging trip, particularly through the Australian outback. On her return she discovered that her husband had "run off with a news desk assistant at TV-AM, where he was working. I had put my job before my marriage, he said". She also thought he was resentful that she appeared to be edging up the career ladder faster than he was. Her news was noticed by her colleagues: "I detected more than a frisson of *schadenfreude* amongst my workmates in the reporting pool when they heard about the end of my marriage".

When Diana was sent to Beirut in 1984 as what was then termed a "fireman reporter" to help report on the relentless civil war, some BBC listeners wrote in to complain, with one saying that it wasn't right to send a woman into a war zone as then men would feel obliged to protect her and they would therefore have to stop what they were doing. Diana thought this ludicrous, "considering that some of the men were really quite weedy Englishmen [and it] always made me laugh, you know, because I was a reasonably strong, healthy girl from Gisborne". The BBC replied rhetorically to one letter writer saying, "Can you imagine the *chagrin* of a journalist debarred from the big story on the grounds of sex?".[2] Diana gave an interview to *Company Magazine* in 1984 on her return from Beirut saying she had just thought, "How wonderful- a really challenging foreign assignment".[3] Diana had in fact already been in a conflict zone for a "File on 4" programme about the Iran-Iraq war, although on that occasion she was the producer, not the reporter.

---

[2] Diana Goodman, "In the Midst of Beirut Horror", *Gisborne Herald*, March 24, 1984.

[3] Jenny Danks, "How to Be a Watched Woman", *Company Magazine*, November 1984.

When asked if she saw any other women as role models, she talked of devouring the work of female correspondents from the time of the Second World War, such as Martha Gellhorn and Clare Hollingworth. From more recent times, she singled out Julia Somerville, "who had run the gauntlet of the reporters' pool" to her aforementioned prestigious post. According to Diana there were no female editors in BBC Radio News at that time, although she mentioned a senior producer—Jenny Abramsky, from the World at One, who "at that time was very supportive of women". She said she admired the on-air presenting talent of Susannah Simons and Sue MacGregor, particularly the latter who "was given a tough time by the male presenters on the Today programme". Outside of the BBC she mentioned the *Daily Mail*'s Ann Leslie and the *Guardian*'s Hella Pick—both of whom had had experience of battling for recognition which "[left] my generation of journalists in the shade". She noted that when she met Hella, she found her expressing regret at not having had a family life alongside her career.

In the same 1984 article in *Company Magazine*, Larry Hodgson, editor of BBC radio news claimed that there were so few women reporters at the BBC because "They don't apply. Lots of women don't want to be reporters. It's a hard life with a lot of time away from home. Two of our women reporters had nasty experiences covering the miners' strike". He added that he thought that one area where he might consider "the sex of a candidate" for a BBC position was as "foreign correspondent". He said:

> The BBC has never had a woman foreign correspondent. The difficulties are considerable. A woman of suitable age and experience is likely to be married with kids. How can she uproot herself and go and live in Delhi?"

When the interviewer asked pointedly, "What if she's single?".

'Then there would be no difficulty', Larry replies, adding a strong hint that the BBC might appoint its first woman foreign correspondent soon.

Diana was subsequently heartened when she found that within national Radio News "some senior managers were moving with the times and were open to the idea of appointing a woman to a foreign posting". Larry Hodgson became one of them. "Also, after observing my colleagues, I decided I didn't want to be still sitting in the reporters' room at their age and the prospect of running a foreign bureau was very attractive". She noted that there was no mentoring scheme as such, but rather "it was a matter of one step leading to the next—just driving myself forward". When Diana was appointed to her first staff overseas posting as Bonn Correspondent in 1986, there was a flurry of press coverage. An article in the *Sunday Times*, titled "Bonn for Diana"[4] started with the line,

> "Another bastion of male domination has fallen at the BBC. The corporation has appointed its first ever woman foreign correspondent -- Diana Goodman, who is going to Bonn for BBC radio news. Ms Goodman already has the distinction of having been the first BBC woman journalist into Beirut, but this is her first permanent posting abroad."

In the article Larry Hodgson also said that Diana was "the best candidate for the job" and Diana went on to explain that she was "single, which helps. I suppose some women wouldn't be able to go that easily".[5] Diana said that in another interview, where readers were assured that I was "unassuming and unaggressive", I stated: "I can't imagine getting married again for a while. I've got too much to do". They were comments that very much reflected the times.

Diana remembered there being six male candidates for the vacancy, and when she came out of her interview one said, "Well, I guess I should have worn a skirt if I wanted the job". At this point, according to an interview in *Prospero*, she also received letters from other women in News and Current Affairs (NCA), thanking her for banging a crack in the glass ceiling.[6] She said, "In the years that followed, trying to live up to that vote of confidence was quite a responsibility". A couple of weeks after Diana's appointment, the BBC announced that Elizabeth Blunt (*see next chapter*) had got the staff job of West Africa Correspondent.

---

[4] "Bonn for Diana", *Sunday Times*, March 23, 1986.
[5] "Bonn for Diana".
[6] "Cracking the Glass Ceiling", *Prospero*, August 2016.

When Diana headed over to Bonn she already spoke some German and she had a sister and her family living in the country. She inherited her predecessor's apartment in Bad Godesberg, a Bonn suburb close to the Rhine. David Smeeton was surprised to see a woman succeed him, and handed her a briefing folder he'd compiled which included advice "to your wife", on "expatriate women's organisations and where the shops were—that kind of thing. The incoming correspondent was also referred to as *he* throughout". Diana's familiarisation visit to Bonn didn't last long. On the second day she was dispatched to Tripoli to join the BBC team reporting on America's air strikes against Libya. In Bonn, she worked alongside an NCA stringer, Anna Tomforde, who also wrote for the *Guardian,* but she was otherwise alone apart from some students who came in to help for a few hours every week. For big events, such as elections or for documentaries, a producer might be sent from London.

Early on in her posting she covered the historic visit by the East German leader Erich Honecker to West Germany in September 1987. This was the first visit to West Germany by an East German head of state. Along with his official meetings with West German leaders and dignitaries he also met up with his sister and visited his parents' graves. At a reception during his visit, Honecker said, "The day will come when borders no longer separate us, but unite us, just like the border between the German Democratic Republic and Poland". Some media outlets selected the first part of this sentence (while erasing the reference to Poland) as indicating improved relations between the two German states but, as Diana attests, his visit was really to cement the "recognition of East Germany as a separate state [and] his vision certainly did not include the sudden fall of the Berlin Wall, which happened just over two years later".

During this posting, Diana remembers covering the return of hostages from Lebanon at the US Air Force base in Wiesbaden. She also reported on stories outside Germany, in particular in Austria and Romania (Fig. 1). She recalls following the election of Austria's president Kurt Waldheim in 1986 and then two years later conducting a sit-down interview with him (during the investigation into his war-time record as a German intelligence officer in Greece and Yugoslavia). She thought he had aged a great deal in his two years in power but remained

Fig. 1 Diana Goodman pictured in front of a tank in Romania (1989)

"extraordinarily confident in his ability to reject the accusations against him".

From her journalism at this time Diana is particularly proud of a documentary she made for Radio 4 in January 1988 called "Children of the Reich", which explored the legacy of the Nazi era on the "second generation" who grew up after the war.[7] Listening to a recording provided by Diana her clear, modulated voice had the international quality of a person who has lived in many places. In the documentary she interviewed the grown-up children of Nazis who had reacted differently to the predicament of their parents' tainted past. The interviews were astonishing. Niklas Frank was the son of Hans Frank, who was the Governor-General of Nazi-occupied Poland during the war and who was executed in 1946 for his part in the death of millions of Jews. Niklas was reflective about his own generation:

---

[7] Diana Goodman, *Children of the Reich*, BBC Radio 4, 1988.

I think that my generation failed. We never asked our parents really what happened? Why, but especially you, my dear father, my dear mother, why were you weak in this time? Why were you a coward? What did you really know about the Jews in your village, in your town, in your city, in your neighbourhood? What happened to them?

Martin Bormann was Adolf Hitler's private secretary and he was presumed dead at the end of the war. His daughter refused to think badly of her father:

My father was a good father, regardless of what everybody says about him. Yes it's true, he did have a bad temper, but he was also very caring. I've always wanted a husband like my father but I've never found him. If you ask me if I can be held responsible for what he did, well the answer is no. And anyway, he just tried to do his best. That is how it is in life. If you don't act first, then you'll be the one who is devoured.

In late December 1989 Diana was sent to cover the revolution in Romania. She drove through the night and argued her way across the Yugoslav border. When she arrived in Timisoara she found a city "in complete disarray, with armed revolutionaries manning checkpoints and Securitate snipers, loyal to the old regime, randomly shooting people dead in the streets". She gave me a sense of the terror of the situation and her professionalism under fire:

In the midst of the mayhem I was able to record the sounds of a rapidly unfolding revolution, including a scene where furious and frightened local citizens had a Securitate sniper trapped under a bridge and were arguing about whether or not to string him up. Other snipers started shooting into the crowd which began to flee in terror. I managed to keep my tape recorder (a cumbersome Uher in those days) running and record the uproar and the sound of bullets ricocheting around. The immediacy of radio meant that BBC listeners could get a tangible sense of what the Romanians were going through.

During this period in Timisoara it was very difficult to source phone lines to file her stories. She ended up sleeping on the floor of the telephone exchange and on another occasion the radio station. On a personal level, those reports reached the ears of another New Zealander, Roger Wilde, whom she had recently met in London. After a brief courtship this fellow journalist and photographer decided to move from the UK to Germany to live with her. They married in 1991.

Although she expected that her next posting would be Jerusalem, the rapidly changing situation in the Eastern bloc led to her being asked to set up the BBC's first bureau in East Berlin in 1990. From here she took on the job of Eastern Europe correspondent. Her first big story upon relocation was the East German election in March 1990. Exit polls predicting a centre-left win proved wrong. In the end the East German branch of the CDU, West German Chancellor Helmut Kohl's party, led the centre-right to victory and reunification was guaranteed. Diana was not surprised. While doing election vox pops she discovered that East Europeans were often reluctant to disclose their voting intentions, relishing the fact that democracy meant they could have a secret vote. "At midnight on October 3rd, less than seven months after that election, fireworks exploded over the Reichstag and the two Germanys became one. I filed by phone from the top floor of an East Berlin office building overlooking the old death strip—and the Reichstag".

After reunification, expectations among East Germans were that their lives and their state owned factories would be "hauled up to West German standards [and that] capitalism would improve their lives". Instead, vast numbers of people working in old factories lost their jobs when the Treuhand government agency started privatising or closing production plants rather than modernising them. She noted:

> In 1991 I went to Zwickau in Saxony to see the last Trabant—East Germany's iconic 'Duroplast car' with a two-stroke engine—roll off the production line. It was painted a striking shade of hot pink. A year before, more than 11,000 workers had been employed at the Zwickau plant. Now they were unemployed. When East German factories closed, the workers didn't just lose their livelihood, they lost the sporting and cultural facilities which used to serve the whole neighbourhood.

Diana noted that some correspondents covered the story from West Berlin, where it would have been logistically much easier. But Diana thought it more authentic to have both her bureau and her apartment in the East. She said, "It was necessary to be in the thick of it. To deal every day with non-functioning phone lines, broken-down lifts, and brown tap water. To have friends in the East and to talk to people one encountered in the course of daily life, who were dealing with rocketing rents, likely unemployment and the closure of most child-care centres". Diana recalled observing the former East German leader Erich Honecker in court, when he was charged with manslaughter for the shoot-to-kill order at the state's borders:

> Seeing him in court, by then a frail, sick old man, it seemed astonishing that he had held an entire nation in a grip of iron. The same was true of Erich Mielke, the brutal former head of the Stasi, who was both ailing and allegedly senile. He claimed not to be able to understand the court proceedings going on around him.

Covering the Stasi files became another story for Diana. She acknowledged that it must have been hard for East Germans to refuse to comply with the Stasi's demands for information "under threat of losing their jobs or their children being refused entry to university". Nonetheless the stories from the Stasi files shocked the population:

> One of the first East Germans to see his Stasi file was Gerd Poppe—a former leading dissident. There were 50 boxes of papers relating to him and his wife. Nearly half of the main members of their opposition group were Stasi informers, along with 60 friends and acquaintances. Poppe said that when he was reading his files he had to stop, until a wave of nausea passed.

From time to time Diana would interview a quiet young East German woman who had just entered politics: her name was Angela Merkel. Dr Merkel had a PhD in quantum chemistry and yet her West German mentors regarded her as a token woman and a token East German. "Chancellor Kohl even called her *'mein Mädchen'*, meaning 'my girl'. Her political colleagues had no inkling that she would push them all aside to become the most powerful politician in Europe". In her office building there were correspondents from the *Daily Telegraph* and *The Times*. She had a full-time office assistant who looked after administration and planning in the Eastern bloc. There was no resident producer but visiting producers would come in for big events such as elections and assorted reunification ceremonies. She believes the news production could have been improved:

> The situation is quite different now regarding bureau-based producers. At the time, there was a senior editor on the foreign desk who foolishly thought that sending producers to help correspondents was tantamount to "nannying" reporters in the field—even though two pairs of hands would have increased output considerably.

During this period Diana interviewed all the big names, including the last president of Czechoslovakia Václav Havel. She recalls the difficulties the former Czechoslovak dissident had had managing the transition from the "Velvet Revolution" to a democratic market economy. She remembers that in person he was an exhausted, chain-smoking and jumpy man, but full of charisma. The first democratically elected president of Poland Lech Walesa, on the other hand, she thought was "notoriously tricky to interview, with a wildly idiosyncratic style of speech that proved a challenge for even skilled interpreters". Despite being "rather short and dumpy" he liked to flirt with the BBC Warsaw office assistant. Once when Diana compared notes with another journalist who had interviewed him on the same day, she discovered that "he had deployed the same 'spontaneous' jokes and mixed metaphors in his answers".

Diana worked hard to reflect the experiences of ordinary people in a world that had suddenly been turned on its head. There was the joy of living in a free country but there were also economic difficulties and many setbacks:

> It was exciting and I also feel privileged to have been on the spot when history was being made. When I counted up, I realized that I had covered the end of four different countries: October 3, 1990, the night of German reunification, when East Germany ceased to exist as a separate entity. The declaration of independence in Slovenia on June 25, 1991, which

began the breakup of Yugoslavia. December 25, 1991, in Moscow, when President Gorbachev resigned, followed by Red Square on New Year's Eve six days later, when the dissolution of the Soviet Union took effect. New Year's Eve 1992 in Prague, when Czechoslovakia broke into two separate states.

In 1994 Diana moved to Moscow. She had already worked there, filling in for previous correspondents' absences. In Moscow she, her husband and son Harry lived in a foreigners' compound called Sadovaya-Samotechnaya (Sad Sam). It was a Stalin-era apartment building that the BBC had occupied since 1963. Other media companies such as the *Daily Telegraph*, the *Financial Times*, *Reuters* and the *New York Times* were also based there. Diana was then the first female foreign correspondent at the BBC to take up a foreign posting with a child. At Sad Sam there were other expatriate families and their children and even a small parent-run kindergarten, run by two Russian teachers. However, there was nowhere for the children to play outside, apart from "a dusty park" although eventually the teachers "paid a bribe to the headmistress of a nearby school for use of her playground".

This move to Moscow coincided with the rise of Jenny Baxter, who was appointed to the BBC's foreign news (FN) department, first as a deputy foreign editor and then as the head of foreign news. She was "the first woman to hold that job. Her appointment brought a less macho approach to dealing with foreign correspondents. It also signalled a change across BBC News, as Fran Unsworth […] was the first female home editor at the time. All of a sudden, there were two women in senior news positions".

Meanwhile a new Russia was being born—one that included Chechen mafia, future oligarchs and Western and Russian businesspeople. This Russia nestled uncomfortably alongside the poverty that still pervaded President Boris Yeltsin's regime. According to Diana it could be hard to reconcile the demands of the news desk in London for up-to-the-minute official information when often it wasn't available or old-school propaganda tactics were still being deployed. So-called "reliable sources" could simply not be trusted and getting to the truth was often impossible. She said, "Moscow was also frustrating because Yeltsin's precarious health and the war in Chechnya made it difficult to get away from the office to visit other parts of Russia".

When she did get away she found another world. She remembered in particular Murmansk in the Arctic Circle, and the small village of Privolnoye in the south of the country where she interviewed the childhood teacher of Mikhail Gorbachev. The teacher, "Martha Ignatenko, was poverty-stricken, barely able to survive on her meagre pension that was supplemented by keeping chickens and a small garden. On hearing of her plight, the owner of a motorcycle shop far away in Sydney, Australia, was moved to send her regular payments". She interviewed a famous photographer, Yevgeny Khaldei, who was also reduced to extreme poverty, and who told her about how his mother had been killed in an anti-Jewish pogrom in Ukraine in 1918. His father and sisters had been murdered by the Nazis in 1941. This man received no royalties from his time at the Soviet news agency TASS; he had been dismissed in 1947, he thought, because he had got on too well with the Western photographers he'd met at the Nuremberg trial and because of his Jewish heritage.

Diana's biggest audience response to a story was one on the plight of disabled children in "a bleak and badly under-funded Russian orphanage" or internat. At the time ninety-five percent of disabled children were abandoned by their parents in Russia and faced with a grim existence in a state-run home. As a mother she felt particularly affected by the suffering children "kept in cold, inhumane conditions, with little treatment and no stimulation". This 1996 report titled "Few comforts for Russia's abandoned children", which summarises the script broadcast on "*From Our Own Correspondent*" (FOOC) is still available on the BBC website.[8] Following the broadcast, donations poured into the BBC from all over the world. The report dealt with a cold-hearted system, corruption and despair and it focused on a young girl:

> Closest to the door was Carina, a four-year-old girl who was born with twisted legs because her mother had syphilis. She was the size of a normal one-year-old. As she whimpered, she continually clenched and

---

[8] Diana Goodman, "Few Comforts for Russia's Abandoned Children", *From Our Own Correspondent (FOOC)*, December 12, 1996, http://news.bbc.co.uk/2/hi/programmes/from_our_own_correspondent/fooc50/4163954.stm.

unclenched her hands. When I lifted the covers on her bed I found she was naked below the waist and was lying on a cold rubber sheet with not even a cloth to catch her excrement. When I stroked her hands she unclenched her fists and stopped crying. She listened intently as I talked. When I moved away she was quiet for a moment, then she realised she was alone once more and started to weep.

Nobody knew how to help in this situation where donations would get siphoned off by the authorities, but she found one Moscow-based institution run by expat volunteers which was giving its children some love and comfort and trying to get them fostered or adopted. She finished her report with these lines:

Each night now before I go to sleep, I think of the pinched and lonely little faces of the children at the internat as they lie staring into the darkness in their narrow beds. Sometimes I get up and sit by my own son's bed and pray that nothing similar will ever happen to him. And I remember the smell which hung over the home. The smell of disinfectant, urine and death.

Other stories that have resonated with her down the years include a visit to Volgograd (formerly Stalingrad) on the 50th anniversary of one of the bloodiest battles of World War II. In Budyonnovsk, on the Steppes of Southern Russia, she covered a story about Chechen separatists who had taken 1,500 people hostage in the local hospital. After a battle with Russian forces, more than a hundred civilians and soldiers lay dead and several hundred were wounded.

By the end of Diana's posting in Moscow, all was not well in her personal life. Her husband, Roger, a "trailing spouse" had largely put his own career as a journalist and photographer on hold to juggle a lot of the childcare while Diana worked and travelled. She acknowledged that this was difficult for him. She had been warned about "the Moscow curse" whereby "the pressures of work, alongside the idiosyncrasies of life in a post-Communist state caught between two worlds, meant that many, or even most correspondents' marriages did not survive". Diana was burnt out and suffering from exhaustion and on return to London, the couple separated. She believes she was lucky on two counts, firstly, there was growing recognition of the need to support good mental health amongst staff and secondly she had an empathetic foreign editor, Jenny Baxter, who helped her navigate a path ahead. Diana moved into a communications role in BBC Newsgathering management, where her work included helping to edit two "rush books" for BBC News: "The Day that Shook the World",[9] about 9/11, and "The Battle for Iraq"[10] about the 2003 fall of Iraqi President Saddam Hussein.

After that she was ready for another change, and she decided to take early retirement: "And that transition led quite naturally to my decision in 2005 to return to New Zealand with my son" in conjunction with her former husband who also settled there. Subsequently, Diana decided to take things more slowly and move away from news. She did more book editing, wrote about wine and architecture, and interviewed leading advertising creatives for a global website. In recent years she has been transcribing letters written by her six great-uncles who were killed in World War I, and her grandfather who survived. In an interview for an article in the *New Zealand Listener*[11] Diana said she doesn't talk much in New Zealand about her career covering Eastern Europe as people don't seem to want to know and she thinks "it can be interpreted as somehow being boastful when all one is doing is just talking about life". In 2016 she was awarded an honorary doctorate by Massey University in Wellington.[12]

Looking back over her career as a correspondent, Diana believes there can be occasional upsides to being a woman that make it easier to work as a foreign correspondent. For example sometimes interviewees are more willing to talk, believing women to be more sympathetic. Also some men in authority don't feel threatened by "a mere woman" and so access can be easier. Nonetheless she often found deep prejudice, especially in some former Eastern bloc countries, which hadn't caught up

---

[9] Jenny Baxter and Malcolm Downing, eds., *The Day That Shook the World* (London: BBC Worldwide Ltd, 2001).

[10] Sara Beck and Malcolm Downing, eds., *The Battle for Iraq: BBC News Correspondents on the War against Saddam and a New World Agenda* (London: BBC Worldwide Ltd, 2003).

[11] Goodman, D. (2016), 'It was like another foreign posting, really' in the *NZ Listener*, pp 37–8.

[12] Clare De Lore, "'It Was like Another Foreign Posting, Really,'" *NZ Listener*, November 12, 2016.

with movements such as feminism. She said: "When I was introduced to the president of Romania, Ion Iliescu, as the new Eastern Europe correspondent who would be covering the country's post-Communist transition, he insisted: 'We'll need a proper correspondent, a very important reporter'—meaning a man". In terms of facing danger, Diana reiterated years later that women can be just as brave as men.[13] "Sure, being under fire was frightening for all of us. But as a generation of younger women has proved in various conflicts since, courage is not related to gender. I can only observe their work with enormous admiration".

Regarding some of her colleagues she is sanguine:

Journalism is a very competitive field in which to work. And the further up the ladder you go, the more competitive it becomes. Other women can be just as rivalrous as men. For me, that came as something of a surprise—I guess I expected more female solidarity—but that's the reality in most professions. These days a number of the BBC's female foreign correspondents have children. Yet, just a few years ago a childless former colleague publicly lashed out in the media, questioning whether women could really manage the pressures of the job while raising small children, even with the help of a partner. She would never have spoken about male correspondents in the same way. I didn't ever tell my husband Roger about my colleague's surprising outburst before he died. As a supportive spouse, he would have felt very unfairly attacked. Of course, some of the male correspondents were pretty preoccupied with besting each other.

She went on to explain that on one of her postings two colleagues embarked on an arm-wrestling competition while drinking in a nightclub.

An old dog, younger dog scenario. The old dog ended up with a broken arm. The sound of the bone snapping was so loud that it stopped the club's jazz band mid song.

---

[13] Diana Goodman, "Speech to J50 Dinner" (Massey University, November 26, 2016), https://www.massey.ac.nz/massey/learning/colleges/college-business/school-of-communication-journalism-and-marketing/news/events/journalisms-50th/diana-goodman-j50-speech.cfm.

She recalls good male friends in foreign newsgathering, for example Christopher Wyld, the foreign editor of radio news and Misha Glenny, whom she knew as a stringer for the *Guardian* in Vienna, and later as "the BBC's collegial Central Europe correspondent". In terms of the agency she had to pursue her own stories, she said decisions on which stories to cover were taken "in conjunction with London". She also tried not to get drawn into the hang-up surrounding being "big-footed", (a process in which a senior correspondent or presenter is sent in to do live presentation for a programme or to report on the top story). She thought sending in back-up "was often the right decision". She remembers one of her colleagues in Moscow insisting that as a resident correspondent he ought to be allowed to anchor at least some of BBC World's live coverage of an election rather than John Simpson who had been flown in. She thought, "John was a consummate live performer, which was why he was there, but he rather graciously stepped aside". She said, "A more pressing issue for me was putting up with resentment about my 'big footing' resident correspondents or BBC stringers on big stories. In some cases, they were not only unhelpful, but deliberately obstructive. One of them wrote to me years later and said she felt terrible about the way she had behaved".

Diana insisted she had never came under any pressure from the Foreign Office to report a story in a particular way, while working abroad, but she did sometimes hear from one or other British embassy who might suggest that "we were giving more importance to a story than was perhaps warranted". She is adamant that in the more than 40 years that she was a reporter, she was never once pressured "to write on political grounds". She added:

> And in my experience, the BBC fiercely resisted attempts to influence its news coverage. As a result, of course, it knocks heads with critics of all political colours. It was ever thus. During my time at the BBC, the only area where impartiality was not required was in covering apartheid in South Africa. Being anti-apartheid was regarded as a given.

She would occasionally get letters of complaint. One man wrote repeatedly because he was offended by her pronunciation of "war";

another thought he could detect a German accent. At other times letters arrived proposing romance or marriage.

I asked if she had ever checked to see if she was being paid the same as men, and she answered that it would never have occurred to her that that might not be the case. She admitted she was surprised by the recent discovery of pay inequality between men and women: "Earlier on, of course, BBC employees were paid according to their grade and that made pay scales pretty equitable. I can't remember when salaries became negotiable". In terms of race, class and sexuality, she thought the BBC had achieved "admirable diversity way beyond anything we could have imagined back then". She was also encouraged by the BBC commissioning local stringers to spread their wings and offer radio and television packages that would traditionally have been done by correspondents, "But it can't be a universal policy. Not all journalists are good at TV, not all are good at radio, and stringers must have the requisite skills to complement their local knowledge". She was absolutely convinced that there was still a point to having foreign correspondents:

> Without question. Of course. it is very helpful to have local staff or stringers on the ground and advances in technology mean that they are now able to report in quality sound and vision. But foreign correspondents who are working or have worked in different countries on myriad assignments will always be able to provide a wider perspective. They can make comparisons between what is happening on this particular story and events elsewhere. That sort of overview is vital in helping listeners and viewers to understand a story and judge its significance.

According to Diana, the BBC's mission to "inform, educate and entertain" is crucial to international newsgathering. It isn't just about providing information, it is also about throwing light on issues, "And without sounding too high-minded, I would say that we should try to expose injustice and wrongdoing". She emphasised that it wasn't all about covering wars and danger, the job is much wider than that and if it is the excitement of danger that you are seeking, then it's probably better to be based in London as a "fireman" (travelling reporter).

The job of explaining a country, or countries, to listeners and viewers is immensely rewarding. Of course, you'll cover politics, the economy, industrial relations, history, culture, health… But you'll also try to gather up the essence of a country: How do the Russians celebrate New Year's Eve—their most important holiday? What do they eat and how do they spend their summers? How does the high consumption of alcohol affect life expectancy? Why does Germany have so many opera houses? What makes people laugh, or give them pleasure?

Diana's advice to young people wanting to become journalists is: when faced with a brick wall, keep going. Listening carefully to what people are saying is also crucial if you are to bear witness to history, and give a voice to the voiceless. Ask "Why?" when an answer seems incomplete, as it can often draw out the most revealing response. She advises they will need stamina, curiosity, the ability to operate equipment and to not mind missing out on events with family and friends. Nonetheless she thinks she's been "extraordinarily lucky" to see and do the things she has, saying:

> The international media—in particular, the BBC—were respected and valued. I forged lifelong friendships, worked harder than any of us thought possible, and relished the camaraderie that emerged under stress. What an amazing gift: to be tasked with informing and educating the public about what was going on in the world while working with extraordinarily talented colleagues.

In an article in the *New Zealand Listener* she advised young women to not be afraid to call themselves feminists.[14] "Try to retain a moral compass, compassion and a strong interest in humanity. In other words, try to care about what you do". In the same article, she notes she became a feminist in 1972, after seeing Germaine Greer speak at Auckland Town Hall. "It gave us fire in our bellies. At the age of 20, I realised feminism means equality. All the other stuff that has been loaded onto feminism, mostly by its opponents, means nothing. It is about equality for women in political, economic and social terms. I find it extraordinary it

---

[14] De Lore, "'It Was like Another Foreign Posting, Really.'".

is still being argued about 45 years since I embraced it". In the end, she appears to be sanguine about expectations, and says to young would-be journalists:

> Relish praise when you get it, but don't expect it. People in newsrooms are too busy. They will already have moved on to the next story.

References

Baxter, Jenny, and Malcolm Downing, eds. The Day That Shook the World. London: BBC Worldwide Ltd, 2001.
Beck, Sara, and Malcolm Downing, eds. The Battle for Iraq: BBC News Correspondents on the War against Saddam and a New World Agenda. London: BBC Worldwide Ltd, 2003.
"Breaking Glass Ceilings at the BBC." Sunday Morning. Radio New Zealand, May 29, 2016. https://www.rnz.co.nz/audio/player?audio_id=201802485.
Danks, Jenny. "How to Be a Watched Woman." Company Magazine, November 1984.
De Lore, Clare. "'It Was like Another Foreign Posting, Really.'" NZ Listener, November 12, 2016.
Goodman, Diana. Children of the Reich. BBC Radio 4, 1988.
Goodman, Diana. "Few Comforts for Russia's Abandoned Children." From Our Own Correspondent (FOOC), December 12, 1996. http://news.bbc.co.uk/2/hi/programmes/from_our_own_correspondent/fooc50/4163954.stm.
Goodman, Diana. "In the Midst of Beirut Horror." Gisborne Herald, March 24, 1984.
Goodman, Diana. "Speech to J50 Dinner." Massey University, November 26, 2016. https://www.massey.ac.nz/massey/learning/colleges/college-business/school-of-communication-journalism-and-marketing/news/events/journalisms-50th/diana-goodman-j50-speech.cfm.
Prospero. "Cracking the Glass Ceiling." August 2016.
Sunday Times. "Bonn for Diana." March 23, 1986.

Elizabeth Blunt, MBE, West Africa Correspondent 1986–1990, India TV producer 1993–1994 & Ethiopia Stringer, 2007–2009

"And then of course it was quiet and eventually we crept out and there were bodies all over the hallway and the washrooms, everywhere".

Elizabeth (Liz) Blunt was born and grew up in Tooting in South London, the daughter of an English father Frederick Harden and a Scottish mother Margaret Tulloch. Her father trained as an engineer but due to an engineering slump in the early 1920s his firm shut down and subsequently he became a copy boy for *Country Life*, eventually rising to become the magazine's Art Editor. Her mother did clerical and accounting work in an office but stopped after she got married, except for a stint during World War II when she worked for *Homes and Gardens* magazine, a sister paper of *Country Life*.

Liz attended her local state primary and then a girls' grammar school in Camberwell, the Mary Datchelor School. Liz excelled at school and went on to read modern and medieval history at New Hall in Cambridge where she became involved in amateur dramatics. She also wrote occasionally for *Varsity*, the university magazine. At the end of her studies she applied to both of the main BBC trainee schemes. She didn't get onto the one she dubbed "the high flyers one", but she thinks that due to her backstage drama work she succeeded in getting onto the "External Services Scheme" for studio managers. According to Liz, "some people who ended up very high up in the BBC actually came in that way". As part of her training she spent six months at Bush House, the home of World Service radio, and six months at Broadcasting House (BH), the home of national News and Current Affairs (NCA) where she stayed for a while after qualifying.

She worked on a wide range of programming, including attachments to the arts programme "Kaleidoscope" and the children's TV programme, "Jackanory". These didn't lead to permanent positions as the programmes tended to run on work carried out by those on attachment, with new posts opening up only every three or four years. She worked at BBC Bristol for a while as a studio manager and worked a summer at the Edinburgh Festival one year. As she was on BBC staff, she could move freely on attachment but she still retained her salary as a studio manager. She remembers that when TV staff went to the posh restaurants for lunch, she would order an omelette because she wasn't earning as much as them.

All of a sudden her life took a sharp turn and in quick succession she got married, resigned from the BBC and followed her husband, a town planner, to Tanzania where he had secured a job. Speaking in her determinedly matter-of-fact manner, she said that shortly afterwards her husband ran off with somebody else. Liz took stock and weighed her options. She had packed up her home and rented it out, so she decided to stay and get to know Tanzania. When she returned to the BBC a year later, the corporation had "too many studio technicians" so she moved to the Science Unit at Bush House for a while and wrote scripts for translation, mostly on current affairs topics. Then the Africa Service offered her a writing contract, which turned into a permanent job as a writer and producer. In this job Liz wrote four-minute current affairs scripts in English that would then be translated into Swahili, Hausa and Somali. She also worked as a producer on the "Network Africa" and "Focus on Africa" programmes.

During this time she travelled on several programme-making trips to West Africa, Ghana, Nigeria and Burkina Faso. She said these trips tended to come up at the end of the financial year, when there was money left over in the World Service coffers. Eventually she got promoted and became a senior "talks writer". She recounts that one day somebody had the bright idea that Bush House needed to be mixed up a bit and the newsroom "ought to talk to the rest of the building". So she was picked "as a guinea pig" and sent off to the newsroom for six months as a sub, where she and others "were received with great suspicion". Looking back she said she was fairly miserable because the newsroom was pretty hostile to anybody coming in from "programmes" and anyone who they thought "wasn't a real journalist".

> I'd already run up against this prejudice (when I was in Bristol trying for jobs in local radio and there were so many jobs I didn't get) and they would say 'Oh, you were at Cambridge? How do you think you can talk to real people in Bristol?' So I learned quite quickly to shut up about the fact that I was at Cambridge, and in the newsroom to shut up about the fact I was at university at all really. So anyway, there I was sitting behind a pillar, occasionally for the whole shift without writing anything. But sometimes I had things to write.

After six months the West Africa correspondent job became free and she applied for the post. "To everyone's enormous surprise I got the job and it was considered what they would call 'a bold appointment'". According to Liz, everybody was confounded by this news as Barnaby Mason had been in the running, as had Lyse Doucet. She said, "I felt very sorry about getting it over Lyse as she was already in Abidjan and knew the job". According to Liz, the consternation was not so much because she was a woman, but because she "wasn't a proper journalist", and hadn't done her time on local papers. She was also from "programmes not news" and had been to university. However, as she pointed out, she "knew her stuff". She had been to the area on reporting trips, and had been producing the programme "Focus on Africa" every day for three or four years. She thinks there was a generation gap in terms of the employment and promotion of women. At this time there were some senior women who had climbed the ranks and worked at Bush House as duty editors, and they were about to retire. It was time for her generation, who were children in the 1950s, to break through the glass ceiling (Fig. 1).

Fig. 1 Liz Blunt and Diana Goodman, the first two women foreign correspondents, photographed outside the BBC in London (1986)

She was appointed within a couple of weeks of the announcement that Diana Goodman had been made the Bonn Correspondent. In a BBC press release on 3rd April 1986, she is quoted as saying she was looking forward to her new role: "Of course I would have been proud to be the first woman appointed, but I am delighted to be the second. A growing number of women have been applying for such jobs in recent years, and I think this is now being reflected in the appointments".[1] The BBC reminded journalists in its press release that Liz had made frequent

---

[1] "New BBC West Africa Correspondent" (BBC Press Office, April 3, 1986), Telex, BBC Written Archives Centre.

visits to the region to make documentaries and had covered the last two Nigerian general elections. In another press release published four days later the corporation reported on the meeting of the two new correspondents and quoted them as saying, "We're delighted to have got the jobs and proud to be the first women the BBC has ever appointed to them".[2]

At 40, Liz set off for her new job in Abidjan, in the Ivory Coast. In the end she stayed for four years. According to Liz, the West Africa job was based in Abidjan rather than Lagos in Nigeria, because Ivory Coast had a convertible currency making it possible for the reporter to travel elsewhere. Ghana was not selected as it was suffering from a financial meltdown and the phones didn't work well. "You couldn't make international phone calls from Ghana on a Sunday unless they'd been pre-booked during the week".

On her arrival the previous correspondent wouldn't talk to her, took his contact book with him and left her nothing. He kept telling her he wasn't ready to speak to her yet and he booked her into a hotel on the other side of town. "Lyse [Doucet], bless her, came and visited me. I was fairly miserable". Liz said that on reflection she thought the previous correspondent had been okay with women as girlfriends but not so okay with women as colleagues.

Hers was a staff position and her brief was "to report anything for anybody who wants it". She reported for national radio (NCA) as well as for the World Service—programmes such as Woman's Hour, the Morning Show and The Today Programme. She could do voice tracks over television agency pictures, but she didn't have a camera for filming, "But most of my work was for World Service Radio and particularly the African Service". She started out with a Uher cassette recorder, because the BBC had finally moved on from reel-to-reel recorders at this stage. She had a telex machine to send text and an analogue telephone.

> During my time there I got given what they called a 'Tandy', which was a sort of prototype of laptop computers. And there was a way in which you could attach it to a phone line and send squeaks and whistles down

---

[2] "BBC's First Women Foreign Correspondents" (BBC Press Office, April 7, 1986), BBC Written Archives Centre.

the phone line which would be reassembled at the other end into news copy and somewhere in Fleet Street there was a 'receiving office' which reassembled it. I think it was over the Reuters office where they had copy takers and that was where the bleeps and squeaks were changed back into words for all the people who subscribed to the service, which included the BBC.

Liz had 20 countries inside her area of coverage and her editor in London thought it a good idea that she should travel to all of them in her first year. She said, "I was encouraged to go out and learn. I was based in Abidjan in the Ivory Coast. I had everything south as far as what was then called Zaire, Democratic Republic of Congo and everything as far north as Mauritania. And on the eastward side as far as the eastern border of Chad, which was the border with Sudan". She was advised to get to know the countries and meet people, get contacts and find out what was going on. During this time she was not under too much pressure to file regular stories, but she did. She got to all the bigger countries "on her patch" and the ones that spoke English and French, but didn't manage to get to the smaller Spanish or Portuguese speaking ones. She said that in those days she was left very free to find her own stories and cover them.

I asked her how the system worked if, for example, she had wanted to go to Mauritania. According to Liz:

> Well, I would call London and say something interesting is going on in Mauritania and I think I ought to get there. And they would say, yes. It's got much more difficult since. These days I would be expected to give a complete costing before I went. I would be expected to tell them exactly what stories I was going to file and who for, so they could share out the bill. But in those days as I say, my boss encouraged me to go and see what was there. And there was always something happening. There were always stories.
> Me: Did you have to say—it's going to take me five days, and I'll give you three stories?
> Liz: Well you would tell them what you planned to do, yes. And there were things where it was marginally cost-effective. I never got to Timbuktu. There was a good story there about a bad locust year in the Sahel. But the planes weren't flying at that point, and it would have taken

me something like three days to get there and three days to get back, even if there were no hitches. And really it also, apart from not being cost-effective in terms of how many stories I did, I would have been completely out of touch and unable to cover other stories in the region. And as I was the only BBC [staff] reporter for the whole of West Africa, having me out of touch for more than a week didn't seem like a good idea. So I never got to Timbuktu.

Liz worked out of her flat, which doubled as an office in Central Abidjan. During the day she had an assistant called Salifou Ouedrago who would operate the telex machine and file stories that came off it. If important people came to visit the BBC office, then they had to sit in her living room.

The story with which Liz is most associated began in earnest at the end of 1989 in Liberia. By the new year, rumours were swirling and the government was shouting that there had been a coup and so she headed over the border. She found out there had been attacks on the border and, when police had left their positions, the rebels had pushed on. She later met one of these rebels back in Abidjan, who said he wanted to return to join the fighting and suggested she should pay his bus fare back to Monrovia. "When I pointed out that this wasn't quite the thing for the BBC to pay for him to go back to fight the next-door country, he accepted with quite good grace".

Apart from the rebels, Liz was also getting information from the French and American embassies as they "were in fairly vigorous competition in West Africa at that time. So, if you wanted to know what the Americans were doing, you would ask the French and they'd probably tell you and vice versa". However, she adds, she did not always find that the embassies were that well informed. Liz made several trips to Liberia between January and September 1990 as the war gained momentum and the rebel groups, under Prince Johnson and Charles Taylor, advanced to the outskirts of the capital. In July a massacre took place at St Peter's Lutheran Church in a suburb of Monrovia; some 600 men, women and children were killed by government soldiers. Following the massacre, a group of countries banded together and formed the multilateral military force ECOMOG—the Economic Community of West African States Monitoring Group.

Liz lobbied the President of Nigeria to be allowed to go into Liberia with Nigerian troops. In September she got permission to board a merchant ship in Freetown, Sierra Leone, that was supplying oil, petrol and diesel to the expedition. On arrival in Monrovia she stayed in an empty American embassy house used by USAID, which the embassy was allowing journalists to use. There had been other journalists using the house, but by the time Liz had arrived there was nobody else there and she was alone. That night there was a lot of gunfire around the ECOMOG camp, situated on an island in the port area, where the bridges were closed. The next day Liz headed to the ECOMOG camp to find out if rumours were true that two of their people had been wounded. She entered a main building and asked a young Nigerian press officer if she could speak to the Ghanaian force commander. She was accompanied by a BBC stringer from the Hausa Service. The press officer headed upstairs. Suddenly chaos descended:

> The first thing that happened was that the president arrived. And people said, oh ECOMOG must have known that he was coming. I'm absolutely convinced they didn't know he was coming. It was a Sunday morning. Everything was very quiet, it was a complete surprise. This motorcade arrived and it's the president and his people. So, he comes in and we saw him—and the other journalist and I saw him come in the door and go upstairs to the commander's office.

President Samuel Doe didn't speak to them but they waited at the foot of the stairs with their tape recorders in case they could grab a few words from him on his departure.

> And then there was another commotion and the rebel leader [Prince Johnson] arrived with his people. And there was an awful lot of shouting and stamping about and trying to go upstairs and being persuaded to come back down or whatever. Then we could hear the sort of click of people pulling back the safety catches of their rifles. And at that point I left the main hallway and went into a side office to get out of the way. I left my portable recorder recording on top of a filing cabinet. And then

everything started happening and there was about an hour and a half of gunfire and shouting and shooting and everything.

Two of the ECOMOG troops came into the office with Liz, and barricaded the door. The other journalist had gone into another room.

They decided their job was to protect the BBC correspondent, which I was, and not go out and fight the rebels. Anyway, I was quite grateful for that. I was lying on the floor barricaded in behind furniture and things and all this was going on outside. I was thinking, this can't be real, this is like a movie, it's not happening. And then at one point I heard what I'm sure was the president's voice outside in the forecourt, outside the window saying, 'please I beg of you, you are embarrassing us'. Seems an odd sort of thing to say, but that was what he was saying. And then the sound of engines and vehicles roaring off. And in fact, that was him being taken away by Prince Johnson's people. And then of course it was quiet and eventually we crept out and there were bodies all over the hallway and the washrooms, everywhere. The Nigerian journalist, he'd gone into a different office but he was all right. We both emerged.

In the midst of the chaos, somebody had taken the tape recorders so there was no recording of what happened. Liz estimated there were about 70 bodies lying inside and outside the building. When she asked an eyewitness what had happened to President Doe, she was told the rebels had taken him away—in fact they had carried him away and he was bleeding quite heavily from upper leg wounds.

She was hustled onto a nearby Nigerian ship and made to sit there as it was the safest place. Eventually she found the car she had come in that morning, which was miraculously not riddled with bullets: "We found the driver who was the car owner's nephew. The soldiers had hidden him in the camp kitchen under a pile of saucepans and he was all right". She went into town and got hers and her colleague's stories out via an early model of satellite phone at the British embassy, where she then slept that night.

Liz still has copies of the telexes of the stories that she sent that day. The first one reads[3]:

> CUE: The President of Liberia, Samuel Kanyon Doe, has been wounded in an hour and a half long gunbattle at the headquarters of the West African peacekeeping force in the port of Monrovia, and taken into custody by rebel leader Prince Johnson. West Africa correspondent Elizabeth Blunt was there during the dramatic events.
> STORY: Fighting broke out in the headquarters office of the West African peacekeeping force at about half past one, after the president arrived with his escort to visit the force commander, General Arnold Quainoo, closely followed by Prince Johnson and a group of his followers.
> A quarrel began between the two groups, and soon rifle, machine gun and grenade fire was blazing around the headquarters building.
> An eyewitness said that President Doe was wounded in the legs and taken away by Prince Johnson and his men. When the firing finally died down, the area around the building was littered with bodies. Most of the 64 men killed belonged to the Presidential bodyguard. Liberia's acting information minister Paul Allen was among those wounded.
> General Quainoo said afterwards that both President Doe and Prince Johnson came to his office without any warning. The day's events, he said, would only complicate the task of the peacekeeping forces.
> According to unconfirmed reports, President Doe was taken to Prince Johnson's base camp on the outskirts of Monrovia, where he was seen being questioned by the rebel commander.

In the second story[4] "President Doe Shot, Abducted and toppled" (TV) she updated on further fighting in the capital and on Prince Johnson saying he would court martial the president and rule the country himself. The next story reported, "President Doe shot, abducted and overthrown",[5] and updated that President Doe was a captive of the rebel warlord Prince Johnson. During the next 48 hours Liz did many

---

[3] Elizabeth Blunt, "Doe Captured in Gun Battle" (BBC News Telexed Story 491, September 9, 1990), Telex, personal archive, E Blunt.
[4] Elizabeth Blunt, "President Doe Shot, Abducted and Toppled" (BBC News Telexed Story 492, September 9, 1990), Telex, personal archive, E Blunt.
[5] Elizabeth Blunt, "President Doe Shot, Abducted and Overthrown". (BBC News Telexed Story 493, September 9, 1990), Telex, personal archive, E Blunt.

updates—some straight news, others "colour pieces'" By the following day, Liz recounted that eyewitnesses were saying "the president is dead", and that his mutilated body was on display at the Island Clinic, a small hospital nearby.[6] An extract of her report was replayed on the BBC's digital audio app BBC Sounds in 2020. In it she sums up the escalating fighting after the news of the president's death:

> With President Doe dead and his closest associates frantically negotiating to get out of the country, the remains of the Liberian army has come under fire from Prince Johnson's rebel forces. Firing could be heard all morning from the area around the barracks. There were a few louder explosions as the troops inside the mansion used heavy cannon to bombard places on the other side of the Mesurado River where Johnson and the other rebel leader Charles Taylor have their positions. Rockets also fizzed overhead.

She filed this last story after talking to numerous people back in the port area. When she reported this to the newsroom in London she reached a very sceptical news editor who asked who these people were, stressing "You can't just go on what they say. Were they diplomats or government officials?" Liz replied that they were different groups of ordinary people but their accounts matched. In the end the BBC announced that the president was dead on this sourcing and not on the more usual "two agencies and a correspondent" criteria. Some reports said that his hands had been injured, indicating torture. Liz said a recording of him being "tormented" had done the rounds but thinks that he probably died from loss of blood due to his leg wounds.

In the days that followed, there was chaos in the capital. Liz helped the correspondent from the Hausa Service to get a voiced report out via a satellite telephone, as the phone service was down and there were no mobile phones. Everybody was very worried that the soldiers would riot. There was confusion as to who was running Liberia—was it the army chief? Was it Prince Johnson? Where was the other rebel leader, Charles Taylor? At one point three separate people were claiming to

---

[6] Elizabeth Blunt, "BBC News Story (No Title)" (BBC News Telexed Story 496, May 10, 1990), Telex, personal archive, E Blunt.

be the president of Liberia. Liz said there was very little movement in Monrovia "beyond what you could do on foot, because even if you had a car, there was no petrol. So people who had cars took the wheels off so that they couldn't be stolen". People trekked about looking for food and exchanging information. Down at the port strangers told her that they had heard what was going on from listening to her on the BBC. And as she was the only white woman in that part of town they were in no doubt about who she was and they would come and tell her information.

She had no international competition for listeners, as the Voice of America correspondent, a China specialist, happened to be still very much caught up in China news, post Tiananmen Square and he "really wasn't very interested in West Africa. The last thing he wanted to do was get mixed up in a war in Liberia". Liz busied herself filing for the BBC, ABC, CBC and NZBC. "Sometimes they would ask for a specific thing. You know, there are some Canadian nuns who had been caught up in the conflict. They wanted their own piece so I would do it for them". As always she travelled without a camera and without a phone, because taking photographs often got you into trouble and she didn't need photographs at the time, although nowadays of course in the internet age she would need both. After a few days, Liz took an American evacuation helicopter out of the country.

Liz continued to cover the civil war in Liberia until she returned to London. She worked hard as a correspondent, with occasional extra work for Commonwealth stations. She would talk to the News Intake Desk, which was staffed 24 hours a day. Sometimes on quiet weekends they would call her up asking if she had anything to offer:

> I fell afoul of some of my local colleagues over that because the Agence France-Presse (AFP) bureau and the Reuters bureau were both headed by Frenchmen. And every Sunday they and their families went for lunch at the beach. So, I didn't know but they had a pact that basically there was no news out of Abidjan on Sundays. And one Sunday morning I got a call from the boss saying, it's deathly quiet, is anything happening? Well I said, there's a small something in Ivory Coast. I can't remember now what the story was but [I said] it'll make a piece for the news. So I did it, and the other two got call-backs and they were furious.

During her time as West Africa correspondent, Liz worked around half her time off base and a lot of that time was spent in Nigeria. She travelled light: it was just her and a portable recorder, without producers or camera operators. When something big happened, she was able simply to call the News Desk and take off. On one story related to a contested candidature for leadership of a Sunni caliphate in Nigeria, Liz predicted there would be bloodshed. She informed the desk and then got on the first flight to Lagos. She said: "I travelled up to the north the next morning and they were burning the place down and I got there before Lagos-based correspondents did. So I was quite proud of that".

When Liz returned to London, she became caught up with the start of World Service Television, which she said was "very exciting" The station sent her out to Delhi for a while to see if she would be able to source television pictures locally and persuade older radio correspondents such as Mark Tully to record voice tracks for pictures. She said she found this new job only "quite interesting". She thought her career had reached a fork in the road at this time, explaining that another of "those BBC silos and cultural problems" was that if you were a "Bush person" like her, then you usually did a tour as a foreign correspondent and then you came back into the newsroom and served your time before being sent anywhere else, whereas the television culture was, "once a correspondent, always a correspondent". She dearly wanted another correspondent job, but there was nothing available at the time: "And I had to go and be a producer for people who actually weren't as good as I was". She thought some were good, but "I had a couple of real sort of twerps". She was in India during 1992 and 1993 and went on producing trips to Pakistan. At the time she wanted to do the reports herself, but now she is sanguine:

> So the result of being a good sport is that I had a long, varied and interesting career. I never succeeded in being 'a big hitter'. But you know, you try not to be temperamental.

Liz would occasionally go back to fill in for periods when correspondents were away. She did a stint when the BBC was in between Mark Doyle and David Bamford in West Africa in 1996. For a while, she was "a sort of London-based foreign correspondent in the newsroom. So I could do tracks and things based in London and I would go and fill in for people". She worked in Turkey for a while and in Lagos for a summer. She also worked on the Intake Desk and later the Intake Planning Desk. She said she enjoyed getting home and hearing or seeing pieces that she'd helped set up earlier. She stood in as a manager for a while, but didn't enjoy that as she thought it was boring. Later her father died and then her mother got sick up in Aberdeenshire and she took some time out to look after her. Thinking again about the arc of her career she returned to the sporting metaphor.

> In one way I benefited from being a safe pair of hands and a good sport. At other times I think, you know, if I'd been a bit more of a prima donna, I might have got further but then I might not have lasted as long.

She believes she may not have got some of the jobs she went for because she was a woman, but she also believes that there were other things that might have been held against her, including her degree from Cambridge. She believes class still played a part in the hiring process, and that when the BBC had a big push to get more racial diversity, she thought beneficiaries were still mostly private-school educated and were generally quite posh. So many silos. She pondered whether perhaps the World Service was better at promoting women to senior positions than the rest of the BBC. With regards to pay equality, she thought that in her time there were grades for jobs with transparent salary boundaries so that you always knew where you were, and that it wouldn't have occurred to her that men might have been paid more than her. These weren't the "personal salaries" which she thought "Carrie [Gracie] had done a splendid job" in uncovering. In referring to Carrie's case against the BBC [See Chapter 7] she thought a large part of the unfairness had been because salaries varied across the BBC between the national radio and TV services and the World Service, and because people in the latter generally earned less money than their counterparts.

Much later in her career, before she retired, Liz was asked to go out in the field again, this time as a BBC freelance correspondent based in Addis Ababa. In 2007 Liz travelled to Ethiopia to work as a "sponsored stringer". She brought forward her retirement from her staff job and moved to Addis Ababa. Ethiopia was seen as a tricky political story, and throughout the years several BBC reporters had been deported. Again, Liz reckons she was seen as a "safe pair of hands". This time her brief was just the one country.

> I covered everything—whatever came up. Addis Ababa was a great source of boring, international organisation sort of stories, because it's a big diplomatic hub. And they have a lot of conferences. It's got the UN agencies, and it's got the African Union. So that was a lot of bread and butter, some Ethiopian politics, which is very arcane, and then lovely cultural stories, because Ethiopia is so interesting.

In terms of technology, some things hadn't changed very much since her posting to Ivory Coast. Email was still only by "dial up", and there wasn't access to the proper internet. There was also only one provider which was Ethiopia Telecom. Broadband cost $1000 a month and was aimed at international organisations only, as "they [Ethiopians] didn't want their citizens getting onto the internet". There was also no text messaging service.

She did however notice some changes to "Newsgathering". It was no longer, "Well we haven't heard from Harar for a bit, so why don't you go there?" Now it was, "Well if you want to go to Harar, how much will it cost?" Newsgathering wanted to know detailed costings, which stories she would do, which programme she was doing them for, and who was going to pay for the trip. As most of the interesting stories were outside Addis, this could be annoying, even though it was "do-able". On the plus side, there were many more BBC outlets to approach as a freelancer.

The other difference she noticed was the growing role of online news. She used to dread this because if mistakes were made they were much more obvious than with a radio broadcast, where people might think they had misheard.

> The moment it was in print on news online, it was there for [the Ethiopian government] to pick over at their leisure and find things they didn't like. And like most bits of the BBC, [BBC News Online] had very little money, so, what they would do, they would take something you had sent for radio, they would squish it together with some reports from news agencies, they would stick their own headline on it and they would put it out and then my phone would start ringing with people complaining.

As these stories had her name on them she would sometimes take some flak.

> So, I did have a former colleague who by then worked for the Ethiopian Foreign Ministry who was an early riser. I remember him calling me early in the morning and saying, 'Huh? Have you seen what BBC's got online?' And I'd go, 'no, tell me'. He said, 'did you really mean to say *that*?' And I would look at it and think, 'oh god, no'. And something had been put in that I hadn't written or an unwise headline. He said, 'I think you might want to change it before people get into their offices here'. And since nobody had the internet at home normally, as long as you got it changed by sort of nine or ten in the morning, people wouldn't notice.

Over the years Liz has had reason to remember her reporting of Liberia. First of all, her accounts of the massacre at St Peter's church and of the gunbattle in which President Doe was abducted and later killed have been accessed by lawyers and interested parties who pursued some of the key people involved in these events into legal tribunals. In 2018 she was called on to testify in person in the case of former Defence Minister Jucontee Thomas Woewiyu. Her recordings of Mr Woewiyu talking about how President Doe "had to go" and that his faction would "go down to Monrovia and get him out" were played in court in Philadelphia.[7] Jackson Kanneh reported from the trial saying,

> "Blunt was a major figure in the coverage of the civil war. As a correspondent for the BBC during the early years of Liberia's civil unrest in 1989 and 1990, she braved the storm to report on the civil war that killed thousands. Her reports for the popular BBC's 'Focus on Africa' programme were one of the most reliable coverage of the war era".[8]

---

[7] "Trial Monitoring: Thomas Woewiyu", Civitas Maxima: Independent Legal Representation of Victims of War Crimes and Crimes Against Humanity, January 30, 2014, https://civitas-maxima.org/trial-monitoring-thomas-woewiyu/.

[8] Jackson Kanneh and Tecee Boley, "Former BBC Reporter Elizabeth Blunt, Ex-US Sec of State to Testify in Woewiyu Case", Front Page Africa, June 12, 2018, https://frontpageafricaonline.com/liberia-war-crimes-trial/former-bbc-reporter-elizabeth-blunt-ex-us-sec-of-state-to-testify-in-woewiyou-case/.

Her script archives were also consulted by a group in the US who brought the civil prosecution for the Lutheran church massacre. In 2021 a Pennsylvania court found Colonel Moses Thomas liable for the killings. She also gave "timeline evidence" in a preparatory case against Charles Taylor's ex-wife, Agnes Taylor, and would have given evidence but the case was dismissed.

The other legacy of Liz's years covering Liberia was the centrality of her role in reporting it for the local population. After she returned from Ivory Coast to London she heard one day from a man called the Reverend Anthony Mbolanda that he was going to open a school and would she mind if it were named after her. Liz said it was an honour and gave her permission. She would hear from the Reverend from time to time, and the school often bore the brunt of the continued fighting in the capital. Eventually the BBC's correspondent Mark Doyle tracked down the school and handed over some money and teaching materials from Liz. In return Liz was happy to see the kids outside a building called the "Elizabeth Blunt School". She formed a committee and for the next three decades they supported the school through fund-raising for scholarships and to buy books, footballs and build and maintain classrooms. Despite the endless bad news from Liberia there are small moments of hope. Liz recounts excitedly how one primary school scholarship pupil called Rita eventually made it through to university after traversing many obstacles.

> She obviously was extremely bright. She then went to the University of Monrovia and studied mass communication. I paid her fees and she earned her keep trading in the market with her mother—braiding hair, dressmaking, anything she could do. And then the university kept opening and closing. They had university strikes, they had Ebola, they had this, that and the other and finally, finally she has graduated. She has got a job stringing for 'Voice of America'. Wow. She's getting married. Gosh, she's a lovely girl. Very, very nice girl. So if we did nothing else other than educate Rita, we have done something.

Liz was never one to overstate her role or that of journalists. I remember an occasion in the BBC World newsroom back in 1992 when she incurred the wrath of the programme editor of a review of the week as she had edited off the pieces to camera (PTCs) from the BBC's journalists around the world showing them in situ. When asked why, she announced that she didn't believe in "the cult of personality". This approach to her job and the dangers involved can be perceived when she listened to a recording of one of stories from Liberia and reflected back on her career for a programme on "Focus on Africa" in 2020:

> "I might say I'm surprised how brave I was but there was nothing else you could do really, except shut your eyes, try and keep calm, and wait for it to be over and not be a nuisance to anybody. These days, the reporter would be a very dramatic figure. But at that point we understated ourselves. I tried to keep myself out of the story. None of this, 'There I was the gallant girl reporter hiding under a table while the President was captured'. It was all very plain, very low key."[9]

In retirement Liz has helped out with various charities associated with Africa. She has returned to the continent many times as part of an international election observer group called "Democracy Volunteers". She is an active member of her local community and a volunteer gardener at Kew Gardens. Her other great love is drawing and painting which she does regularly with a London-based arts group, and she travels to painting classes abroad whenever she can.

References

"BBC's First Women Foreign Correspondents." BBC Press Office, April 7, 1986. BBC Written Archives Centre.
Blunt, Elizabeth. "BBC News Story (No Title)." BBC News Telexed Story 496, May 10, 1990. Telex, personal archive, E Blunt.
Blunt, Elizabeth. "Doe Captured in Gun Battle." BBC News Telexed Story 491, September 9, 1990. Telex, personal archive, E Blunt.
Blunt, Elizabeth. "President Doe Shot, Abducted and Overthrown." BBC News Telexed Story 493, September 9, 1990. Telex, personal archive, E Blunt.

---

[9] "Elizabeth Blunt Looks Back at Her Career Reporting on Liberia", *Focus on Africa*, 2020, Programme no longer on website.

Blunt, Elizabeth. "President Doe Shot, Abducted and Toppled." BBC News Telexed Story 492, September 9, 1990. Telex, personal archive, E Blunt.

Civitas Maxima: Independent Legal Representation of Victims of War Crimes and Crimes Against Humanity. "Trial Monitoring: Thomas Woewiyu," January 30, 2014. https://civitas-maxima.org/trial-monitoring-thomas-woewiyu/.

"Elizabeth Blunt Looks Back at Her Career Reporting on Liberia." *Focus on Africa*, 2020. Programme no longer on website.

Kanneh, Jackson, and Tecee Boley. "Former BBC Reporter Elizabeth Blunt, Ex-US Sec of State to Testify in Woewiyu Case." Front Page Africa, June 12, 2018. https://frontpageafricaonline.com/liberia-war-crimes-trial/former-bbc-reporter-elizabeth-blunt-ex-us-sec-of-state-to-testify-in-woewiyou-case/.

"New BBC West Africa Correspondent." BBC Press Office, April 3, 1986. Telex. BBC Written Archives Centre.

Lyse Doucet, CM, OBE, Chief International Correspondent
Previously worked as a correspondent in Ivory Coast, Pakistan, Afghanistan, Jordan and Israel

"It was a time where you could take out a map, and say right, where does the BBC not have anybody?"

I arranged to meet Lyse Doucet outside Broadcasting House in Central London. It had been more than 20 years since I worked with her last and we live in different countries, but we have kept up with each other via social media. It was a warm spring day, and the BBC piazza was bustling: a number of people came up to shake hands with her from both inside and outside the building. Lots of them congratulated her on her recent coverage of Ukraine. And among the people who were delighted to say hello was Paddy O'Connell, presenter of the national Radio Four programme "Broadcasting House". Lyse had been a recent guest on the programme talking about Ukraine and he wanted to have her on again. They swapped possible dates and then he asked what we were doing loitering around out there. Lyse explained that we were hunting for a quiet spot to do the interview. "Go to the BBC Club" he insisted. God bless Lyse: she didn't even know where it was. Paddy took us around, swiped us in, and dropped us off at a quiet table near the bar.

© The Author(s), under exclusive license to Springer Nature Switzerland AG 2025
C. Murrell, *BBC Women Reporting the World*,
https://doi.org/10.1007/978-3-031-85198-8_5

Lyse is known in particular for her decades of frontline reporting, her commitment to countries such as Afghanistan and her still strong Canadian accent. She addresses the last of these without my even mentioning it: "I would be an unlikely and—in the early years—a very undesirable person to work for the BBC. I'm not British, I don't have a British accent and that did matter in those years. Probably it still does matter a little bit. But I think the numbers now are insignificant. It's not an issue anymore, but it was back then". She said that when she was growing up in Bathurst, New Brunswick, Britain was about cultural references such as Mary Poppins and the Beatles, which were all very far away and exotic.

Lyse's ancestors were Acadian and Irish, and she grew up in an Anglophone household. The small community was 60% English speaking and 40% French and it was "a very egalitarian place". Her life was secure and bound by "a benign religious ethos" which included the presence of such institutions as the Catholic Women's League and the Knights of Columbus, whose members made tea and sandwiches at funerals. She and her sister were "altar boys"—as she describes them—before the Pope said that was acceptable. She was from a family of six children, all of whom, like her, would go on to be high school presidents. In her primary school she had been part of a "naughty gang" influenced by their older siblings and there was a lot of drinking, even in grade six, but she pulled herself out of this circle because her family was hardworking and committed to education. She believes her family values were "probably middle to working class". Her father was a mill supervisor, and her mother didn't work. One of the things she recalls at school was being the first to borrow a book from the new library and one of her first tomes was called "How to be a Journalist".

After school Lyse went to Queen's University in Kingston, Ontario. "It was a very posh university" which took in the sons and daughters of rich families and prime ministers, and she considered this was the biggest culture change she had ever experienced, even up to today. At Queen's she studied politics and political science, graduating in 1980. After Queen's she proceeded to the University of Toronto where she enrolled in an MA in International Relations, "and somewhere along the way, I decided I wanted to be a journalist" and to work in foreign news.

Toronto opened up her world to "infinite possibilities as it was very international". She even found herself taking a module in African agriculture. One of her early role models was Ann Medina, the American Canadian foreign correspondent for the public broadcaster CBC who reported from all over the world including from Northern Ireland, Nicaragua, and Lebanon. Another woman she admired was Barbara Frum, a presenter of the current affairs programme, "The Journal". After university, she joined the Canadian NGO "Crossroads International" where she made lifelong friends and signed up to become an NGO volunteer "somewhere in the world". Because her name was French and she spoke some of the language, she was sent to Côte d'Ivoire (Ivory Coast). In 1982 she packed her flip flops, some sandals and a backpack and settled in Abidjan.

Almost immediately she started to freelance as a journalist from there and also from Senegal. She had her first article published in the "West Africa Magazine". The article was about the establishment of the Pan African News Agency. A short while later she returned to Canada and was interviewed in 1983 for the African Development Bank which brought her back to Ivory Coast, and it was there that she met the BBC West Africa Correspondent Alexander Thomson. This was the first time there had been a BBC bureau in Abidjan and the post covered 20 countries. Lyse set out to freelance alongside him, covering the second-tier stories while he did the headline ones.

She laughed saying, "I always joke and say, there I was, wrong accent, wrong CV, wrong ancestry. And, you know, God came down from the heavens and said, you know, give Lyse a job. And really if anyone looked back at that, you know, they would never have hired me". She thinks she was in the right place at the right time but doesn't say she was "lucky" because "you make your own luck". The BBC office was next to Reuters, so she began to work for the news agency as well. Later *The Independent* opened and it had "a mission to have African news on the front page and not on the inside pages". Lyse was able to help with that mission because there was so much African news—from a drought in the Sahel to a string of political coups.

Her broadcast stories provoked a myriad of complaints to the BBC concerning her accent, along the lines of, "Can't you find people with

British accents?" It was around the same time that the BBC was experimenting with putting Scottish and Welsh newsreaders on air for the first time and Lyse thinks she slid in comparatively unnoticed because there were audience ructions all round. There were also plenty of complaints when she did a story on erectile dysfunction and said the word "penis" on air. Alexander Thomson had "conniptions" and told her this wasn't allowed. But Lyse assured him that African listeners enjoyed it and thought it hilarious. Lyse continued to work from Abidjan after Liz Blunt became the West Africa Correspondent (see Chapter 3) and to conduct coverage from nearby countries, including Nigeria.

After five years based in Ivory Coast, she decided to head to London for a while to work in the Bush House World Service newsroom. However, visas proved to be a challenge and securing a work permit was much harder than she had imagined. Eventually the British Deputy High Commissioner in Lagos talked to the Home Office (without telling her), and she got sponsored by the "West Africa Committee[1]" to work in London for six months. Twenty years later in Jerusalem she met the British ambassador to Lebanon, a woman who told her that she was responsible for sponsoring her. According to Lyse she has often been helped in her career by "the kindness of strangers" and she tries to return that kindness whenever she can.

Lyse remembers herself as "shiny eyed" to be in the British capital where the radio used to incant "This is London". Lyse completed her six months of writing and reporting, including working on UK-based stories. She was asked to extend her stay but decided it was time to go back in the field. Her heart was set on Pakistan, which she researched whenever she had the time. She went to the Persian Service, the Urdu Service and the Pashto Service offering to do stories for them, but they all told her they had people in situ already. This didn't stop Lyse and she headed off to Karachi to freelance again.

> It was a time where you could take out a map, and say right, where does the BBC not have anybody? And I remember sitting in an office

---

[1] The West Africa Committee was formed in 1956 to aid economic development in English-speaking West African countries.

and thinking OK, they have a correspondent in Islamabad, but there's nobody in Iran and there's nobody in Afghanistan. So, I started plotting to get to these places. Call it the foolishness of youth or whatever. Then I settled on Quetta, in [Pakistan's] Baluchistan province and there was nobody there.

Lyse started freelancing from Quetta in 1988 and the World Service foreign language services in Bush House started using her pieces and she was getting great feedback. In Quetta she met Hamid Karzai and other Afghan notables who would later form a government in Kabul. She was sent to Peshawar to report on the Afghan war and covered the return of Benazir Bhutto to Pakistan. Then one day an editor back in London asked her pointedly if she'd ever thought of working for the American channel National Public Radio (NPR), as he considered "that might be better in the long run". She couldn't believe that after all the risks she had taken, this person was encouraging her to work for another organisation. She called a more senior manager and asked if they wanted her to stay or if she should stop taking the risks and return to London. This person insisted that she stay, and so this became her policy thereafter whenever she encountered colleagues who said to her that she wasn't "good enough, or senior enough or didn't sound the right way". She would go over their heads and check out what the policy was and how much news management wanted her.

When the BBC Pakistan correspondent job became vacant, she threw her hat into the ring, even though it was "too senior for me at the time". She didn't get the job but hoped the BBC would make a new Indochina correspondent post and her next plan was to apply for that. According to Lyse, when the new Pakistan correspondent arrived, he said to BBC management that he didn't want Lyse in Pakistan as he wanted his partner to do the available freelancing. He asked them to "get her out". Again, what Lyse refers to as "the kindness of strangers" came to her rescue. She lobbied somebody at the UN who had a word with the Afghan president's International Affairs Adviser to see if she could get a visa to Afghanistan. The BBC hadn't had a visa for a decade and all of a sudden Lyse had secured one. Lyse flew into Kabul on Christmas Day

1988 and found herself in the middle of a huge international story – the Soviet troop withdrawal from Afghanistan. Apart from reporter Nik Gowing (then with ITN) there were few other journalists there at the time.

By January 1989 she was being urged by the British embassy to leave Afghanistan, or she risked not being able to leave later. She paced the floor of her hotel room wondering what to do next. Other journalists who were there were also deliberating. The Irish head of UNICEF in Kabul said to her, "the Mujahidin are coming—they will rape and kill you. You'd better not stay". But she decided to ignore this advice as she was keen to remain. By February 1989 the Soviet withdrawal was "the biggest story on the planet and I was the headline story every day". The British foreign secretary Geoffrey Howe said in parliament that he had been listening to her on the radio.

> But by then I had fallen in love with Afghanistan and there was nothing in me that felt scared of staying. And also, the BBC was listened to by about 95% of the population in the refugee camps, which was by then around six million refugees. And there was a story, I don't think it was apocryphal, that at night in the war the frontlines would fall silent because both sides would listen either to BBC Persian or BBC Pashto on the radio to find out who was winning the war. And so of course all my dispatches were being translated. And you had a real sense of purpose and meaning. It is every journalist's dream to be right smack in the middle of history, to do journalism which has meaning to where you are broadcasting -- to the world and in Afghanistan.

Not long afterwards a Moscow correspondent turned up in Kabul insisting that from then on he would be taking over and reporting from Kabul instead of her. Lyse turned again to the BBC managers back in London and they supported her, "saying no doubt—never mind the funny accent, Lyse is going to continue to report" and he would too. Lyse then applied successfully for the new position of "Indochina correspondent", but before she took up the post she found out that the correspondent in Pakistan was leaving and so she reapplied for that job, insisting that if she obtained it she would be the correspondent for Pakistan *and* Afghanistan. She was successful and after a short break back

Fig. 1 Lyse Doucet dressed as a man in order to travel to the frontline in Afghanistan to meet Mujahideen Commander Jalaluddin Haqqani, pictured on the left (1991)

in Canada to see her family, she moved to Islamabad in 1989 where she remained reporting on the two countries until 1993. During this period, she also visited Iran which was added to "her patch" as there was nobody else there from the BBC. Meanwhile she kept lobbying on the BBC's behalf to open a bureau in Tehran (Fig. 1).

In a film called "No Man's Land" by Shelley Saywell (1994) Lyse was one of a handful of women journalists profiled.[2] She came across as passionate, committed and determined. The narration stated, "At 35, Lyse Doucet is single and nomadic, often living out of a suitcase for months at a time". It examined her dangerous assignments in multiple locations and then added, "But it's Afghanistan that has stolen her heart. She comes back often because she can't leave the story or her friends".

---

[2] *No Man's Land: Women Frontline Journalists*, 1995.

In one memorable scene she walked into the base camp of Gulbuddin Hekmatyar, the renegade prime minister and former Mujahideen leader, who stood accused of responsibility for the rocket attacks on Kabul that had caused the deaths of thousands of residents. She confronted him head on about this and about the many threats he had broadcast against BBC journalists. She asked him if he had lifted the death threats against her BBC team, while his men looked increasingly tense. He replied, "there is no threat" and she countered by challenging that he had made them on his own radio station. He replied "No"; and she countered, "You deny it?" Later she is seen on this film whispering to the BBC Pashto journalist Mirwais Jalil. She can be heard saying about Hekmatyar, "he never admits to anything". Mirwais agreed. Two weeks later Mirwais was killed, after returning from another visit to Hekmatyar, this time in the company of an Italian journalist. He was kidnapped and the next day his body was found in the outskirts of Kabul.[3] David Loyn in his book, "In Afghanistan" (2009) goes as far as to write he was "murdered on Hekmatyar's orders".[4]

After her posting to Pakistan and Afghanistan she returned to London for the obligatory "get to know the newsroom again" tour after yet more visa and work permit problems. The BBC at this point had to justify to the visa authorities why it needed Lyse in London. She laughed, venturing they might have said "she was the best thing since sliced bread". She worked for BBC World TV as a reporter, filming TV packages and doing two-ways. She also returned to cover Iran from time to time, until the fatwa on Salman Rushdie,[5] when this then became impossible.

It was around this time that the BBC announced it was going to open an office in Jordan. She didn't think this would be particularly exciting, but she was interested in the larger Middle East sphere and particularly

---

[3] "A Bullet Aimed at the Media", *New Straits Times*, October 7, 1994, Google News, https://news.google.com/newspapers?nid=1309&dat=19941007&id=mzhOAAAAIBAJ&sjid=UxMEAAAAIBAJ&pg=1960,2982932&hl=en.

[4] David Loyn, *In Afghanistan: Two Hundred Years of British, Russian and American Occupation* (London: St Martin's Press, 2009).

[5] Salman Rushdie is a novelist whose fourth novel, *The Satanic Verses* (1988), incurred the wrath of Iran's leader Ruhollah Khomeini who issued a public 'fatwa' calling for his death.

in the Israel-Palestine story. She was successful in her application and went out to Amman to open the bureau in 1994 with a roving brief for the region and she covered the start of the Jordan-Israel talks.

Within six months a Jerusalem job came up. By then she loved her life in Amman, and she noted that there were a lot of candidates for the Jerusalem job. A number of people from the bureau said to her, "You know Lyse, you should stay in Jordan. Jordan is such a good thing". Lyse let the deadline go by, but then one evening, while having dinner at the American Colony Hotel in East Jerusalem, she was persuaded by BBC producer Jane Logan and CTV reporter Paul Workman to apply anyway. Between them they convinced her Jerusalem would always be "the most important place on earth" and that there was no comparison between being in Amman and being in Jerusalem. They argued she would always be doing "the second or third story" or "doing the Jerusalem story from Amman". Lyse said she had a feeling that London wanted the post to go to a man. In the end the deadline was reopened for her, and after being asked during the board "to pronounce Israel" a number of times—checking once again on her accent—she got the job and relocated in 1995.

She ended up working in Jerusalem alongside Jeremy Bowen, Stephen Sackur and later Paul Adams. By this time BBC World TV was at full strength and Lyse decided to carve out a niche, doing some presenting and leaning on her strengths in this competitive environment. She maintains she has a very good short-term memory and can memorise a half hour of scripts without any autocue. She loved the challenge of live TV and radio and that became "her thing". Not being British, she didn't focus on what ITN was doing and was more interested in what CNN was doing. Again, she wasn't obsessed with which reporter was chosen for the "Nine O'clock News" (then the main bulletin on the BBC national TV channel), and she was also aware that there was an editor on the Nine who "preferred a British accent". But she threw herself into the Israel story and spent the next few years reporting from Jerusalem and sometimes from Afghanistan. By this time Hamid Karzai, whom she had met a decade earlier in Quetta, was the leader of Afghanistan. Meanwhile she continued to make significant connections in Israel and loved the variety of stories concerning everything from religion, to culture and conflict.

On the other hand, the suicide bombings meant that there was a constant flow of hard news and everything in her life got interrupted. Some four years after arriving she decided she needed a break from travelling and from the constant fear of bombings.

In 1999 she headed back to the UK and applied for a full-time presenting role on BBC World TV. She said she "wasn't your classic presenter but they were looking for people who had correspondent experience". At first, she simply enjoyed being back in London, reading, walking, visiting friends and family and living a fairly normal life. However, when the Syrian President Hafez al-Assad died in 2000 she picked up the phone to Damascus to ask for a visa and went off to cover the funeral. Then 9/11 happened and Lyse spent three months shuttling back and forth between Pakistan and Afghanistan. Following this change to her working schedule, her role transformed into the roving job, based in London, that she has done ever since: visiting and revisiting conflict zones. A few years later, at the instigation of a BBC editor, she acquired a new title—Chief International Correspondent, which she admits can be handy. At first, she dismissed such a need but then later thought,

> Once you have a title, you have a chair, and no one can take that chair from you. And I think maybe I understood that that would be a vulnerability for me going forward. So, I now have this bit of furniture, and I don't wear it on my sleeve. And in the same way I don't use OBE or Order of Canada. I don't use those things.

Lyse prefers a philosophy of "by dint of what you do, you will be judged". In her current role she is often returning to places where she has spent time before such as Israel and other countries in the Middle East. This means that having lived through some of a place's history she can draw on contacts and context and "add to the BBC's coverage: not subtract from it". But this doesn't stop her going to new places and employing "a fresh eye". She gives the example of Georgia in the Caucasus, saying she demurred when she was first asked to go there in 2008, when Russia invaded parts of the country. She argued there were better people to go than her, correspondents who had more knowledge and spoke the language. But when she agreed she was pleased as,

"Every place you visit, it changes the map of your mind. Because I understood Russia through Afghanistan or through its relationships in Africa. And suddenly my map expanded a bit more and I saw these countries—Afghanistan, Central Asia, Georgia—differently".

Over the past two decades she has reported from the majority of the world's most significant trouble spots—in particular Afghanistan and more recently in Ukraine, Israel and Sudan. She covered the Indian Ocean tsunami in 2004 in both India and Indonesia. She won an Edward Murrow award for coverage of the Arab Spring for her reporting in countries such as Libya, Egypt and Tunisia (2010–2012), and an Emmy in 2014 for coverage of Syria. Again, Lyse had secured a visa when others at the BBC couldn't, because of her lifetime of networking. Over the years, apart from her day-to-day reporting, she has also done a number of set piece documentaries and podcast series. The topics she has covered include children in Gaza, Syria, and two rounds of a five-part series of interviews with remarkable women called "Her Story Made History" (2018 and 2019). Lyse reported daily from Kabul during the Taliban takeover of Afghanistan in August 2021, and then recorded a 10-part podcast series called "A Wish for Afghanistan" (2021).

By February 2022, she was presenting, reporting and doing lives from a hotel roof in Kyiv, alongside fellow BBC reporter and presenter Clive Myrie. Once again, they had to decide if they would stay or leave, and again they decided to stay. Women journalists came to the fore in this war with reporters such as Sarah Rainsford and Orla Guerin in particular doing outstanding coverage. In February 2023 I took a screenshot of my TV screen on finding three senior women sharing a split screen and all being interviewed—Katya Adler (Europe Editor), Sarah Smith (North America Editor) and Laura Kuenssberg (Political Editor). While it has become increasingly normalised to see one woman at a time being interviewed from the field, this was the first time I had seen an entire set of senior women editors debating the topic of war and its reverberations.

When the conflict in Gaza erupted in October 2023, Lyse was there again. She reported from close to the Gaza Strip and from Jerusalem. This has been a frustrating war for foreign correspondents as the Israeli authorities have refused them access to Gaza except in embedded trips, accompanied by the army. Instead the war inside Gaza was reported by the BBC's Palestinian reporter Rushdi Abualouf (who was later brought out of Gaza with his family) and other brave and talented local reporters who remain behind. The BBC is one of 60 broadcasters and news organisations from around the world who have signed a letter calling for access to Gaza.[6]

Aside from her Canadian heroines Ann Medina and Barbara Frum, Lyse hadn't grown up with British touchstones. Since becoming a journalist she has also spent most of her career on the road, not even being able to see BBC news programmes. But she admits she loved Jeremy Paxman for "his questions and his curiosity" and Owen Bennett-Jones, for what Paxman once described as "the danger in his interviews". Regarding herself, she says she is endlessly curious, always reading, and never being able to say no to more learning. Her earliest plans involved wanting to go to as many different places as possible and to learn about all their different cultures.

She has more latitude now in choosing her stories, because the BBC knows that when, or if needed, she will agree to stay three months in Kabul or Jerusalem or six weeks in Ukraine. When she is at home, she likes to live "a local life", catching up with her close friends such as Channel 4 News's Lindsey Hilsum, walking by the canal, going to the gym, and meditating. She works a lot, but she also likes time to unwind, to read books, and to listen to language tapes. She makes space for the important things—such as her mother's 90th birthday celebrations—and she can sometimes afford to say no to work. She adds that both the strength and the weakness of the BBC is that "there are far too many of us. Like I say regarding Lindsey—At Channel 4 News—there are four people covering the world. But at the BBC there are four people, most of them white, middle-class men, chasing after the same story". She believes she is open about her intentions with editors of Newsgathering about where she is planning to go and expects them to be equally open with her. She works her contacts methodically, saying she won't disrupt other people's plans and always states her intentions. However, if someone does

---

[6] "Open Letter Published from News Organisations Calls for Access to Gaza", Sky News, July 11, 2024, https://news.sky.com/story/open-letter-published-from-news-organisations-calls-for-acc ess-to-gaza-13176605.

stab her in the back, they can expect this to be reciprocated "and I have better contacts".

There is a hierarchy at the BBC that is hard to appreciate from outside the organisation. A reporter can become identified with a particular programme or radio station and then they aren't seen as being suitable for another. At the BBC it is often accepted that the pinnacle of a day's reporting on BBC1 is the Ten o'clock news bulletin followed by Newsnight (perhaps before the recent cuts in 2024). On Radio 4 it's the Today programme, followed by The World at One and PM. BBC World TV and BBC World Service Radio are different beasts: they used to be seen by many in NCA Newsgathering as the poor relations, but this is meant to be no longer the case. In 2023 BBC World TV was amalgamated with BBC News 24 to become the BBC News channel.

Along with the big title, Lyse was also given a permanent producer. The first of these, Melanie Marshall, had very good connections to Newsnight. So, Lyse would prioritise BBC World and Newsnight for her films and the pair performed extremely well. At the end of their first year together Newsnight Editor Peter Rippon wanted to put their work forward for an RTS award, "but then the men freaked out", according to Lyse. When the war in Syria began in 2003, many "big name" male reporters at the BBC began chasing Syrian visas, but the Syrian government contacted Lyse to offer her one. A senior news executive later said to the Newsnight Editor Liz Gibbons that they had given the visa "to the wrong person". The Newsnight Editor meanwhile thought she had the right person.

Lyse insists that so much in journalism comes down to contacts as "access is the big thing in journalism". She always stays in touch with people. Also, she often swaps contacts and information with trusted friends, and she believes good karma sends her information back. She and Lindsey Hilsum, whom she describes as her "journalistic twin" have for years shared contacts and visa workaround information. "She started out in East Africa, and I started at the same time in West Africa". This collegiality works well for them, and they have each other's backs. They have also faced many of the same challenges within workplaces and out on the road.

Lyse operates well with many other BBC correspondents and mentioned particularly in our interview Shaimaa Khalil, Orla Guerin and Secunder Kermani,[7] now with Channel 4 News. She explained how she and Secunder split the workload in Kabul in 2021 so that they could service the BBC World TV audience properly, "because the BBC World audience really matters". They agreed to take it in daily turns to do lives (for World TV) or packaging. This was uniquely egalitarian and "the BBC was thrilled". She doesn't like it when somebody tries to impose a hierarchy: "You know titles are great, but we're all journalists". She acknowledged, without naming names, that some reporters will "grab the lives" on the Ten O'clock domestic bulletin. But Lyse argues that "you have to create space for the new ones coming through".

The business of her accent is something that Lyse has returned to repeatedly. She feels that when she started out, it was problematic because it wasn't seen as English like most other people's English. She has had it mentioned to her many times over and people on interview boards have asked her to pronounce certain words to make sure they find it acceptable. Lyse was sent to voice lessons with "a Henry Higgins character" who decided not to change her accent but to work on her emphasis and to make sure that it always spoke to her understanding in a sentence. For example, he would say to her it's not, "In *the* elections held today in Lagos", instead it is "In the elections held *today*, in *Lagos*..." She made sure she always remembered this and took her time to get things right. She thought the man was very kind, and that "he knew what was happening to me". She remembers quizzing one of the editors when she didn't get a posting she was after. She asked him if he had wanted a British accent. He confirmed that "yes", he had wanted a British accent. But sometimes her lack of a British accent helps her disorientate the unfriendly, because people can't immediately place her by class or where she'd grown up or gone to school. Lyse says she came from a remote place and with an unconventional background, and that (like Diana Goodman, see Chapter 2), her accent put her outside an easy to define class and background. She also feels that Canadians don't have the same constraints of British culture where there's an unspoken rule that you

---

[7] Secunder Kermani is now a foreign correspondent for Channel Four News.

must stay in your lane, and not rise above yourself. Once in Pakistan when another British correspondent was moaning about having to do the BBC Radio 4 piece that night, Lyse offered to do it for him because the story was fascinating. She said, "I'll do the story if you don't think it's worth doing, or if you're a bit tired". He immediately stopped her and said, "Oh no, no. They want *me* to do it". After that, with her "blunt Canadian" persona, she would call people at their word, playing dumb and exposing the fallacy in their arguments.

Lyse tells young journalists that they have to know *why* they are doing what they're doing if they come to the BBC as they are going to face a lot of challenges. It might be class, it might be race, colour or accent. She believes they need to understand that it must be worth it for them. For Lyse the goal was all about the journalism and for her, the BBC was a passport to doing the kind of reporting she wanted to do. She confirmed she had never been stopped by the BBC from going anywhere because she was a woman, unlike female reporters she knew in other places, such as ABC America. But for her the problem was often her male colleagues—people who tried to undermine her or argue that *they* should do a particular story when they knew she was pitching it. She is a spiritual person, taking in parts of many different religions as her belief system and she believes in karma. She theorises that when people undermine you it will ultimately come back to bite them. She also thinks that good karma (and excellent connections) have helped her to access stories, visas and useful connections. When something doesn't appear to work out to her advantage, she is resilient and finds that something good always comes from a strange turn in fortunes.

Lyse argues that although journalism is "very, very competitive", you have to enjoy the journalism, and often you get better access or stories when working cooperatively with others on the ground. She gives an example of helping others, like the photographer and writer Nick Danziger, when she lived in Kabul and was based in room 136 at the Intercontinental Hotel. It was almost impossible to get phone calls in and out of Kabul in 1988–9 and the handful of calls a day had to go through "the Glasgow [telephone] exchange". In the end they knew her so well, that when people asked the Glasgow Exchange to put them through to the foreign ministry in Kabul, the exchange knew that wouldn't work, so they would put the caller straight through to Lyse at the Intercontinental. When Nick Danziger called, needing a visa, Lyse put in a local call to persuade somebody at the foreign ministry to issue one. Then when Iran's Ayatollah Khomeini died in 1989, Nick returned the favour and they worked together to secure flights to Bandar Abbas, where Nick knew you didn't need a visa if you landed on a particular day at a particular time.

She has also observed how journalism can make people behave badly and thinks that sometimes media outlets—she mentions the *New York Times*—seem to actively set correspondents against each other, believing it will bring out the best in people, but she surmises it often has the opposite effect. "It makes you competitive. It makes you look over your shoulder. It makes your success contingent on the failure of others". She thinks she is highly competitive when needed but hopes her focus at the BBC has been to find the countries to work in which are often unpopular, difficult or where she has particular contacts and context. When she has hit roadblocks, she has tried to manoeuvre around them through negotiation. "There have been different moments when I could have been knocked off course. And you know, fast forward 30 plus years and you know, like I'm part of the furniture".

She has always taken calculated risks and repeats there would be no journalism at all without kindness. She also believes you should remember all the other members of the team—such as producers, fixers, camera operators—because she wouldn't be where she is without them.

> First of all, the people like me get far more attention, I mean here you are interviewing me today. And the people who are down at the coalface on the technical side, get far *less* attention in every single way. So, you know, the Persians have this expression about the tree with the greatest amount of fruit should bend the lowest.

People tell her they think she's extraordinarily brave, but she replies that the Ukraine production manager Kate Peters is every bit as brave, as are the whole team who stayed in Kyiv to keep the show on the road.

This is the best job in the world. Obviously, journalism is defined by the questions we ask or don't ask. We all get interested in different things and they define us over a career—what I have looked at or not looked at, what Orla [Guerin]'s looked at or Caroline Wyatt has looked at, the places we went, the stories we did. But the fact that we can go anywhere in the world, knock on a door, and say 'Hi—I'm Caroline Wyatt, Orla Guerin or Lyse Doucet from the BBC and can I ask you a question?' And they say 'yes'. And if they say 'no', well that's a story too. And I just think we are incredibly privileged to work for the BBC, which as I said, has been my passport to travel. [...] But I have to be clear, it's great that people recognise my name, but it's connected to what I do with the BBC, and if I left and went freelance, it wouldn't be that simple. Let's be clear eyed about this—it's the combination of being who we are and the weight of the BBC. You know you're only ever as good as your next story.

Lyse has thought long and hard about the question—do women cover wars differently from men? She acknowledges that because people still ask this question, there must be something in our culture that shows that this is still not resolved, and that people are interested in how women report on war. She assures me there are as many women who are interested in ballistics, bombs and bullets as there are women who are interested in "the human element". At one point during the war in Ukraine she remembers "someone on the Ten" noting that it was Lyse, Orla and Sarah (Rainsford) who were in Kyiv and it was Mark Lowen and Fergal Keane who were covering the refugees. She thinks that these days the human story is always front and centre in the way that wars are covered.

> Because every war is a humanitarian catastrophe, and the tactics of wars, the siege, etc., is a story about a human cost, a terrifying human cost. So, it's part and parcel of the main story.

In countries such as Afghanistan, where men control access to people, she has often had to negotiate for hours with village elders to meet women. Once, when she finally got through, she encountered feisty women who wanted to get their stories across and be heard. This, she thinks, is why men try to control women—because they know they might criticise them or have strong opinions. In societies that aren't as strict or "traditional" as Afghanistan but where there is a "certain amount of bravado or machismo and it's war and men have to be really, really tough" she thinks men can be much more open with women reporters. She has had a number of African army commanders and NATO commanders reveal surprising stories about themselves and then break down crying in front of her. She believes they can talk to women more easily and show vulnerability.

She also underlines that women, even in societies such as ours, would be much more open to talking about the awful things that have happened to them or to other women than they would be in talking to men, "unless perhaps it is men like Fergal Keane or Allan Little" who have covered very dramatic stories very sensitively. She references Allan Little's extensive coverage of rape as a weapon of war in the former Yugoslavia. But otherwise, she thinks that female reporters' abilities in securing and conducting interviews is not so different from men; it's just part of their character's makeup, just like there are some people who are friendlier than others or some who are more interested in other people. She generally has a friendly approach and thinks that is fine as long as you don't pull your punches. She does tend to ask a president about their partner and family and is happy to make small talk before beginning an interview, while appreciating this approach is not for everyone. She wonders whether being Canadian may be partly related to her general friendliness in these matters. Over the years, Lyse's brief has morphed from pure field reporting to more analysis and also "live two ways". She says Orla Guerin and Jeremy Bowen are more focused on the packaging of TV stories whereas she likes to try different things and works across all programmes in both the national and World Service programming. She repeats that one of her best talents is her formidable short-term memory which allows her to be an "explainer-in-chief".

Lyse, like Kate Adie before her, has had to renegotiate her salary over the years, a long time before Carrie Gracie took the BBC to court over equal pay. She said the problem was working out what other people—especially men—earned. She decided when she started being a presenter for BBC World TV and radio (and also for the Ten and the Today programmes), that the person who was most like her was probably Nik Gowing and so she would go into negotiations asking that she be paid in a similar way to him. She felt that several of her bosses obfuscated on this front, and she was told several times that she couldn't go abroad until she'd signed her new contract. In the end, armed with her self-respect, her sister's advice, the Harvard Business School's book "Getting to Yes" and having a financial number in mind, she would be more demanding. When Richard Sambrook took over as head of news, she demanded a 20 + percent salary increase, which he agreed to but had to take to the board. Several other managers tried to talk her down. She stuck to her guns. She thinks women don't like to talk about money because it makes them look like they're doing the job just for the money. But she believed that she had to do it for other women. In later years (when Carrie Gracie took up the cudgels), she said lots of men did finally reveal what they earned. She recounted that Allan Little would show them his P60s, and reporters such as Wyre Davies were also open about the unfairness of the system. She categorises herself as having "velvet elbows" in the fight for better pay.

Lyse has won many awards over her lifetime and has a long list of honorary doctorates from British and Canadian universities. She has an OBE (2014) and an Order of Canada (2018). Yet she is adamant that she doesn't see journalism as a career, because "journalism is not nine to five, journalism is a way of living, it's a lifestyle [...] because when you start travelling, you don't know when you're coming back. Go to Ukraine, you don't know when you're coming back, because the story will stay with you. And you will stay with the story". She thinks there is a passion about journalism, and it becomes part of who you are. Lyse doesn't talk about partners or children that she might have had, but she does address the latter through discussing a friend of hers, an ABC correspondent called Deb Whitman. Deb chose to give up her job in Jerusalem and return home and have children. She has since pondered with Lyse if she could have kept her job back then and had her babies, wondering if she "left too early". There are lots of women who felt they had to make a choice between two lifestyles that weren't compatible. Lyse says that when she talks to younger women there seems to still be an assumption from newsroom editors that once they have children these women won't want to travel any more. "There are society assumptions" that put pressure on women she adds. But many do, and she cites Clarissa Ward, Anna Foster and Christiane Amanpour as foreign correspondents who have juggled childcare but do leave their children with family and go on the road for weeks when necessary.

Lyse is happy with her current mix of work. She returns to Ukraine often where she finds there is incredible resilience, patriotism, and hope. She believes that even in the worst moments of war she also sees the greatest of humanity in the way that people help others. She has also spent a lot of time covering the Israel-Gaza war, mostly from Jerusalem and the West Bank. She doesn't want to keep seeing dead bodies and charred streets, but it comes with the territory. She tries not to dwell and is not depressed:

> I still think that it's an incredible privilege. I haven't lost that. Or the excitement of it. I love live TV, and I love explaining things. I love the storytelling and still feel it's an incredible privilege. So, I'm not jaded, and I haven't lost hope.

In the summer of 2024, she presented a number of domestic news programmes, including The Today Programme on Radio 4, where it can seem strange to hear her saying lines such as, "The face of the [UK] high street is changing". In June 2024 Lyse was awarded an honorary doctorate in law from Concordia University in Montreal.[8] In her address to the graduating cohort she summarised her life experiences after leaving university and reminded those present to take risks, as she had. She quoted Seamus Heaney "The way we are living, timorous or bold, will have been our life".[9]

References

Loyn, David. *In Afghanistan: Two Hundred Years of British, Russian and American Occupation.* London: St Martin's Press, 2009.

---

[8] *Lyse Doucet, 2024 Concordia Honorary Doctorate*, 2024, https://www.youtube.com/watch?v=uv52pIOnTC0.
[9] Seamus Heaney, 2014 "Field Work: Poems".

Lyse Doucet, 2024 Concordia Honorary Doctorate, 2024. https://www.youtube.com/watch?v=uv52pIOnTC0.
New Straits Times. "A Bullet Aimed at the Media." October 7, 1994. Google News. https://news.google.com/newspapers?nid=1309&dat=19941007&id=mzhOAAAAIBAJ&sjid=UxMEAAAAIBAJ&pg=1960,2982932&hl=en.
No Man's Land: Women Frontline Journalists, 1995.
Sky News. "Open Letter Published from News Organisations Calls for Access to Gaza," July 11, 2024. https://news.sky.com/story/open-letter-published-from-news-organisations-calls-for-access-to-gaza-13176605.

Orla Guerin Senior International Correspondent based in Istanbul. Orla has worked as a BBC correspondent previously based in Los Angeles, Rome, Jerusalem, Johannesburg and Islamabad

"Do not take no for an answer. Just do not".

I first met Orla some thirty years ago on Grafton Street in Dublin. I was with a friend and former ITN colleague Jarlath Dolan, who later died while working as a foreign correspondent for the *Irish Times* in South Africa. Jarlath introduced her as being "RTÉ's Europe Correspondent" and I asked her where she was based. She replied, "In Dublin", to my surprise. There followed an informative discussion about RTÉ's stretched finances. We headed to a pub, but Orla didn't follow us. Instead, she touched her "pledge badge" on her jacket which showed she didn't drink, and we went our separate ways.

I am meeting her now on Zoom—it is late in the Covid era, and Orla has finally agreed to give me an interview after two years of lobbying: she says in the end she was impressed with my patience. These days she does her foreign corresponding from a base in Istanbul and is speaking from a beautiful book-lined room in an apartment in the heart of the old city. From there, as the BBC's senior international editor, she reports on Turkey and across the region and beyond.

She grew up in Whitehall on Dublin's northside. She has one sister, and they were a tightly knit family unit. At four years old, she went to the Holy Faith neighbourhood school for primary and then for her final years of secondary schooling she continued her studies at a place called "Whitehall House", which ran a leaving certificate and a commercial course. She thought the school had very low expectations of girls at the time, and believed they were just "funnelling people into the commercial course" as there was no expectation you would go on to college. "I remember things being said like, 'Well you'll just work for a year or two and then you'll get married'. That was the horizon". She thought some did find their way into nursing, but she couldn't remember any discussions about girls wanting to be doctors or accountants. Ever the journalist, she said she'd be interested in going back and finding out how many of her fellow schoolmates did end up going on to third level studies. It certainly wasn't the norm either in her school or at home, where both her parents had left school early and gone out to work.

Orla has no idea how or why she "had the notion to become a journalist" but it was something that she hit upon as a teenager.

> I did the usual stuff, like wrote letters, looked for any opportunity I could find to write about something and get it into print. I badgered local free newspapers, I badgered everybody. And I knew about the course in Rathmines, which at that stage was still the recognised journalism training programme. DCU [Dublin City University] at that time was only postgrad.

Orla figured that with this route she would be finished in two years and would then be qualified to be a journalist. She enrolled at the College of Commerce in Rathmines as a 17-year-old and was finished by the age of 19. She had a Saturday job working in Penney's Department store from the age of 16, which she kept throughout college. She also freelanced while studying, "getting little bits of stuff done here and there", including for trade papers such as a business magazine and an insurance magazine. She couldn't recall if it was during or after college that she started doing book and film reviews for the *Evening Herald*, helped in this by writer (and later filmmaker) Ferdia MacAnna who "put some work [my] way". Back at Rathmines she did her first placement at the *Sunday Tribune* under Vincent Brown "the legend", and the second one, which she found herself, was with "It Magazine". After college she picked up a short contract with the *Sunday Tribune* and then her first staff job from a new paper in Limerick—the *Limerick Post*. The paper was just starting out and so she went off to that city on what she describes as a big adventure "in its own way".

Not long after she started her new job, her father passed away suddenly and she felt she needed to get back to Dublin quickly, and so she ended up working for the *Irish Medical News*, followed by the *Irish Medical Times*. She remembers it as an interesting period to be doing health stories as there was a lot of AIDS research coming out in Ireland. The country had one of the worst infection rates of HIV due to the high level of drug addiction in Dublin's inner city, so she found there was plenty to write about. During this period she was also freelancing for the *Herald*. In 1987, RTÉ (Ireland's public broadcaster) advertised for journalists in the Dublin newsroom. She applied, even though she hadn't ever planned to work in broadcasting, but the opening was there. She was invited in for writing and broadcasting tests and to her great surprise was offered a job. At 21, she was one of a few new hires that included Fionnuala Sweeney, who went on to be an anchor at CNN, and RTÉ reporters Bob Powell, Eoin Ronayne and presenter Anne Cassin. They were assigned to *Two FM* radio shifts:

> So basically, it was rip and read. You wrote your own bulletin, and you read the bulletin every hour on the hour for like eight or nine hours. And you did overnights, and you did early mornings, and you did the whole thing. And that was good training. And after a few months of doing that, I was moved on to the TV reporting desk, which was kind of hilarious because I had no idea. I'd never done television, we never trained for it in college, there was no notion that people were going to go off and be TV reporters. And in RTÉ at that time, I'm sure it's very different now, there were no producers. So, there was nobody to tell you 'this is how a TV piece is done'.

She took to her new job like a duck to water and loved that every day was different, and you never knew where you were going from one moment to the next. She remembers covering education, fisheries, agriculture and conducting lots of court reporting. The last of these was fascinating as there were plenty of very high-profile extradition cases in the courts at the time. She ended up "slightly specialising in court reporting" and really enjoying it. A short while later, RTÉ advertised for a London correspondent, and as there were very few foreign jobs at the time at the station, she decided to apply. She chuckled, "I only had my foot in the door [when I applied] which caused jaws to hit the floor in the newsroom". She didn't succeed but was told she came second, which she found encouraging. Then in 1990 in "a kind of delayed response to the Berlin Wall", RTÉ decided to create the post of Eastern Europe correspondent. She applied and was successful and in no time at all she set off for Vienna, the old "listening post" for the Soviet bloc. After spending a short time there, she argued with her managers back in Dublin that the story was really in Moscow rather than Vienna and that she should relocate and so off she went to Russia, aged just 23.

It was while she was over in Moscow, scoping plans for a proper bureau and tackling the bureaucracy of the fading Soviet era, that the broadcasting environment changed back in Ireland. Legislation was brought in to make way for commercial competition and a cap was introduced on RTÉ's advertising revenue that resulted in a loss for RTÉ of between £Ir 10 and 12 million Irish pounds.[1] Money became tighter and one of the first things to go was the budget for the Moscow office. For the next four years, she travelled for her job from a Dublin base. She is sanguine about those years underlining that they were extraordinary—Yugoslavia started to fall apart and within two years her focus had switched from the former Soviet Union to the fighting in the Balkans. Overall, she believes it worked out fine and RTÉ was very supportive, and she doesn't remember being turned down for any trip she wanted to go on. She travelled light—hiring local crews and local translators in situ. Occasionally she was able to have an RTÉ crew for making longer programmes, for example, for a documentary on Sarajevo. But otherwise, she said, she had to go around with her begging bowl.

---

[1] Paul Cullen, "RTE Cap 'almost Destroyed' Ad Industry," *Irish Times*, November 10, 2000, https://www.irishtimes.com/news/rte-cap-almost-destroyed-ad-industry-1.1114836.

And you know, particularly in Sarajevo, I remember getting immense help from the BBC and ITN. Both of them, you know, who would agree to stick my track on the end of a satellite feed, do a free piece to camera for me, let me come in and see their filming so I could script to pictures that I knew would make their way to Dublin. And it was a great experience, and it was really challenging, and I definitely didn't know what I was doing. But that way of having to work—of not having resources and not having a team. You know, that was one of the reasons why, in the end, I thought I want to move beyond RTÉ. It wasn't that I didn't enjoy it. I did. I really enjoyed it very much, and I have very fond memories of my time there. But I just thought I can't go around the world doing foreign news, you know, begging for TV feeds and all of that […] In those days it was kind of—go out with your notebook and see how many free facilities you can get your hands on.

She believes that the people in charge of newsgathering—Rory O'Connor and then Joe Mulholland—made the best of a tough situation. In 1992 she received a Jacob's Award[2] for her reporting from Eastern Europe. She was away often, and sometimes, when back in Dublin, she would co-present RTÉ's main morning radio show "Morning Ireland". She enjoyed working with people such as David Hanley and she relished the live aspect of it: "But it won't surprise you at all to learn that my style was quite abrasive".

When the BBC's Moscow Correspondent job became free in 1987, she applied but it went to Diana Goodman (Chapter 2). Once again the BBC managers were "very nice" to her and told her to keep in touch. She wasn't successful either in a second application to the BBC, but again was told to keep in contact. Then in 1994 the BBC let her know that there were "UK news jobs" coming up and she was advised to apply. At this point, she was on leave from RTÉ, after what she laughingly calls her "spectacularly successful political career" when she stood as a Labour Party candidate in the 1994 European Parliament elections but didn't win a seat. She was half-way through a master's degree in film at UCD and an EU course in film production. She had set up a film company "on paper" and was hesitant about applying for the job. On top of that

---

[2] Jacob's awards are Irish Television Awards which began in 1962.

she says she didn't know a lot about British domestic news. However, the BBC waited for her to finish her course, and she set off for London in July 1995.

On arrival in London, she spent a few months "on the taxi rank" doing either national radio or TV reporting and by Christmas she found herself once again in Sarajevo, covering the war in the Balkans. Following this trip, she did an overseas stint in Los Angeles for six months. While there, the Southern Europe correspondent job came up, and she applied and was successful. The role at that time was based in Rome, but the main news story was in the Balkans. This was her first of six overseas posts, and she has never really returned to London since for any length of time. In Italy Orla covered a wide range of stories, including political ones but these were the more staid years of Prime Minister Romano Prodi (rather than the Silvio Berlusconi era) and "Italy was being very grown up". With the country fairly quiet, she spent a lot of her time away.

When Orla first went to Sarajevo while working at RTÉ, she had never been in an active combat zone before and there was no specific training. The Security Correspondent, Tom McCaughren, advised her to go to the army's headquarters and pick up a flak jacket. She was given one, but was informed that she couldn't have the plates "because the plates are an item of ordinance, and we can't just give them to you". When she arrived at her destination an American colleague rubbished her jacket saying it was only good for stopping a cold. She would "bum a lift" from the BBC or ITN, usually from Split in Croatia. She remembers that back in those days in Sarajevo nobody had armoured vehicles, and people kept getting killed in soft-skin cars.

> It was very dangerous on the main street in Sarajevo because you had hills on which there were Serb positions. And you had the city down below. And it was basically like shooting fish in a barrel. 'Sniper Alley'—you know, it was, it was very, very dangerous.

Orla did her first proper safety training on arrival at the BBC. It was a "Hostile environment First Aid Training" course (HEFAT), which also comprised information on disaster coverage, dangerous situations and what to do if kidnapped. As a journalist who ventures overseas, you have to repeat it every three years, and when I interviewed her, Orla had recently returned from completing a two-day refresher for her Ukraine reporting assignments. "God forbid, you ever need it. It's very practical". These days the course also includes a section on psychological trauma (PTSD) and on cybersecurity.

She thinks the way that her job is done now is 100% different to the way she first carried it out.

> And in 'Category One Countries' (the most dangerous), you know, we're always working with the safety advisor, and they are physically present on the ground and going out with you every time you film. And that's non-negotiable, that's the way it works. And in the Beeb, we have this form called a 'Risk Assessment Form', which is the bane of the producers' lives because they have to complete it, which has to be done in advance, even in war-like situations. In fact, especially in war-like situations.

These days in Ukraine, you can no longer just decide that there might be a story in Bucha, you have to plan in advance and get it signed off as "editorially worthwhile" and "being hopefully possible from a safety point of view". The paperwork now goes through a series of senior editorial managers, and the High-Risk Department in London.

> So, the top people in Foreign News and High-Risk would be signing off on that form. And there's also input from the high-risk advisor on the ground. And always it's discussed with the team. Like it's always a team decision about, what do we think, do we try and go here? Or do we try and go there? And you always have to be prepared to abandon the plan halfway through if it just doesn't seem safe. And my policy, 'touch wood' over the years, has always been that, you know, everybody else's instinct is as important as mine. And sometimes, you know, somebody just gets a feeling. And that's that.

She recounted an anecdote about approaching a particular Ukrainian village on a trip that they thought had been cleared of Russian fighters, but in the end they weren't sure. Their very calm "fixer-translator" became increasingly nervous about the expedition, feeling that it might be dangerous and so they turned back. Another journalist she spoke to afterwards had gone further down the road before also turning back for the same reasons. He said it was the emptiest road he had ever seen in his life. She added that two weeks earlier, they had met a celebrated Ukrainian journalist, Maks Levin, who had then been killed in a similar situation. Levin had been covering the war in Ukraine since 2014 when it started in the East. He was always on the front line, travelling to similar villages where the Russians had apparently been pulled out. Then one day he went missing:

> Everybody had a bad feeling from the beginning, you know, for this guy to disappear off the grid, it just wasn't going to have a happy ending. And the area where it was, was so contested that the Ukrainians couldn't even go in for about two weeks to try and find him. And it looks like he [and his friend] were caught by the Russians more or less immediately and were executed and just dumped.

She reflects that quite a few journalists were killed in the early phase of the war, while doing things that were no more dangerous than she and her team were doing. She noted there is "always a degree of risk, and it's a calculated risk, and you hope your calculations are correct. But of course, you know, there's no guarantee". These days this kind of reporting is very different to previous eras when you could have been out of touch with head office for days at a time. Today there are WhatsApp groups for communicating with other correspondents and colleagues and you have open-source intelligence, access to eyewitness video, new tech and artificial intelligence (AI) for sourcing new information and fact checking. All of these resources mean that you can be available 24/7.

The BBC had a large newsgathering operation in Kyiv back in 2022 that had a producer in charge (I-C) of the whole operation.

> And that person in the first part of the war, for the first few months, that was our bureau chief from Moscow, Kate Peters. Obviously she knows the region like the back of her hand. So, she was doing it for the first few months, and [has been doing it since], in a rotation with other people.

Initially, the BBC had teams in a number of different locations including Kyiv, Lviv and Odessa. They also had teams in Dnipro and

Mykolaiv at different times. After a while the main base became Kyiv, with teams travelling out from there to different stories. There was also a base in the east of the country, and the BBC base changed, depending on where the story was located. When I spoke to Orla initially she had just returned from a month based near Lviv. In terms of daily production, the I-C dealt with London every day and also with the teams on the ground. A field producer would be in touch with the I-C the night before, revealing what they intended to do—the kinds of editorial ambitions that were in play for the next day. "The I-C would be talking to London, and we would also be talking to London, but the I-C has to know what you're up to and is the main point of contact, and then people just go out and get on with it".

Orla explained that there had been a system in place for which person was offering on a particular day so that everybody's material could get on air and the Ukraine stories "wouldn't be drowning each other out". To begin with in Ukraine there were lots of stories every night and the TV bulletins were co-presented from London and Kyiv. It was the I-C's job to make sure there was a pipeline of stories—with everybody getting a chance to go out and bring back strong pieces and not all reporters offering on the same day. Orla might offer one on a particular day, Jeremy Bowen might offer the next day and Sarah Rainsford the day after that. She said, "We were trying very hard to not have a traffic jam of Ukraine stories", in particular because people were taking risks to go out and gather that material. The editors back in London wanted to make sure the work got showcased separately and was given the kind of airtime it deserved.

When asked to pick out the stories that resonated the most with her in the conflict in Ukraine, Orla selected several TV news pieces that reflected incredible personal suffering of the kind that reduced elderly men and even soldiers to tears. The first was two weeks into the conflict when the BBC team was trying to get as close as possible to Kyiv's commuter town of Bucha.[3] The town was occupied by Russian soldiers and people on the outside understood terrible things were happening

---

[3] *BBC News at Six* (BBC 1, March 11, 2022), Box of Broadcasts, https://learningonscreen.ac.uk/ondemand/index.php/prog/3BF08012?bcast=136349192.

inside, but nobody knew just how bad it was. The team interviewed a pensioner turned soldier who could barely find the words to explain the horror of the fighting before starting to weep. They passed accidentally through the last checkpoint, which was empty, and realised they were in no man's land and there was an active sniper in the area.

> But as we were standing there, this lone old man [Anatoly] goes by with a shopping cart, an empty shopping cart, making his way up the road. And it was just so surreal. And we went over to speak to him, and I said, 'Look, where are you going?' And he said, 'I'm going to try and find fuel. It's so cold in my house'. And he burst into tears. And then was apologising for crying. It was absolutely heart-breaking.

A second story concentrated on Irpin,[4] where old and young were attempting to flee the town by crossing a broken river bridge that the Ukrainian forces had blown up to stop the Russian advance. The camera focused on an elderly man who was slipping on a wooden plank, thrown hastily across the bed of the fast-flowing river.

> And he almost fell, and he kind of crouched over and he was on the wood. And you could see he couldn't really move. He looked like somebody who had difficulty walking at the best of times. And somehow, and I don't know how, he summoned his courage. And he managed to stand up and you could see the huge effort. And he shuffled. I mean, he literally shuffled inch by inch by inch across that wood and got to the other side. But that was harrowing.

In the last story Orla selected, she went to Lysychansk in a Ukrainian army convoy to rescue civilians.[5] If the soldiers hadn't stopped for a couple of minutes of morning prayers, then the shell that exploded in front of their convoy would likely have killed them. They filmed people packing up their belongings and a father grieving over the body of his adult son. All of this was accompanied by sounds of mortars landing.

---

[4] *BBC News* (BBC News Channel, March 8, 2022), Box of Broadcasts, https://learningonscreen.ac.uk/ondemand/index.php/prog/3BF07FB8?bcast=136397864.

[5] *BBC News* (BBC News 24, June 23, 2022), Box of Broadcasts, https://learningonscreen.ac.uk/ondemand/index.php/prog/3BF7C576?bcast=136965402.

And the last family that we picked up that night was a woman and her four daughters. And they had spent four months under the ground. And they came out and they were almost blinking in the light, the kids' faces were all dirty, because they had no running water. And there was a girl of about 12. And she was helping her mam, she was carrying the bags, she was picking up the little sisters, she was doing all of that. And then all of a sudden, she just stood stock still and burst into tears. The weight of the whole thing just kind of crashing down on her. And then they were put in the back of the truck.

For Orla, when she is in these stark and bleak situations, she often asks herself how she would cope with these circumstances: "Would you be a stoic as many people are? Would you be as strong? You know? Would you have the humanity and the compassion that people are showing each other in that situation there?" She is very impressed by the Ukrainians' bravery and resistance, especially considering the constant shelling in places such as Mariupol, Lysychans'k and Sievierodonetsk. "The playbook doesn't change—it's shelling them into oblivion, and then when there's only rubble left, march in and take control. I mean, it is very clear that there is no shortage of brave men and brave women in Ukraine. That's not the issue. The issue is that they are outgunned still".

From her base in Istanbul, she travels a great deal and not always in the direction you'd imagine. In the past few years, alongside Greece, Ukraine and Azerbaijan, she has also travelled to Colombia, Venezuela, El Salvador and Brazil and during Covid she went to India and Algeria. She has worked on stories related to post-ISIS Iraq and retains a keen interest in Libya, a country she returns to when she can. She reports frequently in the Middle East, including in Israel, particularly since the Gaza conflict erupted in late 2023. But it hasn't always been plain sailing.

Orla thinks she was busiest in a 24/7 way when she was a Middle East correspondent, based in Jerusalem. She had always wanted to work in the Middle East and her time there coincided with the second Palestinian Intifada. She arrived in 2000 and for the next five years she covered the occupied West Bank and Gaza. She admits it was "very intense" and that she had never worked harder. "We were out from seven o'clock in the morning and finishing at midnight". Although she did manage small bursts of travelling in the region, she was mostly confined to the West Bank and Gaza Strip due to the uprising. In 2002 the BBC complained to the Israeli government after Orla and her team were pinned down by Israeli fire while filming a demonstration in the West Bank.[6] According to the BBC, "They made the point that they had been on legitimate business, on press business. They were filming a peaceful demonstration".

Despite her busy schedule, Orla did find the time to fall in love and marry Reuters correspondent Michael Georgy in 2003. Working in Israel was tough, and her reporting was under constant scrutiny from both the Israeli government and the Palestinian authorities in the West Bank and Gaza Strip. In 2004 the Israeli government wrote to the BBC accusing Orla of antisemitism, and "total identification with the goals and methods of the Palestinian terror groups" following her report on a 16-year-old would-be suicide bomber.[7] The complaint was investigated and dismissed. When reports surfaced in the press that Orla was being 'pulled out' of Jerusalem and moved on to Johannesburg in 2006, the BBC vigorously denied this and pointed out that Orla had been moved as part of a normal staff rotation, and that she had stayed in Jerusalem for two years extra to her posting.[8] Orla argues that the Israeli lobby is much stronger than any Palestinian lobby,

> My feeling when I was based there, which I'm sure is still the way my BBC colleagues are operating, is that we have to call it the way we see it, you know. We go out and report what we see, and what is actually taking place.

From Johannesburg, Orla covered all of sub-Saharan Africa. When I researched some of Orla's TV stories from this time, I found her as far away from base as Chad, where she uncovered deceptive practices by a

---

[6] Ewen MacAskill, "BBC Protests after Crew Caught in Violence," *The Guardian*, April 3, 2002, https://www.theguardian.com/media/2002/apr/03/israel.bbc.

[7] Chris McGreal, "BBC Accused of Bias against Israel," *The Guardian*, April 1, 2004, https://www.theguardian.com/media/2004/apr/01/bbc.israel.

[8] "BBC Pulls Guerin out of Israel," *Broadcast*, December 1, 2005, https://www.broadcastnow.co.uk/bbc-pulls-guerin-out-of-israel/1032900.article.

French children's charity.[9] Back home, she was constantly examining the divisions inside South Africa. A 2007 story showed Orla reporting on the national side's victory in the Rugby World Cup, and she headed to Soweto to find young black children training barefoot on a football field, demonstrating amply the country's two-tier race reality.[10] From her base, she also covered politics and elections in Zimbabwe, focusing on the lack of social care, poor health services and the shocking human rights issues in the country. Although the BBC was banned from reporting from Zimbabwe, Orla sometimes went undercover to speak to voters who had been intimidated by government officials or to see isolated and poverty-stricken parts of the country the authorities didn't want the outside world to know about.[11] On another occasion in 2008 Orla was the only British TV journalist to get inside the national ceremony to witness President Robert Mugabe's handing over of some power to opposition leader Morgan Tsvangirai.[12]

At the end of three years in South Africa, she moved to Pakistan in 2009, where she remained until 2013. She landed at a time of bombings, violence and suicide attacks. She said it was "Just relentless. It felt like it was all the time and every day". Nonetheless, she thinks Pakistan was the place she loved the most and she found the people "absolutely extraordinary" and even more hospitable than in the Arab world. Islamabad she thought was generally quiet, but a few hours down the road, you had Peshawar and the tribal areas, the mega-cities of Karachi and Lahore, and "fascinating places like the Swat Valley". In an interview in the *Sunday Times* in 2011,[13] she said:

---

[9] *Question Time Extra* (BBC News 24, August 8, 2007), https://learningonscreen.ac.uk/ondemand/index.php/prog/0074D601?bcast=27781146.

[10] "Springboks' Victory," *BBC Newsnight* (BBC 2, October 26, 2007), Box of Broadcasts, https://learningonscreen.ac.uk/ondemand/index.php/prog/0072D4D0?bcast=27674103.

[11] "Voter Intimidation," *BBC News* (BBC 1, May 6, 2008), https://learningonscreen.ac.uk/ondemand/index.php/prog/00905514?bcast=29274654.

[12] "Zimbabwe Election Results," *BBC News at Ten* (BBC News 24, September 15, 2008), Box of Broadcasts, https://learningonscreen.ac.uk/ondemand/index.php/prog/00B27257?bcast=30356400.

[13] Caroline Scott, "Another Day, Another Taliban Bomb," *The Times*, February 27, 2011, https://www.thetimes.com/article/another-day-another-taliban-bomb-cxhbmk960fx.

"There are periods of relative quiet, then it feels as though there's a Taliban bomb attack every day. I drive around Islamabad doing my shopping, but I wouldn't walk alone, because women don't. And there are places, like the tribal area along the border, where as a westerner you just cannot go. Every journey I take is evaluated carefully in advance".

She also made some forays into Afghanistan, to enable the Kabul reporters to take a break or return home for a while. She really enjoyed those trips, even though she regretted not being able to travel beyond Kabul. Among Orla's TV reports from this period was a story profiling suicide bombers in Lahore, and a report on the death of Pakistan's most wanted terrorist, Baitullah Mehsud. From Kabul, she reported and did "two-way" interviews on numerous car bombs and killings.

After Pakistan she returned to being a Middle East correspondent again, this time from Cairo (2013–2019). For the first two years she mainly covered Egypt, but for the second two, she travelled further afield as "it got harder and harder to actually report inside Egypt". She visited Yemen to cover the war there and considers it to be a very under-reported story, partly because it is so hard for reporters to enter the country. In 2016 she was in Libya with the Tripoli coastguards reporting on African migrants" dangerous journeys by sea. A year later, she reported from the frontline between Iraqi forces and ISIS militants in Mosul, and also from Kirkuk in Northern Iraq on the Kurdish border. In 2019 she made a final move to Istanbul, from where she operates as a travelling international correspondent.

Looking back over her career, Orla rules out any pre-ordained logic to it, but thinks that she simply followed the big news destinations:

I suppose I've been drawn to areas where the story was kind of tough and interesting. It hasn't been Paris and Berlin and Sydney—you know the places that would be lovely to live in […] It was never a case of deciding I want to do X, Y and Z bureaux. It was a case of what looked interesting and what came up and so on.

She never had a mentor as such, although she has taken advice from other people throughout her career. She remembers Kate Adie as being someone whose work she was aware of when younger and calls her "an absolute legend", reiterating she has huge respect for her work. She acknowledges that women of Kate's generation did "have to be three times as good to get half the chances". She recounts how Kate was very kind and supportive of her when she arrived at the BBC. "Some of the guys were terrified of her, but I never felt that way because I found she was always really encouraging". Now she acts as a mentor to some of the younger reporters and loves the opportunity to help. "There is a really brilliant young generation, particularly of women in Foreign News now. They're absolutely superb correspondents and a lot of them have been on the Ukraine story". She also didn't feel like she'd been an oddity or a pioneer "as a woman doing foreign news" when she entered the job market, because there were other visible women and she mentions Lindsey Hilsum, Lyse Doucet, Christina Lamb, Christiane Amanpour and the late Marie Colvin.

She still believes that women don't get the same opportunities at the start of their careers, adding that building your experience by going on big stories is how you manage that, and women often miss out on being selected. She became aware recently that many of the men that she started out with used to go drinking in the bar after work with the bosses (what she called "the Boys" Club'), and that they were able to share what they wanted to do regarding their careers and where they wanted to go. But on the other hand, she also believes that "you have to make your own luck, and you have to make your own opportunities, and you know if you're determined, you'll get there […] but there is still more, let's say 'unconscious bias' than we realise".

Orla credits her own early experiences as being vital to her career trajectory. She thinks that having already done foreign reporting at RTÉ, before landing at the BBC, gave her an important advantage, because at the time there were women at the BBC who were finding it "very hard to get into Foreign". She believes that her overseas experience perhaps gave her an opportunity to "leapfrog a few stages". These days she maintains there are still ongoing related problems. One is "discrimination or a lack of opportunity between men and women with children". She could only think of two current women foreign correspondents with children and named the Europe Editor Katya Adler and Anna Foster who reported from the Middle East. She is sure the default setting for colleagues in overseas bureaux is still the man who is married with kids, and whose partner may have had to give up a job in order to allow him to take up his post. She wonders if women with children feel supported or encouraged to go for these bureau roles, "and that's something I don't know about directly, one way or the other. But just looking at the numbers, the numbers are not there. There are not many women with children". She admits that the Europe Editor Katya Adler stands out as unusual in this regard: "She's an amazingly talented professional. When she's not interviewing European leaders, she's presenting the *Today* programme. So, you know, she has done it. The numbers are not the same between men and women".

The other burning question is the issue of equal pay (covered in more detail in Chapter 6 of this book). She has found the whole business disheartening:

> And I think when that came to light for me, in the BBC, it was a shock. Because I believed, wrongly as it turns out, that all of those battles had been fought and won by the very brave generation of women who came before me. And you know, women in Irish journalism, women in British journalism. It just never crossed my mind when I started working, never dawned on me for a minute to think that I would be paid less than a guy or that any woman would be paid less than a guy […] And, you know, the truth of that has come out and slapped us all in the face in recent years, and not only in the BBC. So clearly, there is work to do. And I think that's work for everybody to do, not just women. But men as well, you know?

She also believes there still aren't enough women progressing into senior management roles and thinks this may also be down to there not being enough early opportunities. Within the BBC Orla thinks she is typecast as being "a TV person" which she feels is a little unfair, as she has done "extraordinary amounts of radio over the years". She is also an avid radio listener, whose radio is always switched on, tuned into either RTÉ, the BBC World Service or Radio 4. But she does love TV the most and a lot of this is down to the teamwork involved in television newsgathering and how stimulating that can be on the road. In particular she relishes working with really great camera operators. In 2012 while reporting from Israel she gave an interview to Quentin Letts of the *Standard*:

> "It takes about 10 people to get me on screen. I am currently one of five BBC reporters here and I am lucky to work with two incredible cameramen, an Australian called Sarge and a Palestinian called Jimmy".[14]

These days the BBC is very "digital first" and it can be challenging on a busy day to file 800 words alongside a TV piece for the 10 O'clock news bulletin. She says she envies the journalists of the *New York Times* and their sole mission of filing one 1000-word written piece a day. She explains that on a hectic day, it can be radio that loses out, especially recently in Ukraine:

> I'd be out all day, we'd be doing a TV piece, and I'll be recording radio as I go along. And the cameraman will be filming. And obviously, at times, you know, I'm doing an interview with him. But you know, he's also filming other shots, and when we get back it is a race against time. And I'm literally handing the radio material that I've gathered to my wonderful producer, who will go off and do that edit on her own. She has to, as I can't be in the radio edit, I have to be in the TV edit, because I have to lay down a voice track […] Sometimes I can't even listen to the [radio] piece before it goes out because there isn't time. Now, that's not ideal. But that's the reality of news gathering on a busy news story (Fig. 1).

She has been very happy with her team in Ukraine. Her female producer is Wietske Burema, who is a long-time BBC foreign producer. Her camera "shoot-edit" is a Turkish man, Goktay Koraltan, who is also a long-time BBC employee. In answer to a question about whether or not it is better to employ local people to cover a country's stories than foreign correspondents, Orla is adamant this is not a binary question. She thinks that local journalists will always have contacts, insight and knowledge that outsiders will never have: "With the richness of the World Service, the BBC is able to cover the world, and many of those journalists, most

---

[14] Quentin Letts, "The Woman with a Bias towards Bloodshed," *The Standard*, April 12, 2012, https://www.standard.co.uk/hp/front/the-woman-with-a-bias-towards-bloodshed-6304024.html.

Fig. 1 Orla Guerin pictured in Eastern Ukraine (2022)

of them are people living in their own areas". But she also sees the importance for an international audience of the outsider's different perspective, and thinks the BBC is lucky to have both. Inside the BBC, she notes, all the different parts of the corporation are under the same roof and can feed off one another—she cites BBC Monitoring, the World Service language services and "News Content" (formerly BBC Newsgathering). It is the same in large bureaux abroad:

> When I was based in Pakistan, our little kind of BBC English gang was based inside the bureau with BBC Urdu and BBC Pashto. It was their bureau, and we were kindly given some space. And they were absolutely superb journalists and some of the best in the country, and some of the most generous, kind colleagues, and I've benefited hugely from being able to work with them.

In December 2024 Orla received an honorary doctorate from University College Dublin. The day after the ceremony I got a chance to ask her again about the future of international reporting. She admitted that attitudes are changing about the notion of foreign correspondents. She hoped this wasn't a "self-serving argument" reiterating that there is still a role:

> You need to be looking at things as an outsider. You want to have a level of expertise and knowledge and that's why people go and spend a few years in a country. But it's also why typically people would leave after a few years and be rotated out and somebody is brought in. Because at a certain point you start seeing it as an insider. So I think there is a value in bringing experience and a different frame of reference from the outside. But equally it's extremely important to have good local journalists on the ground. And even when we are going to a bureau and coming in for a few years, there is an abiding presence of our local teams.

In our previous interview she noted that when she was in the Middle East for five years she could feel herself beginning to operate with just such an "insider perspective", seeing checkpoints as entirely normal and not noticing their strangeness for an international audience. "But the upside is that you can build extraordinary expertise in a region if you stay there for a very long time. So, it cuts both ways".

Like Lyse Doucet, Orla is frustrated that she is still being asked the question: "Do women cover wars differently?" She laughs thinking about how she and Marie Colvin shot this down in a BBC Woman's Hour programme in 2001.[15] But then she adds, "But now I'm at this point in my career, part of me feels like probably we do still need to be talking about this". Again, she stresses this issue isn't binary and deplores the cliché that gets peddled that women always cover the personal side of things and men will cover the bombs and the bullets.

> I think you can't cover a war without covering the mechanics of a war. And any journalist covering a war will do that. And that involves being on

---

[15] "Women War Correspondents," *Woman's Hour* (BBC Radio 4, October 5, 2001), BBC Archives, https://www.bbc.co.uk/radio4/womanshour/2001_40_fri_01.shtml.

the frontline and covering the conflict aspect of it. I think it is absolutely also true that war affects people. And the way you reach an audience, I think, is by telling stories that are personal that they can connect with. […] When you have the opportunity to tell the story of one family, people do relate to that. And I think good journalists, male or female, will follow the story, whether that's in the hospitals, or on the frontlines, or with the troops, or with the families, and the best pieces will often have elements of all of that.

Journalism for Orla is the best career under the sun. She would advise young women to never take no for an answer and to aim high with the view "why shouldn't it be me?" She acknowledges she was bold back in RTÉ when she put herself down for the Southern Europe Correspondent job but "RTÉ took a chance on me". She believes that younger people have more confidence these days and perhaps will also not feel they have to "bide their time". Her advice is "apply and keep applying". She singles out Donie O'Sullivan at CNN as a young Irish reporter making an incredible contribution to journalism, especially during the Capitol riots on January 6th, 2021.

Orla professes she has no great burning desire for a particular posting as she really enjoys being based in Turkey. What she wants is to stay on the main stories:

> To me, the war in Ukraine is a very irrational war. It's illogical. It is damaging for Russia over the longer term. But none of those things appear to matter to Vladimir Putin, who seems determined to prosecute this to the limits of his power. And I personally don't think he will stop in Ukraine, and I don't think he will stop at the borders of Ukraine. I think he'll keep going.

She returns often to Ireland, in particular to spend time with her sister and her family. She sees herself in the future retiring in Ireland but thinks perhaps, "it'd be nice to have one foot in Ireland and one foot somewhere else", although she hasn't planned anything along those lines yet.

> The Ireland of today is wholly different—in ways that are only positive—to the Ireland that I left in '95 […] It's a hugely changed country, and

it's far more progressive and modern and inclusive and confident. Which is not to say that we don't have our issues, but I think there's been a kind of almost unrecognisable change in Ireland and in the Irish psyche. And we're a different place. Now, we're a different place with different people, or new people.

For the time being this woman with multiple honorary doctorates is happy to keep up her frenetic reporting pace, while also helping to mentor the next generation of young journalists. To this end she has taken up an honorary professorship of international journalism at the University of Galway. In her downtime in 2024 Orla has been doing plenty of outreach work—giving a talk at Downing College, Cambridge, on her career in international news. On 19th July 2024 she was interviewed at length by RTÉ Radio on the consequences of a potential wider war in the Middle East. Orla has recently been reporting from Israel and from Lebanon, including from the "Blue Line" on the Israel-Lebanese border where she visited Irish UNIFIL peacekeeping troops. While nothing is certain about the current escalation of the conflict in Israel, Syria or the wider Middle East, what is certain is that Orla will be there.

References

BBC News. BBC News Channel, March 8, 2022. Box of Broadcasts. https://learningonscreen.ac.uk/ondemand/index.php/prog/3BF07FB8?bcast=136397864.
BBC News at Six. BBC 1, March 11, 2022. Box of Broadcasts. https://learningonscreen.ac.uk/ondemand/index.php/prog/3BF08012?bcast=136349192.
BBC News. BBC News 24, June 23, 2022. Box of Broadcasts. https://learningonscreen.ac.uk/ondemand/index.php/prog/3BF7C576?bcast=136965402.
Broadcast. "BBC Pulls Guerin out of Israel." December 1, 2005. https://www.broadcastnow.co.uk/bbc-pulls-guerin-out-of-israel/1032900.article.
Cullen, Paul. "RTE Cap 'almost Destroyed' Ad Industry." *Irish Times*, November 10, 2000. https://www.irishtimes.com/news/rte-cap-almost-destroyed-ad-industry-1.1114836.

Letts, Quentin. "The Woman with a Bias towards Bloodshed." *The Standard*, April 12, 2012. https://www.standard.co.uk/hp/front/the-woman-with-a-bias-towards-bloodshed-6304024.html.

MacAskill, Ewen. "BBC Protests after Crew Caught in Violence." *The Guardian*, April 3, 2002. https://www.theguardian.com/media/2002/apr/03/israel.bbc.

McGreal, Chris. "BBC Accused of Bias against Israel." *The Guardian*, April 1, 2004. https://www.theguardian.com/media/2004/apr/01/bbc.israel.

Question Time Extra. BBC News 24, August 8, 2007. https://learningonscreen.ac.uk/ondemand/index.php/prog/0074D601?bcast=27781146.

Scott, Caroline. "Another Day, Another Taliban Bomb." *The Times*, February 27, 2011. https://www.thetimes.com/article/another-day-another-taliban-bomb-cxhbmk960fx.

"Springboks' Victory." *BBC Newsnight*. BBC 2, October 26, 2007. Box of Broadcasts. https://learningonscreen.ac.uk/ondemand/index.php/prog/0072D4D0?bcast=27674103.

"Voter Intimidation." *BBC News*. BBC 1, May 6, 2008. https://learningonscreen.ac.uk/ondemand/index.php/prog/00905514?bcast=29274654.

"Women War Correspondents." *Woman's Hour*. BBC Radio 4, October 5, 2001. BBC Archives. https://www.bbc.co.uk/radio4/womanshour/2001_40_fri_01.shtml.

"Zimbabwe Election Results." *BBC News at Ten*. BBC News 24, September 15, 2008. Box of Broadcasts. https://learningonscreen.ac.uk/ondemand/index.php/prog/00B27257?bcast=30356400.

Carrie Gracie
WS China Reporter, NCA China reporter, China Correspondent and China Editor

"They wanted to put women into high profile positions—they just didn't want to pay us right".

Carrie and I met up one rainy morning in Richmond during the dying days of the Covid pandemic. The café was too noisy to hear ourselves and so we repaired to a table outside, wrapping our raincoats tight. It had taken a bit of convincing to get Carrie here and she told me it was the first proper interview she had given since leaving the BBC after an acrimonious battle over equal pay for women. She said she wasn't bitter and had moved on but sometimes her responses revealed that the whole business had left her deeply disappointed with the organisation that employed her for more than 30 years. She started out by saying she was fed up with talking about the struggle that led to her taking the Corporation to court. Later she relented, but we'll come to that.

Carrie was born in Bahrain where her father was a Scottish oil executive and later a diplomat. Her mother taught briefly and then had five kids, after which she didn't work for many years, until eventually becoming a careers advisor. Carrie was the second born and she had three sisters and a brother. As a small child, her family lived in Kent'—where her father was an unsuccessful Liberal Party parliamentary candidate. After that they moved first to northwest Aberdeenshire, where her father stood for parliament again unsuccessfully and then to Glasgow briefly, before returning to Aberdeen. Carrie was sent to a private girls' school but left aged 16, objecting to it because she considered herself a socialist. Thereafter she went to a number of different schools.

She doesn't recall wanting to be a journalist when young, but she was fascinated by her aunt who was a professional interpreter in Russian, French and later Spanish. She had a love of languages, and studied French, German and Latin at school. She was interested in politics, which she puts down to her father, and had a love of acting. Encouraged by her mother, she took part in the National Youth Theatre in London during the holidays. After finishing her Highers (Scottish leaving certificate), she went to Edinburgh University to study History and English. But when her mother died suddenly of cancer, she dropped out and returned home. While there she set up a restaurant, and a year later applied to Oxford where she read Philosophy, Politics and Economics (PPE). She said she didn't think that carefully before choosing PPE, as she was grieving for her mother "and basically living in a field in Scotland with a pony".

After Oxford, and without a career plan, she and her boyfriend set off to teach English in China. She can't recall why she was interested in China, other than that Chinese wasn't one of her aunt's languages and "It was a big mystery place, nothing like today". In the mid-eighties China was barely beginning to open up to the outside world. She didn't know any Mandarin but being a hard worker and competent at languages she mistakenly thought she'd pick it up very quickly. She spent 1985–6 in provincial China, teaching at two universities and travelling widely in the country, including in Tibet. After rural Scotland, Chongqing was an enormous industrial city which she found "so grey, so polluted, there wasn't a blade of grass. It was foggy and cold in winter with zero heating and foggy and hot in the summer with zero air conditioning". She found it challenging but also extremely fascinating. On leaving the country, the pair joined the backpack trail through Southeast Asia and returned to the UK.

Back in Britain they decided to make a film about Oxford, which according to Carrie, was really, "more of a slideshow than a film". They negotiated to put it on in the crypt of St Mary's in the High Street. They projected it onto a wall and ran it twice an hour, charging tourists a pound each to view it. At the time tourists couldn't get access to the colleges and so the film gave them an opportunity to sit down and see behind the walls. "We were raking it in" she remembers. They had fun taking their friends out to dinner and spent all the money "and had no sense of the future whatsoever. Just had a ball". During that summer, she decided to apply to the BBC.

She considers she had a rather eccentric CV that wouldn't have been the normal one for a BBC graduate trainee. She applied for the production training stream, rather than the news trainee stream, and thinks her advantages were that she had a first-class degree, was older than most at 25, and had the China experience under her belt. She was keenest to join the World Service and to work in international news. On the scheme she learned some useful craft skills and got attached to different programmes, "where you had to more or less sink or swim". She spent some time in the African Service which she really enjoyed, and in the Chinese Service "which was less fun". She believes her Chinese wasn't really up to being in that department and that she was therefore more of "a spare part" than a useful addition to the service. She also picked up experience at Radio Scotland and did some reporting in Edinburgh and Glasgow. "This gave me a taste for shoe leather reporting, and actually talking to people and being on the ground. I loved that".

Her last attachment was with World Service Current Affairs, where she stayed after her traineeship finished. She is emphatic that current affairs was considered to be part of "programmes" and was very different to "news". As Liz Blunt had found before her, programme people were considered second-class citizens by "newsroom people". She thinks that all the departments were very male in both programmes and news, but "I don't think we realised that there was this glass ceiling there, but then we met it".

After arriving at the BBC, she had decided to take her Chinese more seriously and enrolled in language lessons at night classes at the Polytechnic of Central London (later the University of Westminster). First, she took a GCSE, then an "A Level" and afterwards she did two years of a degree before becoming a World Service reporter in Beijing in 1991, moving on quickly to become the BBC's national radio and television correspondent. "At the time people didn't trust you to be the voice of the BBC, or the face of the BBC, you were a producer", and it was quite a journey to become confident in herself and for the organisation to get behind her. The BBC job was a staff position and not the usual first posting as a BBC World Service stringer or sponsored stringer, where you had to "semi-resign" and give up your staff position. She said she didn't think she would have done it if it had been a stringer post, "because it's counter factual". Her predecessors in the post were Simon Long and Tim Luard. At the time that she arrived, there was a male "correspondent" who was the principal voice, especially on domestic outlets, and her post was "lower in the hierarchy. I was definitely number two in the bureau at that point, and James Miles was number one".

She thinks that the job was probably for two years, but the BBC needed people to stay longer, "It's such a difficult environment to get people into, and to acclimatise people to that. My experience was that they never wanted me to leave, and they would have chained me to Beijing". She added, with hindsight, "It's like, we've got someone who can do China [...] and they're prepared to do it for half the price of a man—something that obviously they don't know but we know". On reflection, she decides that for her post perhaps that wasn't the case at that time, but that the culture was changing towards "star power" bargaining for on-air "individual deals". She also believes that BBC management did have the tendency to appoint a man if one were available and all else was equal. So, it wasn't just about the money but it was also a case of preferring to have a particular star on air and on the TV.

She observes that Kate Adie was just about the only female face you ever saw doing TV foreign reporting. Overall, she thinks the World Service became better at rewarding women because they worked harder and the women who advanced were "less into the performative aspects of journalism and more into the fact-finding, gritting reality of journalism". She adds that traditionally they had gained experience at tasks that some men might consider were beneath them. Women in the World Service culture took their journalism very seriously and were prepared to put in the hard yards for the sake of journalism "You wouldn't have got many men going to China at that point, not many reporters. It was not a coveted place to be at all".

Carrie set off for Beijing in early 1991. The job was nearly all radio reporting, and they hardly filmed any television at all. The office was one room plus a studio. There was a Chinese "administrator" whose job was to navigate the endless bureaucracy and set up interviews, and there was a driver who wore many different hats. She believes that these two local people essentially worked for the government as they were the only kind of people whom you were allowed to employ. In these pre-internet days, their story options came via a Xinhua text machine (feeding them all the official stories), the Western news agencies, their own sources and their own projects. Their day would start with digesting what was in the Chinese press, as the state media was important "in terms of government signals". After that they got on with their chosen reporting. Recorded radio packages had to be sent back on the plane to London, and as there were no direct flights, they had to go via Hong Kong. Obviously, they could do direct radio interviews with London, and they could "feed the beast" of 24-hour news by means of one or two-minute "voiced up news reports", but for edited packages the route was by plane. Later, in 1993–4 she started doing filmed packages for World Service TV: "I really enjoyed that. I was still pre-children and so I was kind of a workaholic. I just lived and breathed my work and China".

She took a Chinese lesson every morning at 8 O'clock before she went to work and thinks it was "a great brain exercise". She thought some bosses in news didn't get behind language learning; "it was as if they didn't trust people who spoke languages. They'd gone native, they weren't to be trusted. They couldn't see the wood from the trees, blah blah". After a few years in the job, she applied for the "correspondent" vacancy, but she didn't get it. The person who did had more widespread experience, but not local experience. She was annoyed about not getting the job, and the constant fighting between the Chinese authorities and the bureau infuriated her. The Chinese authorities were angry in particular about reporting by a roving BBC reporter, Sue Lloyd-Roberts, who had entered the country on a tourist visa with a hidden camera and had then proceeded to film an organ transplant story involving prisoners acting as donors.[1] In response the Chinese authorities started limiting the BBC bureau's access to stories. In the end she said she felt, "like a pawn in a big game which I had no control over and the people who did have control over the game had no interest in my opinion".

She therefore decided to leave China and the BBC in 1995 and returned to London. At this time she got married to a Chinese rock musician, Cheng Jin, and had her daughter. Alongside this change, Carrie finished her Chinese degree and studied for a diploma in interactive media at the University of Middlesex. She figured that if she went back to China she would go as a freelancer so that then she would be in editorial control of her stories, and "nobody would be able to push me about". Carrie believed that if they did, she could push back and wouldn't "be stuck between these two giants". In the end she returned to China in 1996, with an accreditation for the Irish public broadcaster RTÉ. She pursued her reporting happily until the BBC decided it needed a correspondent to cover the Hong Kong handover in 1997 and the expected demise of China's leader Deng Xiaoping. The BBC offered her the old job back, but she turned it down because her daughter Rachel was very young, and she didn't want to work 18-hour shifts day in, day out, as she had done previously. Eventually she negotiated for a producer from London to work with her, who was then sent from London, and she agreed terms and rejoined the BBC. When Deng Xiaoping died in 1997, she ended up living in the bureau for a while with her baby in a basket. The Hong Kong handover also proved to be an extremely busy time, requiring a lot of juggling.

In 1997 she applied for and secured the job of "Beijing correspondent and Bureau Chief", and by then BBC Beijing was a much bigger operation. They had a camera and a camera operator; the bureau had more staff—two fixers and a couple of foreign producers. The job was challenging and demanding and required a lot of travelling. This was particularly the case when she became pregnant with her second child. When her little boy Daniel was six months old, her daughter Rachel became very sick. The health system in China at the time was "very hit

---

[1] "China, Human Organ Trade, 1994," *BBC Breakfast News,* May 1994, https://www.youtube.com/watch?v=yngV3pNYEho.

and miss" and so she took her to Hong Kong. Her husband, Cheng Jin, wasn't allowed to leave the country and join her in Hong Kong. Eventually she and her daughter were medically evacuated to London and her daughter was diagnosed with leukaemia at Great Ormond Street Hospital. There followed two years of intensive treatment and Carrie had to formally leave China again.

As the main breadwinner she was forced to return to work and so she rejoined the World Service newsroom, working as a radio presenter for "The World Today" and "Newshour". After a while a colleague advised her to be more strategic in her approach to her work hours as she needed so much time off to care for her daughter. This person said: "You need to do the fewest hours you can for the best income you can, and the place to do that is TV presenting". She absorbed the lesson and moved over to work as a presenter on the BBC News Channel and on World TV in late 1999. She professed, "that was not a hard move". She thought that nothing could be as hard as confronting the Chinese police or coping with your child being in hospital with leukaemia.

Carrie worked doggedly on her "fixed shifts" but at least once a year she did "a big China project". These started out as radio features and moved on to filming—such as the ten years she devoted to the "White Horse Village" series (more on this later) and another on the preparations for the Olympics. She always kept her hand in as a reporter but, "being a parent was [her] primary responsibility in those years". The main point of working was to earn money. So, either she did her China projects when they could all go to China as a family, or she would persuade her (by then) ex-husband to come over and look after the children while she flew to China to report. She found both solutions worked.

> It's something I say to other women. Maybe you can't do the big job all the time because you've got this other huge job. And you feel incredibly divided. But sometimes it's better to do an easy job so that you can give more of your energies at home and then like really focus once or twice a year and do something amazing and that shows you can absolutely clean the floor with everybody else. Sorry, that's not a nice expression and I don't mean that. But it's like there's something about that pent up energy and creativity that you're not able to use day in and day out. So, you've

got this kind of frustrated, creative journalist spirit in you. But when you get those tiny windows of opportunity you go out, you grasp it, you do something with it. And that's what I did. And that kind of worked well, because it forced me to be much more strategic than I had been before. I think having kids changed me so massively. And then having a child with leukaemia changed me massively again. […] I just had to get a grip and be a grown up. I couldn't go around just letting the BBC push me around. You know kind of going "yes sir, no sir, three bags full sir". I wasn't that person.

On the News Channel she did a mixture of jobs—mostly presenting in the studio or for outside broadcasts. She also did stints as a radio presenter for "*The World Tonight*" or "*PM*". She found some of her TV bosses hard to deal with and didn't get on so well with one of the people in charge of news, who she said, "wanted [her] off his screen as far as possible". To add to her stress, in 2011 Carrie was treated for breast cancer, and ended up undergoing chemotherapy and having a double mastectomy.

Not long after this, BBC management started talking about having a China Editor because the China coverage "wasn't really cutting through". Fergal Keane was favoured by some for the role. She thought that domestic radio and TV recruitment panels looked down on the World Service, "You know just a bunch of blue stockings who will bore you to death if you give them half a chance". Carrie also had time-related demands based on not wanting to move her daughter twice, due to her schooling. While the project was on hold "due to budget issues", James Harding arrived at the BBC as head of news. Among other jobs, he had been the *Financial Times*' Shanghai correspondent, and he really admired Carrie's coverage and wanted her in the BBC role. On top of that the BBC had been attacked about the lack of women in senior jobs, and in 2009 presenter Miriam O'Reilly had successfully sued the BBC for age discrimination against women after being dropped from "Countryfile". James Harding tried his best to be persuasive, but Carrie held out. However, in 2013 she said yes, because "it was a massive opportunity and privilege to take charge of the BBC's China coverage". The job ad at the time underlined the role's seniority, as Carrie explained in her book (2019: 27):

> The role of China Editor is at the most senior level of correspondent in BBC News, on a par with the World Affairs, Middle East, Europe and North America Editors overseas and the Political, Business, Home and Economics Editors in the UK.

Looking back, at the time she did give James Harding and deputy head of newsgathering Jonathan Munro credit for enabling her to take on the role of China Editor, and for Katya Adler to become the Europe Editor. "They wanted to put women into high-profile positions—they just didn't want to pay us right. And that's the most extraordinary thing—as we subsequently discovered. And I just find that hilarious. That was decided at their grace". She changes the subject to the post in China, which she loved. "I was no longer putting myself down, being the woman who did the kind of background, sweeping up job. I was ready to step up and say, 'I am this organisation's best person to present this story. This was an achievement in vanquishing my own self-doubt'". She likes to think that she did it creatively and assertively and she gathered up her confidence to "just grasp it and go with it". Not all the things that she'd asked for were delivered—such as a producer to work solely with her. So, in the four years that she worked in Beijing this time round, she had to battle to get the production resources that she needed.

She found it hard to schedule in the big projects she wanted to do for a bureau that was really set up to do reactive daily news stories. These projects were stories such as the "Murder in the Lucky Holiday Hotel"[2] (more on this series later), and the "Belt and Road" film series[3] for which she would later travel to five countries to report. These plans didn't always work with on-the-day news editors who needed short news stories. Tussles were part and parcel of this issue, but she did "a lot of paddling beneath the surface" to achieve her goals along with her team.

---

[2] Carrie Gracie, "Murder in the Lucky Holiday Hotel," March 17, 2017, https://www.bbc.co.uk/news/resources/idt-sh/Murder_lucky_hotel.

[3] "BBC World News," *The New Silk Road*, March 17, 2017, Carrie Gracie Webpage, https://carriegracie.com/carrie-gracie---silk-road-bbc-news-film.html.

She thought that the way that China pushed around the international news organisations got worse, but that underneath politically, life in China just continued: "one party, one state remained the same".

Carrie believes that surveillance by the state was actually worse in the 1990s. She wasn't there in the noughties, but considers the authorities were more open in the run up to the Beijing Olympics, but then toughened up after the "Arab Spring" which "freaked them out". Xi Jinping was also much more wary about opening up in general than his predecessor Hu Jintao. How the authorities treated their Uighur minority was a symptom of "how freaked out they were. The decade that we've just lived through has seen a tightening of the screw, and Xi Jinping was a part of that". Carrie recalls having to be tough in her dealings with the government functionaries who were not happy with BBC coverage. She surmises that having had a Chinese husband, Chinese friends and speaking the language had helped her as she "had a lot of friends in the establishment" and "liked sitting around talking to Chinese officials". She points out that at the time "the Foreign Ministry was full of kind of closet liberals" but speculates they are probably all deep undercover by now. She argues that since trade has opened up more with Beijing in recent years it has attracted a lot more Westerners but not ones who will necessarily put in the time to learn the language or understand the country's history or cultural norms (Fig. 1).

Carrie is proud of how she managed her role as BBC China Editor, given the tough political climate under the Chinese leader Xi Jinping, as the authorities always had to be seen to be pushing her around and putting pressure on her.

> It created ethical dilemmas because you know what the Chinese state does is to put pressure on the people whom you care about, when you *don't* do something they want you to do, or you *do* do something they don't want you to. They start hurting you where they can hurt you. All kinds of visas got rejected, and people were held up and their families were affected. And so, all kinds of collateral damage is happening around you, if you decide to take a firm stand on things in relation to China coverage. And that weighs on your conscience and involves difficult decisions and the protection of sources in China now involves very difficult ethical judgements as well.

Fig. 1 Carrie Gracie standing in front of the Forbidden City in Beijing, during Prince William's visit (2015)

She divided each year between London and Beijing, trying her hardest to guide her children through their teenage years while holding onto one of the top jobs in BBC journalism. There were obvious times to be in the UK, such as during Xi Jinping's visit to London in 2015. At the time, British viewers were obsessed by Brexit and Trump, and they weren't that interested in China. She thinks it is important to be in touch with your audience and to continue to understand their interests and obsessions, as well as the people in the country you are covering. This brings us onto the subject of the BBC employing local producers as correspondents. She gives the plan a big tick but adds:

> I think what is wonderful about getting more local talent on air and in production is the really serious commitment to stories, a serious understanding of stories, the enormous creativity that they bring to that. And so, the only thing I suppose then is a challenge is—can they communicate to a different audience that is not their audience? That is what I was saying about having to have both. And they need to get that somehow, or they need to be helped to get that by good production, or by spending time in their target audience. I think in general I really like putting on air people who are from the cultures of the stories that they're telling. I think it has to be done with care. It does take a lot of story-telling talent to communicate with an audience which is not your own.

She adds it would not be possible for the Chinese people who work for the BBC in Beijing to become correspondents because they and their families would come under too intense pressure from the regime. However, she thinks it is a very obvious role for the African journalists the BBC employs in different countries across the African continent, especially those with bilingual or first language English. She likes to hear their voices "bleed through from the World Service and World TV onto domestic radio and onto domestic TV".

During her role as China Editor Carrie did investigative reporting when she could. She said the Chinese authorities didn't get so angry about geo-political stories such as international tussles over the South China Sea; it was more the domestic stories about how they treated the population that upset them. These included stories on removing organs from prisoners "to pass them onto X, Y and Z", or their "oppression of the Tibetans or the people in Xinjiang or their pocketing loads of money and sending their kids abroad. Every China-based reporter knows which stories are super sensitive […] They hated the 'Murder in the Lucky Holiday Hotel' podcast and put us under a lot of pressure over that". In that podcast Carrie followed the true-life story of Gǔ Kāilái, a wealthy and dangerous Chinese businesswoman and the wife of Bó Xilái, (one time Minister of Commerce) before he was convicted on bribery and embezzlement charges.

This lively and provocative series investigated corruption in the Communist Party hierarchy and examined the case of Gǔ Kāilái who was found guilty and imprisoned for the murder of British businessman Neil Heywood. In episode 3, the reporting team is caught up in an angry confrontation with security personnel outside villa 16 in which Neil Heywood died. You can hear Carrie arguing purposefully with them to gain access, which is ultimately refused. This episode demonstrates something of the tension that comes with reporting hot-button issues in China. In episode 5 Carrie goes to the city of Chongqing, which Bó Xilái once ruled, only to find that the sole person in the city of 30 million who had been willing to do a sit-down interview had been warned off by China's propaganda department. Carrie's team is followed, their phones are bugged and their emails are hacked. Conducting vox pops, she finds Bó Xilái is still very popular on the streets and people think he is in prison for political reasons. Carrie believes she was under surveillance for months while conducting this story.

Back in 2005 Carrie had become interested in the urbanisation of the Chinese countryside as villages and small rural towns were transformed into large, industrialised cities. She focused on one village—White Horse Village—as it morphed from a small, insignificant village of farmers in south-western China into a large conglomeration with plenty of opportunities for some villagers, but cutting others out of the transformation. For the following ten years, she returned constantly to chart its stories of change and to profile its winners and losers: from the "restless mother" to the hapless Communist Party Secretary who is ultimately charged with corruption. The "economic miracle" delivered better schooling and more opportunities, but local corruption led to poorly built apartment blocks and forced demolitions. The series, commissioned by Newsnight and World News, won a Peabody and an Emmy. It also gained Carrie many enemies in the Chinese hierarchy.

Carrie made a number of other documentaries during this time, including "The Xi Factor" for Panorama.[4] In this film in which she examined the phenomenon that is the Chinese strongman leader, she is often "joined at the hip" by her minder from the Ministry of Propaganda. As she leaves the village where Xi grew up, she is urged by the minder to "make every single word about Xi positive in the entire film". Carrie does not allow an opportunity to go by without probing people for their views of Xi but the crackdown on dissent acts as a silencer on open or challenging views.

Carrie explained in her book "Equal: A story of women, men and money" and in her interview with me that her world came tumbling down while on holiday in July 2017. The BBC (due its new Royal Charter) had been forced to publish the salaries of its highest earning staff members. Carrie stared at the list: "It turned out that the highest-paid stars were all white men. There were very few women or ethnic minorities on the list at all, and they were mostly clumped towards the

---

[4] "Panorama," *The Xi Factor* (BBC, October 19, 2015), https://www.bbc.co.uk/programmes/b06kvljt.

bottom".[5] Featured on the list were the (male) North America Editor, the (male) Middle East Editor, the (male) Economics Editor and the (male) Home Affairs Editor—but *not* the China Editor, and not the Europe Editor, Katya Adler. She told me this news about her pay versus that of the men dropped out of the blue and "was just so disappointing". She said that if it had just been her, she would have got angry and then probably quit the BBC. However, there was "a bigger structural issue around it" involving unequal pay for women across the organisation. She recalled how she'd been to see the then head of newsgathering, Jonathan Munro, earlier that year and had talked about planning an exit from China, but he had said he couldn't do without her and "'you're so great', you know blah, blah, blah. The BBC can't do China without you". At the same time, as she later found out, he was promising other women more money because they demanded it and because they knew the list was coming out.

In her book Carrie explains that four years earlier, when she had accepted the job of China Editor, she had demanded equal pay from James Harding and had been told she would have the same salary as the North America Editor. Now she discovered that, "the North America Editor was earning at least 50 per cent more—and perhaps close to double of what [she] earned". Carrie was earning £134,000 and Jon Sopel between £200,000 and £250,000. Four days after the publication of the salaries, 44 senior BBC women wrote a letter to the Director-General Tony Hall, demanding equal pay for the same level jobs, and the group "BBC Women" was formed. There was little solidarity from men at the time, she notes, other than from the history presenter Dan Snow, and most of the first people through the managers' office doors to complain about their own salaries were men. Carrie believes that the way that the news came out, and how badly it was handled by management (whose members kept stressing the BBC was better than fellow broadcasters) meant that it was bound "to end in a catastrophe or a major collision". She wrote to Tony Hall in a letter she later reprinted in her book (2019: 35) explaining that she was a cancer survivor who

---

[5] Carrie Gracie, *Equal: A Story of Women, Men & Money* (London: Virago, 2019), 16.

had nursed her own child through leukaemia and hadn't wanted to take the job due to the strains it would put her and her family under.

> I agreed to do the job because I cared about our coverage of China and because I thought the BBC needed older women journalists to 'lean in'. I am bitterly disappointed to discover that my contribution as an editor is valued at so much less than my male peers.

Carrie was of the opinion that it needed "an Oliver Cromwell of a reformer to say 'this makes no sense. This doesn't stack up. We're going to rip it all up and we're going to make it equal'".

However, she added that Tony Hall "wasn't the person to reform the system properly".

A month after the announcement, Carrie sent an email to the BBC's Human Resources department stating she had not received equality of pay and naming Jon Sopel as her "comparator". The BBC said it would get back to her about her case but by September 2017 it still hadn't. In October BBC management offered her a £45,000 pay rise, but according to Carrie, this still didn't give her pay parity with her comparator or solve the underlying issues of unequal pay for women across the corporation. She declined the offer, employed a lawyer and "lodged a formal disagreement" (2019: 91). In her book Carrie details the difficulties that arose over the coming months of the BBC internal complaints process, during which she felt gaslighted and undermined by the corporation and was made to question her self-worth.

Meanwhile in parliamentary hearings the BBC's management claimed its internal review had found it had no equal pay problem, while the "BBC Women" pooled their investigative resources, communicating information by messaging app. Carrie underlines that the BBC had an "ethnicity pay gap" as well as a gender pay gap, with some members of the BBC Women group pointing out that they had been "disadvantaged twice over" (Gracie, 2019: 119). In early December 2017 Carrie resigned as China Editor because she wasn't being paid equally to the men in similar positions and she returned to London to work instead as a presenter and reporter. On 8th January 2018 Carrie wrote an open letter to the *Times*,[6] explaining why she had stood down from her China Editor post. The letter was published in full on the front page. Carrie addressed a number of angles in her writing, stating:

> Patience and good will are running out. In the six months since July's revelations, the BBC has attempted a botched solution based on divide and rule. It has offered some women pay "revisions" which do not guarantee equality, while locking down other women in a protracted complaints process.

She ended with a call to arms:

> It is a century since women first won the right to vote in Britain. Let us honour that brave generation by making this the year we win equal pay.

Carrie's grievance claim was put through a lengthy process, in which at one point it was argued that her pay was different to her male peers because she had been in a "growth and development" phase during her time as China Editor—something that had never been mentioned during the period she held the job. She had, after all, been connected to reporting China on and off for a quarter of a century. It seemed none of the male editors had gone through such a process and all evaluations of Carrie's work had been exemplary, with managers citing her work in public as ensuring the BBC's TV licence was worth paying. She wrote:

> "No one could have been a better BBC China Editor. I was not in development, and I had to turn my anger into effective action in the hope that future generations of women might escape these insults".[7]

When Carrie went to give evidence in parliament regarding unequal pay, supporting her from the audience were veteran correspondent Kate Adie, and Miriam O'Reilly who had successfully sued the BBC in court over ageism. Also in the house were presenter Samira Ahmed who would

---

[6] Carrie Gracie, "Carrie Gracie: Secretive BBC Made Us Feel Trapped," *The Times*, January 8, 2018.

[7] Gracie, *Equal: A Story of Women, Men & Money*, 167.

go on to launch and win her own case against the BBC over equal pay, and Martine Croxall who sued the BBC for age and sex discrimination. At Carrie's hearing the general secretary of the National Union of Journalists, Michelle Stanistreet, testified that the union "had lodged a collective grievance on behalf of 121 members of staff, with more joining subsequently".[8] Over the following months Carrie fought on, turning down a further offer that still didn't meet a threshold of pay parity. Finally, in late June the BBC acknowledged it had underpaid Carrie and agreed to pay her several years of back pay at the same salary as Jon Sopel. The Director-General Tony Hall and Carrie wrote a joint press release:

> "The BBC is committed to the principle of equal pay and acting in accordance with our values [...] Carrie has made, and will continue to make, an important contribution to the BBC. During her tenure as China Editor, Carrie delivered reports, analysis, and work, that were as valuable as those of the other International Editors in the same period".[9]

Carrie had won and she elected to give all the money to the Fawcett Society and the charity YESS Law. This would help the Fawcett Society to get its Equal Pay Advice Service up and running and enable YESS Law to aid low-paid women get access to solid legal advice. For YESS, the priority was to help women avoid litigation while seeking redress of grievances. It had taken Carrie a year to get this resolution and by the time she secured it there were 500 journalists in the "BBC Women" organisation. She credits her years as a foreign correspondent in Beijing for enabling her to take on the fight. In a radio interview in 2022 she said:

> The important thing that I want to say about this experience is that it is the defiance that I learned in China that enabled me to take on the BBC,

---

[8] Gracie, 170.
[9] Gracie, 229.

because I had been forced to think very hard, over 30 years as a China reporter, about what was "true north" ethically for me as a reporter.[10]

In the last pages of her book, Carrie celebrated her win while acknowledging her bosses at the BBC had had "a tough time trying to modernise a venerable national institution for turbulent times" (2019: 251). She wrote that she was grateful to them "for keeping the argument separate from the person making it". At the start of August 2020 her Panorama episode examining "China's Coronavirus Cover-up" aired.[11] Shortly afterwards she announced that she was leaving the BBC. In a way she prefaced this in her book when she explained how she had earlier been forced to take time off work due to the stress of the whole business:

> I now understand why whistle-blowers rarely continue to work for the organisation they call out, often don't work again at all and struggle to recover their trust in people and organisations.

In my interview with her the overwhelming feeling I got was that while her anger may have abated, her disappointment with the whole process had not. Her attitude in advising her children about where they might work in the future sums up how she now feels about employment screening and worth:

> When you look for an organisation, really check out the organisation, the culture of the organisation. And it's not about your job title or your pay, it's about your quality of life and the quality of the future and how much the "values" of the organisation can corrode and poison and change you.

Carrie, she told me she'd "finished with news". These days she volunteers as a bereavement counsellor and spends quality time with her children, friends and a boyfriend in south-west France. Nonetheless, her continuing interest in China reporting came through. For example, with

---

[10] "Sinica Live in London, with Legendary BBC Presenter and China Editor Carrie Gracie" (Sinica Podcast, October 6, 2022), https://thechinaproject.com/2022/10/06/sinica-live-in-london-with-legendary-bbc-presenter-and-china-editor-carrie-gracie/.
[11] "Panorama," *China's Coronavirus Cover-Up* (BBC 1, August 1, 2020).

regards to the Covid pandemic, she lamented: "I really wished I'd been in China at the start of Covid because that was an incredible story, obviously a very problematic story, but I wanted to be there and wasn't". In discussing her ten years of filming of the White Horse Village series, she noted "But someday I'll get my Wellington boots on and get down to that village again".

References

"BBC World News." *The New Silk Road*, March 17, 2017. Carrie Gracie Webpage. https://carriegracie.com/carrie-gracie---silk-road-bbc-news-film.html.
"China, Human Organ Trade, 1994." *BBC Breakfast News*, May 1994. https://www.youtube.com/watch?v=yngV3pNYEho.
Gracie, Carrie. "Carrie Gracie: Secretive BBC Made Us Feel Trapped." *The Times*, January 8, 2018.
Gracie, Carrie. *Equal: A Story of Women, Men & Money*. London: Virago, 2019.
Gracie, Carrie. "Murder in the Lucky Holiday Hotel," March 17, 2017. https://www.bbc.co.uk/news/resources/idt-sh/Murder_lucky_hotel.
"Panorama." *The Xi Factor*. BBC, October 19, 2015. https://www.bbc.co.uk/programmes/b06kvljt.
"Panorama." *China's Coronavirus Cover-Up*. BBC 1, August 1, 2020.
"Sinica Live in London, with Legendary BBC Presenter and China Editor Carrie Gracie." Sinica Podcast, October 6, 2022. https://thechinaproject.com/2022/10/06/sinica-live-in-london-with-legendary-bbc-presenter-and-china-editor-carrie-gracie/.

Sara Beck
Bureau Chief in Moscow, Jerusalem and Singapore, Head of the Russian Service and BBC Monitoring

> *"I was driven by a real passion for a part of the world and the language and the culture and everything that came with that. And then that translated into the journalism".*

It is July 2022 and I am interviewing Sara Beck at the Reuters Institute in Oxford. I had wanted to select a journalist who had worked more on the producing side of news rather than as a correspondent. At some time in a BBC career, everyone makes a decision or falls onto a particular path which takes them towards radio, TV or online, national programming or the World Service, news or current affairs and into reporting, producing or news editing. And even though the BBC would argue these areas are all intertwined these days in one seamless multifunctional news gathering team called "Content", people will always have leanings towards different types of news production, even if they change their path along the way.

Sara Beck, until recently the Chief Operating Officer for the Saïd Business School at the University of Oxford, was born in Yorkshire to a mother who was a primary school teacher and a father who was the director of a teaching institute called Carnegie College. When she was growing up in Yorkshire in the 1970s and early 1980s, the news stories that stuck clearly in her mind were the rise of Prime Minister Margaret Thatcher, the miners' strike and the "Yorkshire Ripper". The hunt for Peter Sutcliffe, who murdered 13 women and attempted to murder a further seven, greatly affected her childhood, because she wasn't allowed to walk anywhere by herself and was always met from school. She noted, "That was a strong story and the reporting of that story I remember really clearly, for those were kind of seminal years". The last murder was of a Leeds University student and it took place behind a Safeway supermarket where Sara had a Saturday job. These were stories in the news that directly affected her life. On the international news side, she remembers the Falklands War of 1982 but it didn't affect her in the same way as the stories closer to home. We shared a memory of the famous phrase by BBC reporter Brian Hanrahan from on board an aircraft carrier: "I counted them [aircraft] all out and I counted them all back" and she laughed saying she was very proud to have worked with him during her career.[1]

Sara studied languages (including Russian) at her state school in Leeds and then went on to read French and Russian at Bristol University. Her first plan was to use her languages to work abroad. In her third year she was finally able to go to the Soviet Union, "And it was just like this door opened into this magical world, that bore no resemblance to anything else. I was transfixed". In her fourth year she slipped in another trip to Leningrad on a cultural exchange and was hooked. After university she got a job in advertising, and from there applied for a "tourist representative" position with one of entrepreneur Richard Branson's companies that had a partnership with the Russian company "Intourist" in Yalta. On completing the interview she was sent off to Crimea for a year. Feeling super fluent in Russian after this job, and wanting to do more, she approached a friend who was in the Russian Service at the BBC. This friend put her in touch with an editor who asked her to do a report for them in Russian, which she did on the annual Notting Hill Carnival. A vacancy as a production assistant came up shortly afterwards and she

---

[1] "Veteran BBC Reporter Brian Hanrahan Dies Aged 61," *The Times*, December 21, 2010, https://www.thetimes.com/article/veteran-bbc-reporter-brian-hanrahan-dies-aged-61-8x8d20kx57b.

landed the job in 1991. At the World Service she worked with Russian broadcasters, editing and producing their radio programmes together. While her friend worked in news, Sara was in Arts where her colleagues were "a group of 1970s émigrés, many of whom were Jewish and highly cultured, wonderful and eccentric". She ended up as a producer for writers such as Zinovy Zinik, who went on to great acclaim. With Zinik she would travel to places such as Edinburgh and New York for literary festivals and to make programmes about Russian artists.

After working for a while in the language services she moved on to the English-speaking section of the World Service and programmes such as "Meridian" and "Outlook". These programmes' essential appeal is that their stories usually unfold gently in an unhurried manner, which couldn't be further from news. She would sometimes commission news correspondents, such as Carrie Gracie (see Chapter 7), who was then the reporter in Beijing, to do arts pieces. She got her first job on the news side when a vacancy came up as a producer in the Moscow bureau for national radio (NCA). She hadn't done much in the way of news, and felt she was a bit "untested". But she was successful and went over to Moscow, and quite quickly she also started doing TV producing, a role she learnt on the job.

One of the major ongoing stories at the time was the first Chechen war, when the Russians unleashed a huge assault on Grozny and then occupied the city. Teams tended to go in from the UK via a base in Nazran in Ingushetia to cover the fighting. Sara also travelled outside Russia to cover the fighting in Kosovo. But this was the Yeltsin era and there were plenty of political and social stories to cover on base. Working with Diana Goodman (Chapter 3) she produced stories connected to the degradation of the Soviet infrastructure and worsening social conditions. Then when President Yeltsin became ill and had a heart operation, the bureau did countless stories from outside his hospital "with zero information". Other big stories she remembered from the time included "gangster capitalism and the crash of the rouble". She recounted that the BBC bureau was put at huge financial risk at the time because "the rouble devalued through our fingers".

She worked happily alongside the TV producer Kate Peters and Jamie Coomarasamy, the World Service producer, whose aim was to become a reporter. Sara did a bit of reporting but believes she didn't have "the blinkered approach" necessary to be a reporter. She got more satisfaction out of getting the team to the right place and making the bigger operation work. She laughed, "It became clear that I was more managerial". During this time she worked long hours, travelling into the office listening to the commercial radio station Ekho Moskvy in the car, and then picking up the latest information from Reuters, Sky and NBC whose correspondents were all in the same building. As the Moscow bureau was ahead of London time, they had time in the morning to plan their day before speaking to the news desk back in London.

> We would pair up with correspondents and support them on their stories, arranging interviews, editing clips and mixing packages. At that time, there was still a stronger [dividing] line between domestic output and international output and there were some turf wars about who would appear on which programmes. Broadly speaking, we managed to keep it harmonious and not waste time or resources. That was mainly down to a strong sense of the team in the bureau, which we worked hard to maintain.

Russia was not the easiest base for conducting journalism. It was always difficult to access verifiable information from Kremlin sources and finding people who spoke enough English for broadcast interviews was also a challenge.

> A lot of effort went into finding English speaking interviewees so that we could create the best possible packages or live guests. It was no mean feat to find Russians with fluent English, an interesting perspective or specialist knowledge. We had a list of 'friendly' English-speaking political analysts who would oblige us by coming into the office and doing rounds of interviews in the radio studios. And we were always on the look-out for more and I nurtured a fat contact book of English speakers and fixers in the provincial cities and towns. They were always at a premium.

At this stage of her career a large percentage of her day was taken up undertaking basic editing jobs, and checking off pieces for each of the radio and television bulletins on breaking news stories.

In the days before digital editing, as a producer I would sit for hours in the radio studio cutting down quarter-inch tape interviews into clips for packages and then mixing it all together with the correspondent's links from tape to tape. For TV, it was a larger team effort. We had really experienced picture editors and camera-crews in Moscow so often I would be editing the radio version and dropping in and out of the TV edit room to check how the editor and correspondent were getting on. It was the most efficient way to get bi-media pieces together. The online versions had yet to arrive to make the versioning even more complicated.

In 1995 the BBC announced it would be interviewing for six bureau chiefs in Moscow, Brussels, Washington, Hong Kong, Johannesburg and Jerusalem. The external candidate who was offered the Moscow job then pulled out, and Sarah was asked to apply in his place. She thus became the only woman out of the six:

And that was a really strong group because they did a very good job of inducting us and they locked us in a basement in Shepherd's Bush for two weeks and kind of did management 101 on us. And the group of six of us stayed really close and supportive.

When you include Monitoring, the Russian language service journalists, drivers, fixers, translators, a cook and weekend support staff, Sara estimated there were around 60 people on the BBC payroll at that time in Russia. There was a lot of coming and going of multiple correspondents and reporters including Diana Goodman, Jamie Coomarasamy, Angus Roxburgh, Rob Parsons and Martin Sixsmith—with Andrew Harding in the Caucasus. Her job was to keep the bureau afloat financially, make sure all the stories were covered and check all the journalists were working well together and weren't "at daggers drawn" as they could be in other bureaux. Overall, Sara worked there for five years including seeing the handover of presidential power to "some newcomer called Vladimir Putin" as the clock ticked over onto New Year's Day 2000. She laughs thinking about how hard it had been to get on a bulletin when this news was announced because of the "Y2K dramas" (when people feared all the world's websites would fail to tick over to the new millennium). The other important fact she remembers is that she went in to Moscow with a partner and came out single.

At this time the head of foreign news, Jenny Baxter, had called her and offered her an interim position as the bureau chief in Jerusalem and so in early 2000 she set off for the Middle East where she was to remain for a year. The job was 24/7. As had happened in Moscow, the Jerusalem bureau also needed to relocate to cope with the growing number of staff. This post she found especially hard at first because the Middle East wasn't her area of expertise; but she did have correspondents such as Paul Adams, who had grown up in the Middle East and knew its politics backwards. In any spare time she had, she would read widely, trying to get her head around the new dateline. She is sanguine about the effects of going from expert to learner:

> I see it much more about stages in your career, because you have to go from specialist to generalist, to scale. I think it's very specific to journalism and the amount of back knowledge you need, particularly for production […] But I think in any career, there's that point where you go from real comfort zone and depth, to having to take that step and make that transition. The same happened later in stepping out of the media and into higher education management.

She gained confidence during her time in Israel and in reference to the newsgathering she argued, "you just need to mainline the story". That year the BBC Jerusalem bureau won the Gold Monte Carlo Film Award for its coverage of the "Second Intifada 2000" story. Within the year Jenny Baxter had called again and said she could stay in Jerusalem or she might want to consider Singapore. Management didn't seem to mind which she did and said it was her choice. In the end she chose Singapore, partly because she felt worn out by Jerusalem after Moscow. Jerusalem was a place where there were no boundaries between work and home life, and she "was not very good at boundaries".

Singapore was very different—there was no "mainlining the [everyday] story" there, instead stories had to be found from across the region. The correspondents were Matt Frei, followed by Clive Myrie. She had a producer at the time called Jeremy Hillman, who used to do the diary. And whereas in Jerusalem the diary was all about what was happening that day close by, in Singapore it could be Tokyo, Manila, "and anything east of Delhi". Sara was based there from 2001 to 2003 and the stories she remembers particularly were the Bali bombings, the World Cup in Tokyo, East Timor independence, troubles in Jakarta and the awarding of the Olympic Games to China. "After Jerusalem it was an absolute shock—we were looking for stories, and they were primarily features". In contrast to working in Jerusalem where she was concerned "primarily [with] safety and who have I got where and a lot of kind of pastoral [work] keeping people on track", in Singapore her job involved visiting the different bureaux and supporting the people and "kind of bureau politics".

After a couple of years, Sara decided that she wanted to return to the UK. She put store by her personal relationships and once again she felt herself adrift. A job on special projects was created for her in Newsgathering (now BBC Content) and she teamed up again with Diana Goodman on some of those. When Jenny Baxter went on maternity leave, she worked with two senior news heads, Richard Sambrook and Adrian Van Klaveren, on planning coverage for a possible Gulf War. Then suddenly in April 2003 she was also drawn into dealing with two deaths of staff members in quick succession. The first was Kaveh Golestan, a camera operator in Northern Iraq who stepped on an antipersonnel landmine. In this incident the producer, Stuart Hughes, was also injured, leading to the amputation of the lower part of his leg. Within a week, a translator, Kamaran Abdurazaq Muhamed, who was part of John Simpson's reporting team in Northern Iraq, was also killed. Sara worked as a family liaison, overseeing the return of the bodies to their families and helping with the funerals. On another front she co-edited a book on the Iraq War called "The Battle for Iraq"[2] with Malcolm Downing and Diana Goodman. This featured articles from BBC teams covering the war from different locations.

---

[2] Sara Beck and Malcolm Downing, eds., *The Battle for Iraq: BBC News Correspondents on the War against Saddam and a New World Agenda* (London: BBC Worldwide Ltd, 2003).

In 2003 the job as head of the BBC Russian Service came up. This job meant being in charge of around 100 journalists in both London and Moscow. This took her into a whole new area of "change management" which meant on the one hand reinvigorating an area of the BBC that wasn't doing so well and on the other hand deciding on cuts in resources.

> The service had run the same way for a long time and I guess it's only to be expected that some weren't looking for the level of change that we brought in. We were under real pressure to improve the audience figures and the quality of the output. We had to look at what we could do differently, and better. We modernised the schedule, and moved more presentation to Moscow to be closer to our audiences. We brought in different formats to add to the traditional translated package from English output, and we expanded the online presence.

This meant many trips back to Russia.

> In addition to putting a focus on the quality of the journalism, we also started to manage performance and behaviours more attentively. Some of the Russian journalists took the opportunity, particularly in the online team, to develop their reporting and profile really well. And several of them moved out of the service into English output roles. I really liked that kind of movement, especially if colleagues then came back into the language service and brought new ideas and ways of doing things. We had some real stars.

In 2005 Sara took time out for six months to study (via a Reuters fellowship at the University of Oxford) and wrote a report on "neutral language" in newsgathering which used the siege of Beslan (2004) as an example. Sara then returned to her Russian Service job until 2006. She brought in new people to improve the editorial and online services and she enabled the department to work more collaboratively with "Newsgathering". In late 2006 Sara was asked to head up the Business and Economics Unit at TV Centre in Shepherd's Bush, "because it needed some changes". She added, "So I kind of moved from this person that had the Moscow connection to being the person that made changes".

She thought that running a bureau was the best training on the job you could get for moving into management.

Along the way Sara undertook more focused training—from within the internal BBC coaching programme and also externally through the "Runge Balliol" management course at Oxford. Looking back, she didn't ever feel like she had to ask, "What about me?" She said she had informal management mentors, people such as Jenny Baxter, Fran Unsworth and Mark Byford. On the topic of equal pay for equal work, an issue that ended up being called the "BBC Equal Pay Scandal" (see Chapter 6), Sara is convinced she was paid less than her male colleagues in several instances. The first time was when she was appointed bureau chief in Moscow. Again, like the other women I have interviewed in this book, she said that when this was happening, "I would have presumed that it was all fair" but she had never questioned her pay. She remembered that when the World News Editor Vin Ray offered her the Moscow bureau chief job in 1995, he told her what he wanted her to do and said:

> 'Just tell me what it is that you want?' And I said 'Just give me whatever I'm supposed to have'. So I had no idea that that was an opener for me to put a figure on the table. So I was an absolute walkover with them. And I know that other bureau chiefs when that moment came, they would put a high number forward and then negotiate on flights and school fees. And I just never did. Plus I was single, so they never paid any of those extra things for me anyway. And then later on in my career, I knew very well that I was undervalued and I challenged it as I was leaving—but I was leaving.

Sara said the issue wasn't so much about the remuneration as she was being paid well, but it was about parity.

> I think it's about fairness and clarity. And the mindset, the reason why the BBC got itself tied into all of that was more about mindset than process or an attempt to be unfair. It was about a kind of understood, in my opinion, an understood value that was being brought. And the issue is that the "understood value" was something that was not fairly consulted or researched, you know, so it was just the kind of accepted view of who was where.

Sara reiterated that she had simply been "very trusting of the organisation that I worked in" and that she assumed that as there were employment bands or grades and they had been creating six bureau chiefs, then obviously they would all be paid the same. She didn't think that any differences would have been down to location of the bureau because "you had your local conditions remuneration" added on to your base salary. "There was this accepted view of who was good and that was strongly male led—you know, who was a good performer".

Later on, the on-screen talent would have their agents negotiate for them, which skewed difference again. In discussing her own case she said:

> What I probably didn't realise is those others that were maybe the bureau chiefs, some of them might already have had more miles on the clock than I did production-wise. So they were probably on a higher salary anyway. And the thing that they didn't do is—they wouldn't have lifted you up to that. And that's why you get caught in a tribunal because it's the same job.

In the interests of full disclosure Sara said she had been in the room, but wasn't part of the discussion, when Carrie Gracie's salary was originally negotiated for the China Editor job. She thinks something similar happened there, insofar as Carrie's salary "was fair in the firmament at that time" and then something moved. Jon Sopel's salary for the Washington Editor's position went up and Carrie's wasn't brought up to equal that.

After working with the business and economics team in TV Centre, she spent the next five years in a range of different management jobs. First she returned to the World Service in 2008 to oversee the 75th anniversary of its founding. She organised large events such as concerts, community gatherings and competitions. She also commissioned a season of special editorial outputs connected to the anniversary. After that she became deputy editor of BBC programmes under Steve Mitchell. This section of the BBC had 1,100 people in it and she worked on the planning side with a £95 m budget. Once again "change" involved getting people "to work more collaboratively and efficiently" and "trying to move some of the programme editors into a different space". Programmes included everything from the *Today* programme on Radio 4 to BBC1's *Panorama*. She was also in overall charge of complaints and the risk assessment for programme deployments abroad. Here she drew on her experience of working in the field in Newsgathering. She was also trying to get "Current Affairs" people to work more openly with "News" colleagues.

Then in 2011 along came the Jimmy Savile scandal,[3] in which the former BBC presenter was found to have sexually abused hundreds of people over his lifetime. Her manager Steve Mitchell was asked to step aside during the investigation and he left the BBC shortly afterwards. The Pollard Report[4] found he had taken a *Panorama* programme about Jimmy Savile off the "risk register" of sensitive programmes, and, according to an article by Lisa O'Carroll had he not done this "there would have been wider awareness of allegations that Savile was a paedophile in the runup to Christmas 2011".[5] In the meantime Sara went on maternity leave until 2013, after which she returned to work as deputy head of Newsgathering. There she worked again on a "change agenda" and oversaw 800 staff in 40 bureaus around the world. This section had a budget of £91 m.

In 2016 Sara's career took off in another completely different direction when she got the job of "Director, BBC Monitoring" which was based in a stately home in Caversham, Berkshire. Here BBCM provided open-source news and information in 100 languages from 150 countries. Monitoring was "a big change job" that had already begun but the person in charge had left suddenly. The funding of Monitoring had been transferred to the BBC in 2013 as part of the government's "2010 Comprehensive Spending Review",[6] and since then the BBC's budget

---

[3] Josh Halliday, "Jimmy Savile: Timeline of His Sexual Abuse and Its Uncovering," *The Guardian*, June 26, 2014, https://www.theguardian.com/media/2014/jun/26/jimmy-savile-sexual-abuse-timeline.

[4] Nick Pollard, "The Pollard Review," December 18, 2012, BBC Archives, http://downloads.bbc.co.uk/bbctrust/assets/files/pdf/our_work/pollard_review/pollard_review.pdf.

[5] Lisa O'Carroll, "Pollard Report: BBC News Deputy Stephen Mitchell Retires without Payout," *The Guardian*, December 20, 2012, https://www.theguardian.com/media/2012/dec/20/pollard-report-bbc-news-deputy.

[6] "Spending Review 2010," Policy Paper (London: UK Government, May 29, 2013), https://www.gov.uk/government/publications/spending-review-2010.

had been cut dramatically. In turn, the annual operating budget for Monitoring had fallen from £15 m to £13.5 m and was due to fall further. Under the cuts, Monitoring had to lose £4.5 m.

Over the course of a couple of years Sara worked with a consulting company called Cognizant and succeeded in reaching the £4.5 m target but this involved making 98 people from Monitoring (in the UK and abroad) redundant. She found this really hard and she did her best to redeploy people to make room for some staff in other areas of the BBC. She added people to bureaux in Jerusalem and Istanbul, but as was acknowledged in an email sent out at the time, 1000 years of experience left the BBC in this move. Sara believes that she did a good job with the brief and at the time that she left, Monitoring was making money, was completely digitised and people were doing "agile working". She had found on arrival that Monitoring had been in a bad way, lacking resources and betraying signs of inefficiency. Under her management the ways of working were restructured, streamlined and additional new technology was introduced. There were "new teams, new values, objectives and key results". In 2019 Cognizant (in partnership with BBCM) won the MCA award for "Transformation Project in the Public Sector". She believes these changes have been shown to work successfully for the department in the war in Ukraine.

Nonetheless managing these changes at Monitoring had been a political hot potato and she and the director of news, Fran Unsworth, had to give testimony before two parliamentary select committees on the planned changes. Because Monitoring also delivered "Open Source" radio monitoring data to government bodies, MPs wanted to know why the BBC was hacking into the department's budget. In one of the Select Committee hearings on Defence, titled "Open Source Stupidity: The Threat to the BBC Monitoring Service" an MP explained that a group of visiting colleagues had discovered some monitors on the Russia Desk in Caversham had been working on a story about the American actor Steven Seagal being given Russian citizenship.[7] They were worried that

---

[7] "Open Source Stupidity: The Threat to the BBC Monitoring Service" (House of Commons Defence Committee, December 13, 2016), https://publications.parliament.uk/pa/cm201617/cmselect/cmdfence/748/748.pdf.

this "popularisation—if not infantilisation—of BBC Monitoring is well underway". In oral evidence Sara replied:

> There are some strands of the work to which Monitoring contributes that might include a piece about Steven Seagal. But if you look at the front page of our portal—our shop window, if you like—today's stories are about the Chinese media reaction to the TPP talks, Ukraine abducting Russian troops, the Yemen truce, and an analysis piece about the Russian weekly programme, Vesti Nedeli. I do think there is still capacity for us to carry on doing that kind of work.

After three years in this role, in 2019 Sara applied for the job of Director of the World Service but lost out to Jamie Angus. The BBC had paid for her to have an external executive career coach when she took on the job at Monitoring as extra support; now Sara began to consider that perhaps her next role might be outside the Corporation as she felt she'd done versions of most of the jobs that might be left inside it. She also put the word out to a couple of friends in her network and was then approached by a head-hunter to apply for a job as Chief Operating Officer (COO) with the Saïd Business School (SBS) at the University of Oxford. In the press release announcing her new role, SBS wrote:

> Sara has an impressive track record in leading change and supporting multi-functional areas through transition and transformation. Most recently, at BBC Monitoring, Sara took her department through a complex restructuring and relocation programme.

In her new job Sara was working with 450 staff and with an annual budget of £90 m. SBS deals with research and training for Oxford University—from undergraduates to MBAs, through to executive education. Sara was brought in to manage the professional services side of the operation and was just getting her head around these new challenges when Covid-19 hit.

> And you know we went into crisis management. But of course, I was very comfy in crisis management, because that's all I'd ever done. [...] Actually, it was a great lily pad to land on. I was very clear, I didn't want

to do comms, because I've got loads of friends that have done comms. And in my discussions with that coach, her view was that in comms, you're completely dependent on the relationship with the CEO. And so, it's a much harder job to have influence and have a say in things, because you're just kind of dependent on that. Which is a bit like working with a correspondent, isn't it? But, in COO roles, you're kind of in the room, and it was much more what I was used to; it's kind of general manager, executive, and it was great.

Alongside this job, Sara also had a board position with Global Canopy, an environmental charity.

When we met, Sara had just resigned from SBS in order to accompany her husband and children to Thailand (Fig. 1). This was the first time she didn't have anything planned ahead in work terms, except for undertaking an executive coaching accreditation with Meyler Campbell while in Bangkok. When I spoke to her again, a year later, she had completed her training and she already had her first clients in Bangkok and elsewhere. In 2024 she returned to the UK in order for her children to begin the GCSE cycle at school. Her client database is going well and she has plenty of work on the horizon.

When she looked back on her career, she thought it had been an exciting one even if she hadn't always been very strategic. Unlike men, she says, she didn't plot where her next job would be, each time she took on a new role.

> I think the Russia thread ran through and was really useful for me, and that's where my heart is. So, it was fine. I think I went with things that I liked doing. I certainly wasn't on the ball about salaries and that final BBC job that I had; I know that I was tens of thousands out from the person before me [in Monitoring].

This thought bothers her because she felt that by that time, she was much more confident in her approach to her work. She thinks her career coaches have helped her with this.

> But earlier on, it wouldn't have crossed my mind. And I think I was very trusting. And I was always looking for excitement. And I would go

Fig. 1 Sara Beck pictured at the Reuters Institute at Oxford University (2022)

> further and further and (unlike some of the others), I didn't have a family. So, they would have been thinking about "where can I put my kids" and that kind of thing. I didn't. I never put that responsibility on the BBC, I brought myself home [to the UK] because I knew I wanted to settle down. And I never asked the Beeb to be part of that. Whereas I know other people did. I know other people would have said, you know, "I need this deployment because of family".

When I asked her if international news was still a good career option for young women, she thought it was, but it was different to when she first went to Moscow because then it was quite the "Wild West" with far fewer safety measures and now there's a more disciplined approach. She believes today there is much more consideration about safety and pastoral issues involved with "post trauma" effects. In the past there weren't so many women in international Newsgathering and not many rules about how things were done. "These days I am forceful in my advice about clarity and about being clear about salary". She thinks it is still an exciting career, but she advises people to have a specialism that lights them up to do it.

> I was driven by a real passion for a part of the world and the language and the culture and everything that came with that. And then that translated into the journalism. And I would say, more or less all of us in that Moscow group, and we were quite tight, and we've all stayed in touch with each other, were doing it because of that. So, I always say when I'm talking to younger people, you need that thing that fires you and energizes and drives you and then you acquire the other skills around that to turn that into something else, to take it further.

She does wonder if young journalists in the future would be prepared to put in the hard yards of experience to get the job they want. She is adamant that nobody mentioned work-life balance in the first 20 years of working, "and you know personal relationships for me crashed on those rocks". She related an incident where somebody from the Moscow bureau rang a London manager to explain how their relationship was splitting up and was asked what number marriage it was, to which the reply was "second". This person in London then replied, "only your second?" And this, she argues, "is horribly accepted". She said that one had to put up with being called out of celebrations, weddings, and holidays. Today she is married with two children and admits that that is still quite rare for women in foreign news.

> It's been a great career—so I'm more accepting of some of the things at the BBC that weren't in place and some of the failures and mistakes that have been made. And I don't think they should be there, and they're getting ironed out, but it was still a great career and I think I was very lucky.

References

Beck, Sara, and Malcolm Downing, eds. *The Battle for Iraq: BBC News Correspondents on the War against Saddam and a New World Agenda.* London: BBC Worldwide Ltd, 2003.
Halliday, Josh. "Jimmy Savile: Timeline of His Sexual Abuse and Its Uncovering." *The Guardian*, June 26, 2014. https://www.theguardian.com/media/2014/jun/26/jimmy-savile-sexual-abuse-timeline.
O'Carroll, Lisa. "Pollard Report: BBC News Deputy Stephen Mitchell Retires without Payout." *The Guardian*, December 20, 2012. https://www.theguardian.com/media/2012/dec/20/pollard-report-bbc-news-deputy.
"Open Source Stupidity: The Threat to the BBC Monitoring Service." House of Commons Defence Committee, December 13, 2016. https://publications.parliament.uk/pa/cm201617/cmselect/cmdfence/748/748.pdf.
Pollard, Nick. "The Pollard Review," December 18, 2012. BBC Archives. http://downloads.bbc.co.uk/bbctrust/assets/files/pdf/our_work/pollard_review/pollard_review.pdf.
"Spending Review 2010." Policy Paper. London: UK Government, May 29, 2013. https://www.gov.uk/government/publications/spending-review-2010.
The Times. "Veteran BBC Reporter Brian Hanrahan Dies Aged 61." December 21, 2010. https://www.thetimes.com/article/veteran-bbc-reporter-brian-hanrahan-dies-aged-61-8x8d20kx57b.

Caroline Wyatt
Presenter on Radio 4 PM. Formerly Berlin, Moscow, Paris, Defence and Religious Affairs Correspondent

"Go heavy on the torture, light on the donkey".

Caroline was born in 1967 in a mother and baby home run by the Catholic Church in Darlinghurst, a suburb of Sydney. She found out later that her mother Irena was from a Polish immigrant family and had just turned 16 when she gave birth, while her Anglo-Irish father Alan had been 18. She was adopted, along with two other boys, by a British diplomat David Wyatt and his Swiss wife Annemarie. They had a peripatetic lifestyle, moving from posting to posting including to Canada, Sweden, Northern Ireland during the Troubles and Berlin during the Cold War. In order to ease the disruptions of uprooting she was despatched to boarding school in Surrey, where she read a great deal and remembers wanting to write for one of her treasured teen magazines.

Before starting university she travelled over to Berlin to spend some time with her father, by then the minister and deputy commandant of the British sector of the military government. Later that year Caroline returned to England to study English Literature and German at Southampton University. During her years as a student she didn't get involved with the college newspaper but said she enjoyed working on a journal devoted to poetry, and literature which was "full of adolescent angst".[1] During her studies she undertook an exchange with Rutgers University in New Jersey where she took a course in journalism, and she interned at *Cosmopolitan* magazine.

After her BA, she decided to pursue further study at City, University of London, where she took a postgraduate diploma in magazine journalism. There her tutor pushed her to apply to the ITN and BBC graduate training schemes. Despite "two horrible interviews" she won a place on the BBC scheme and began two years of news and current affairs placements. Her intake of eight young journalists in 1991 was the first one to include more women than men. After stints on the Six and Nine o'clock TV news bulletins, the Radio Four newsroom, and various regional newsrooms including Birmingham and Newsroom Southeast, she ended up in World Service Television (World TV), which is where I first met her on the smokers' balcony on the fifth floor of TV Centre. I remember her at that time as smart, funny and eager to get on. The newsroom hummed with restlessness: depending on your stage of life and career you were either eager to escape into the wide world, or you were excited plotting the next bulletin. Today she retains her hearty laugh, her resonant voice, a pragmatic approach to life and a fondness for recounting a cracking yarn.

She remembered noting that there were women in interesting and senior positions at the corporation—including Jenny Abramsky who was a senior manager in radio, presenters Angela Rippon and Valerie Singleton, and the roving TV correspondent Kate Adie. She nominated Bridget Kendall and Diana Goodman as people she held to be role models. At the end of her two year contract, Caroline secured a job with World TV, where she worked as a producer, and sometimes reporter. In one job she had to organise the foreign correspondents' work and this encouraged her to try her own hand abroad. She took a punt and applied to become a "sponsored stringer" for the World Service in Berlin,

---

[1] Caroline Wyatt and Scott Hughes, "CV: Caroline Wyatt: Bonn Correspondent, BBC," *The Independent*, February 23, 1998, https://www.independent.co.uk/news/media/cv-caroline-wyatt-bonn-correspondent-bbc-1146423.html.

with the impressive title of "German Business Correspondent". In an interview in 2021 with "Women in Journalism", Caroline said:

> "And so when I decided to go abroad, it was actually to Berlin where I'd lived as a teenager when my father was working for the British military government. So it was a place I knew in a country I knew, and I was fascinated by the history and the current affairs. And so in one sense it was cheating because going to Berlin felt like coming home".[2]

In 1993 she packed a suitcase, popped it into the boot of her car and drove to Berlin where she stayed on a friend's sofa-bed until she found an apartment. Eventually she was able to negotiate with the BBC for an office, taking a spare room in Diana Goodman's[3] East Berlin bureau. She thinks the stringer network worked because it tended to take younger, hungrier journalists. The staff correspondents, generally being a bit older, weren't as interested in scrabbling around creating stories when there were already enough stories in their diaries. Generally the two sides managed to rub along well as neither side was poaching from the other. Correspondents such as Diana Goodman in Berlin and William Horsley in Bonn were on staff and worked for the national news service, "News and Current Affairs" (NCA), while Caroline was working for World Service News and programmes such as "Europe Today" and "Newshour".

Through the deal she was given £1000 pounds per month, guaranteed for a set number of stories. For anything that she did over that she got paid extra: "So you know a 'live two-way' might be £40 and a radio despatch £45. TV paid much more—that was £250 for a voice track or 'track and rushes', because we didn't have VT editors". Because she was working in this casual framework, she felt incentivised to find stories and to get on air as often as possible. While there she was also able to sell her stories to American, Australian and New Zealand broadcasters.

> I just thought this was the best job in the world and I was the luckiest woman in the world. Because it was just my dream job to report from

---

[2] "In Conversation with Caroline Wyatt" (Women in Journalism, April 6, 2021), Item no longer archived, https://www.womeninjournalism.co.uk/.
[3] For more information about Diana Goodman's career, see Chapter 3.

abroad, and to be paid to go and be nosy about what Germany was like after the Wall came down.

She enjoyed in particular going to the parts of East Germany that she hadn't been able to access when her father was with the British military government working as a diplomat. Back then the family had been allowed to cross over to the East to go to specific places like the ballet or the opera, as long as the car was flying the British flag. But now all was open. Unification had led to the joining of two groups of people who culturally and socially had grown up very differently. The GDR was changing from a communist "command economy" with nationalised industries, to one where assets were being privatised and sold off to foreign investors. The pace of change was shattering for many people from the East who were forced to come to terms with the new reality of a consumer-led economy. She remembers being impressed with Chancellor Kohl when he decided the exchange rate would be one Deutsche Mark for one Ostmark so as to make the East Germans feel invested in the change process. On the other hand she later covered many stories on corruption in his CDU party.

As was briefly discussed in the chapter on Diana Goodman, with the fall of the Berlin Wall the Stasi archives were thrown open and terrible information emerged. For some it revealed that family members had spied on one another for the East German state. She remembers in particular the case of politician Vera Lengsfeld who would discover in 1992 that her husband, the poet Knud Wollenberger, had been spying on her throughout their marriage. Caroline also investigated "no-go areas" in the East, which were often full of dumped toxic waste.

The British, American, French and Russian troops left the country between 1994 and 1995 and then new relations had to be forged between Germany and these countries. Because she was working for the World Service, her stories didn't always have to have international significance and could be what she called "German-German" stories. She particularly enjoyed doing quirkier and more exploratory features, for example, about the Leipzig comedy clubs, which had operated as a form of resistance to the East German regime. After a while she found herself doing more television stories and eventually her salary was taken over by World TV and she was able to set up a separate bureau in West Berlin: "So they gave us our own budget to do whatever we wanted, because they were trying to get German hotels and conference venues to put BBC World on air". She and her colleague Mark James had free rein from then on in selecting stories and managing their budgets for news gathering.

By 1998 Caroline took stock of her career so far and decided that she needed to move back onto the regular BBC staff books so that she could get herself promoted. The only way to do this, as she saw it, was to become a "News and Current Affairs (NCA) correspondent", "a real correspondent as the BBC saw it". And so when William Horsley left Bonn she applied for his job and was successfully promoted at the grand old age of 30. She noted:

> By becoming an NCA correspondent, as Diana had once explained to me, you know, you're really only there for the big stories and you're not needing or supposed to be filing every day.

But Caroline, having learnt her trade as a stringer, couldn't help herself and did end up filing most days for either NCA or for the World Service, and she finally got her own producer, Simon Wilson, "who was very keen that I did more for the Nine and the Six". She remembers the 1990s as "a growth phase for news and a massive investment in journalism in Eastern Europe". She thought it a "once in a lifetime opportunity" to have the money for stories that discussed and explained the new Europe. On reflection she believes that the problem today is that "money for despatches or packages or whatever, the rates are still pretty much roughly what they were then. You know, maybe a tenner more. But when you think that inflation has gone up what—tenfold, 20-fold? We expect now that news will be free or cheap".

She explained that the BBC has changed its employment practices many times over the years—finding it in turn better to employ people on staff or as freelancers. When you work in a busy city or region or if there is a war on, then you can make a lot of money. For others who want to stay in one place it has meant constant adaptation: "So someone like Hugh Schofield in Paris has been staff, he's been freelance: he's been staff, he's been freelance".

Overall Caroline lived in Berlin from 1993 to 97, then moved to Bonn in early 1998 only to have to relocate the bureau back to Berlin because the German government was moving cities. Alongside Germany she also covered stories in the Czech Republic, Romania, Slovakia, Bulgaria, Albania and Kosovo and she did bureau "back-fill" reporting in Iraq during the four-day American bombing campaign in 1998 known as "Operation Desert Fox". In Kosovo she and camerawoman Susan Stein narrowly missed getting killed by militia at a roadblock outside the city of Prizren, but they were saved by quick-thinking German soldiers. Caroline later found out that the militia who had pointed guns at them had killed two other journalists earlier that day.

When she realised that her time as an NCA correspondent in Germany was coming to an end, she had to consider where to go to next. She approached the then foreign editor Jenny Baxter to ascertain what would be coming up:

> And she said, "Well, there's Moscow, Johannesburg or Delhi". And I don't like heat. So basically, it was Moscow. So that was it. I was going to go for the Moscow job. And I knew, probably from about a year before I finished in Germany, that that was the job that would be coming up at the right time. And if I was willing to take it, then—not that it would necessarily be mine by rights automatically—but then I was still able to have a good chance of it.

She was offered the job, and after three weeks' study of Russian with a Ukrainian opera singer, off she trotted to Moscow in late 1999. The bureau got busy quickly, with Vladimir Putin's election as prime minister, and then president. The creation of the Putin power structure dominated the four years she was to spend in Russia. She covered stories about his alliances, and his relationships with the oligarchs who were turning over piles of money in the new Russia: "And people who had been mere bureaucrats or civil servants were suddenly buying $5 million dollar flats in the centre of Moscow". She recalls it was an era when the UK government still thought it possible to be a friend of Russia and politicians were generally optimistic. But later when Putin began to clamp down on dissent, the Russian people realised that economic improvements did not always arrive hand in hand with personal freedoms.

A story that also dominated the headlines in the 1990s was Chechnya, a would-be breakaway republic that declared independence from Russia in 1991. Three years later Russia sent in troops. She visited Chechnya initially to investigate stories of human rights abuses by Russian soldiers. Having been refused permission to go in independently, her team eventually joined an embedded mission, only to find that the Russian soldiers were drunk on vodka from morning until night. On a chopper flight over Grozny she thought that the city resembled Beirut after the Lebanese civil war, with buildings lying in ruins but with residents living among them. The Russian government was in denial about the scale of the fighting in the republic.

When 9/11 happened she and her team headed straight to Afghanistan to cover the "war on terror". Over the subsequent years she also travelled to Tajikistan, Uzbekistan and undertook reporting cover for the Jerusalem bureau. When she filed her daily locations for the Russian Tax Office in 2001–2 she discovered that she had changed countries every week for 52 weeks. From Moscow there was a direct flight to Tajikistan, and from there it was possible to hook up with the Afghan Northern Alliance and get a helicopter into northern Afghanistan where the Northern Alliance had its headquarters. It was from this area that she covered much of the American-led invasion of Afghanistan (2001–2), swapping between there and various other BBC houses elsewhere in the country.

Some days she said stories just crossed her path. On one of these the team filmed an old man who had been liberated from a Taliban jail where he'd been tortured. He had walked and ridden a donkey across the mountains for a week until he more or less crawled back into his hometown. The donkey at this point was half dead. When Caroline rang the then editor of the Six, Jay Hunt, she immediately said she'd take it for the bulletin, instructing her to "go heavy on the torture, light on the donkey". During these years Caroline had many close shaves with danger. On one occasion, after consulting their security detail, the team decided not to accompany the Northern Alliance to witness them liberating a town, only to discover later that "the people who did go were all blown up" when the convoy drove over an IED.

Caroline was sent to cover many of the big breaking news stories of the day, even when they were far away from her base in Moscow. In 2001 she spent weeks in India reporting on the earthquake in Bhuj where more than 20,000 people had died. Caroline said her previous jobs as a producer and stringer helped her hugely with her wide-ranging role at the time, and she had also learnt a lot from correspondents such as Diana Goodman and William Horsley. Her job was immeasurably improved by working with field producers and bureau producers—including Chris Booth, Alan Quartly, Steve Rosenberg and Sarah Rainsford[4], two of whom went on to become correspondents in Moscow in their own right.

In late 2002 Caroline was filming stories in Kuwait when it became obvious that preparations for war were advancing quickly. She noticed American military materiel shipping in and bumped into a number of British soldiers. She contacted the foreign editor and said that should there be a war, then she would be happy to be involved, and this is how she was put down as a possible embedded correspondent on the BBC's planning list.

> At this time it wasn't clear or definite that there would be a war or that British forces would be involved, or indeed, how that would work. But the BBC, along with the MOD and others, was already making the preparations and starting to pick out names, and work out the training that you'd need. I don't remember the exact date on which the embedding was formally agreed but I think by February we were already doing training, or even by January maybe. The training involved how to wear a gas mask and what you do—your drill in emergency.

Unlike the previous Gulf War (1991), this time BBC News was a much bigger operation with rolling news channels and multiple websites in addition to its traditional radio and television offerings. The BBC "worked out, in conjunction with the MOD, a hub and spokes system".

---

[4] For more about Sarah Rainsford's career, see Chapter 10.

She was to be based at, "the so-called FPIC" (Forward Press and Information Centre), and noted wryly "there was only one word in that that was accurate and I think it was 'Centre'". She complained that this centre (also known as the Forward Transmission Unit or FTU), was meant to be attached to the headquarters of the operation, but this proved not a very useful place to be. She added that there were very few briefings from senior generals, and most of the filming from the "BBC spokes teams" attached to military units bypassed the centre and was sent straight to London. She is breezily sardonic about some of what happened when the "centre" got moved across the Kuwaiti border and into Iraq, while attached to a British convoy. They were stopped by border guards:

> They said we didn't have the right sort of visa to invade Iraq. And we said "Yes, but we're with these gentlemen with all the big guns" and they eventually let us through [...] And it got more farcical from there.

In the end, despite having had to agree to be embedded for up to a year (due to the training involved), she was only embedded for six weeks. It was a frustrating role compared to the roles of some of her colleagues who were attached to military units. She was glad there were BBC "health warnings" on embedded reports so that viewers could understand the circumstances in which interviews were given, via the military filter. At times she was jealous of the non-BBC journalists who were operating as "unilaterals" and who were totally outside the embedding system. However, the option of working as a unilateral—under conditions where one would have no intelligence about where the fighting was happening—was deemed too risky. The deaths by crossfire of three members of an ITN team meant BBC management refused any offers from its journalists to embark on possibly foolhardy excursions.

> We were inside the camp under the control of the military in the sense that we didn't have our own ability to go out in our own vehicles because they said 'No—you've got to come out in our vehicles or with the press officers'.

In the end the whole FDU system collapsed. She believes this was because it wasn't giving the journalists what they wanted and she wasn't even sure it was giving the military what it wanted. It was only after Basra fell that they were able to get into the town and start filming. At this point they became "unembedded". There were still pockets of fighting going on and there were dead bodies everywhere. One of the first stories she remembers doing inside Basra was about the looting:

> There was an incredible sight of 4x4s speeding down the highway out of Basra just dragging the hospital incubator, the chairs and desks from schools, the lamps. The looting was unbelievable. The electricity pylons, cables, anything that was useful was being taken away.

A short while after the fall of the city Caroline left for Kuwait and her first hot shower in a long time. Looking back she thought that, "we had done what we could within the quite severe limitations we'd been given". She wasn't to return to Iraq until she became defence correspondent a few years later. The next dateline for Caroline was Paris.

Caroline was told before the interview that she wouldn't be the top candidate for the post but she did have a reasonable chance of success. She was open in her application that she only had "O Level French" but she promised to improve her skills if she got the job. She laughs remembering that the men who applied for the job had all said they were fluent in French. In the job interview she was asked to give an instant obituary of President Jacques Chirac as if she were sitting over in Paris in the correspondent's chair. She believes she stumbled through this test only adequately, but as it turned out "none of the blokes actually spoke French—which tells you a lot about the difference between men and women!".

Paris proved to be a fascinating posting during which Nicolas Sarkozy won the French presidential election. She recorded plenty of political pieces, including those related to the European Union (EU) and trade: stories about the wine industry, the fashion business, the champagne trade, and, of course, cheese. She probed areas related to French culture, sport, France-UK and France-Germany bilateral relations. The stories she most enjoyed were the comparative ones which interrogated social customs. Some of these included investigating education, labour relations, the healthcare system and the differences between French and British women's attitudes to relationships. She covered the ongoing issues related to the ban of the hijab in schools and she reported on the riots in the "banlieues" (large housing estates outside major cities). She remembers in particular doing stories about the heatwave in 2003 in which 15,000 people died and the grapes withered on the vines.

Towards the end of her time in Paris, Caroline travelled back to London to speak to the then Foreign Editor Jon Williams about possible vacancies coming up. She wasn't interested in most of the national ones nor the Brussels posting and it wasn't looking great because as Jon said, "you don't do hot places". But he added that there was the defence job, "but you wouldn't want that". On the contrary, Caroline felt she'd been working up to this post her whole life—after a childhood in places such as Northern Ireland and West Berlin, where her father worked closely with the military, she'd gone on to cover the wars in Afghanistan and Iraq and was completely across the armed forces' issues. She landed the job in 2007 and professed herself delighted:

> Because it just meant I could carry on going to Iraq and Afghanistan and actually covering what British forces were doing there. [They] had gone into Helmand in 2006 but they were also fighting in Iraq. And Iraq was not going that well and neither was Afghanistan. It was the era of Blair and then Brown and it was fascinating. It was just the most riveting period of defence stories, because you had everything from the politics of Iraq and Afghanistan, the politics of the Labour Party, international politics and how we were getting on with America.

Caroline was the first woman to take up the role of BBC Defence Correspondent. She thought it was important to maintain good relations with the MoD, with the press office and also with the rotating cast of ministers and secretaries of state. She recounted that one evening the foreign editor Jon Williams had introduced her at a party with the following words:

> There are two types of defence correspondents. There are the ones who want to be inside the tent pissing out and there are the ones who want

Fig. 1 Caroline Wyatt and camerawoman Julie Ritson pictured in front of armoured vehicles in Helmand Province, Afghanistan (2011)

to be outside the tent pissing in. [Here he referred to a previous defence correspondent by name] who was outside the tent pissing in and Caroline is inside the tent pissing out (Fig. 1).

Caroline thought this was a reasonable explanation of her approach as she believed that a good working relationship with the MoD would enable her to get closer to the story and go on more useful trips to places—albeit embedded with the troops. She was also still doing occasional bureau replacement in Kabul, Baghdad and Jerusalem and was sent to cover multiple major disasters. In these roles she did get a chance to meet local people and to follow up on their stories. Overall, she spent seven years travelling constantly to Helmand, Baghdad, Basra and the many other places where there were British troops. There were multiple trips to Wootton Bassett to witness the return of servicemen's bodies from Helmand and to report on medical stories about injured soldiers and their recoveries. She covered defence housing problems and cutbacks and the jockeying for position between the RAF, the Royal Navy and the army.

With regards to the future of foreign correspondence, Caroline is both optimistic and pessimistic. She explained that on the plus side, safety "on the road" had massively improved from travelling to the Middle East with next to no body armour or training, to the situation today in which journalists have to attend compulsory "Hostile Environment and First Aid Training" (HEFAT) and sometimes travel with bodyguards. In an interview with "Women in Journalism"[5] she reflected on the death of Marie Colvin in Syria in 2012, saying: "You can never entirely mitigate [danger]. In order to go and get the story, you have to accept an element of risk". However the training that correspondents now undertake walks them through different scenarios such as how to deal with checkpoints, what to do if kidnapped and how to keep yourself calm.

> In the war in Syria, or even Iraq and Afghanistan, it is very hard to know quite often who is friend and who is foe because sometimes people switch sides or you know, can be your friend one day, and suddenly the amount of money they might be offered for your life is far too tempting.

Here she was focusing in particular to the 2017 kidnapping of *Times* correspondent Anthony Loyd[6] in Syria. Loyd had been betrayed by someone he thought was a friend. Luckily he was wearing a tracking device linked to his newspaper in London, which alerted representatives of the Islamic Front in Syria whose intercession helped lead to his escape.

Caroline's next job was as Religious Affairs Correspondent. This post sat in home news rather than foreign news, but with the understanding that she could also examine the topic through a lens of religion and world affairs. Caroline had been brought up a Catholic at home and at school, but on many occasions over the years of her work in conflict zones she had questioned the existence of God. Speaking in 2022 on a BBC programme called "Faith in Journalism" she recounted how many of the journalists she knew had renounced the faith they were born with due to the horrors they had witnessed. She had had many crises of faith during her time in the field and she said this usually happened in Afghanistan,

---

[5] In conversation with Caroline Wyatt, 'Women in Journalism'. 6 April 2021. https://x.com/WIJ_UK/status/1379429178043297798.

[6] Anthony Loyd, "Kidnapped in Syria: Anthony Loyd's Harrowing Story," *Men's Journal*, December 4, 2017, https://www.mensjournal.com/entertainment/kidnapped-in-syria-anthony-loyds-harrowing-story-20141017.

"where the sheer level of suffering, poverty and occasionally hopelessness made me just come home and think 'no, there clearly cannot be a God of any kind because no God would allow this level of suffering for women, for children'".[7]

When she took up the job in 2014 Caroline found that cuts had affected the role and that it no longer came with a producer. Nonetheless her brief was more than just the usual Church of England beat, because the Director of News, James Harding, was particularly interested in Pope Francis and the internal politics of the Vatican. So she clocked up many airmiles travelling across South America and Africa, following either the Pope or the Archbishop of Canterbury Justin Welby. As one of the "Vaticanisti" or "VAMPs" (Vatican Accredited Media Personnel) her descriptions of travelling as a passenger on the papal plane seem quite similar to the experience of being embedded with the army. It is not that journalists wouldn't ask awkward questions of the host—the Pope—or of his advisers, but that the onboard-the-plane setting of the two-hour press conferences could lead to a certain politeness or deference, especially while being fed delicious meals. Although this papacy was (to her) an improvement on that of Benedict XVI (which was marred by constant allegations of sexual abuse in the Catholic Church), she accepts there remained many unanswered questions.

She also covered Christian communities in the Middle East, ISIS taking over parts of Syria, and the persecution of the Yazidis in Northern Iraq.

> I think in that role I was able to make it much more international. But it never sat easily within the BBC News structure at all. Religion is something that BBC News is possibly allergic to as a subject, because they found it so difficult to categorize. Because on the one hand, it's good and it's diverse—that's good. On the other hand it is a motivating factor for lots of things that aren't lovely and cuddly and involve happily living together.

---

[7] "BBC World Service—Heart and Soul, Faith and Healing," BBC, September 2, 2018, https://www.bbc.co.uk/programmes/w3csxfmg.

The editors on the news desk had taken some persuading to cover the persecution of Christians in the Middle East but they were easier to persuade on the story of the Yazidis as they decided it had an interesting international news angle: "These were exotic people who worshipped a God that we knew nothing about". In other stories she tackled different strands of Islam, for example, to find out what Muslims in the UK thought about British Islamist Anjem Choudary.[8] Choudary was eventually sentenced to jail in 2016 for supporting a proscribed organisation and in 2024 was sent to jail again for a longer period. Alongside these stories Caroline followed the Pope to the Philippines, and her last story on this beat was the canonisation of Mother Theresa in Rome.

By this time she had begun to feel increasingly unwell and had been diagnosed with multiple sclerosis (MS) in late 2015. By mid-2016 she was starting to not be able to use her arms properly, followed by her legs. BBC managers said they would hire her a producer to help with the workload, but she told them it was too late and that she couldn't continue to do the job due to the long hours and the travel. In 2017 she went to Mexico for a stem cell transplant to see if it would halt the progression of the disease. To begin with it seemed to improve her symptoms and she felt like she had a brand new immune system. But after a while the gains were lost.

At the time she was working from home, but five months later she returned to the office to present Radio 4's "*PM*" plus the World Service programme "*The World This Week*" (TWTW). When cutbacks came, she was the only one journalist made redundant from TWTW. After this she put together a portfolio of presenting jobs for disparate radio programmes such as "Saturday PM", and "fill in" for weekday "*PMs*", "*The World at One*" and "*From Our Own Correspondent*". Alongside this varied portfolio, she also pitched for and made documentaries. "All of it involves sitting on my bottom and not using the little energy I have to travel to places and go and stand outside buildings. So it's a very different kind of job".

---

[8] Anjam Choudary was before the courts again in July 2024 charged with directing a terrorism organisation, and being a member of and supporting a banned group.

Looking back, Caroline realises that she had had a number of warning signs about her health from as early as 1991, when she had symptoms such as occasional numbness in her arms, which she put down to chronic fatigue or RSI. She had had an MRI scan back in 2001 when doctors had found one lesion on her brain but had advised her to ignore it—unless she began to have trouble walking. This then came to pass and a brain scan found many more lesions. Since the diagnosis Caroline has been taking part in different drug trials and has become an ambassador and spokeswoman for the disease. Unfortunately these drugs stop large parts of her immune system from working and so during Covid she had to stay and work from home.

Caroline is very certain that she has enjoyed a fabulous career and that when she started out it was a fascinating time to be a correspondent, just after the Berlin Wall had come down. Everything was changing and there was so much to discover while the Eastern European countries morphed into new entities. She counts some of her closest friends as the people she met in these different countries who helped her to understand the background to what was happening. On the other hand just as she arrived back in the UK, her long-term relationship ended with a man with whom she might have had children, plus she ignored her MS symptoms, putting them to one side while working. In the last few years she has been taking care to recalibrate and restore her work-life balance and to make sure that she creates time for her family and friends.

Looking back she believes that she was lucky in joining the BBC when she did. The significant barriers for women correspondents had already been breached when she arrived by the likes of Diana Goodman, Liz Blunt, Ofeibea Quist-Arcton and Bridget Kendall, and the BBC was taking in more women as trainees. She took a punt on becoming a BBC stringer in Germany and the experiences she clocked up set her on a path to later accede to staff positions, to new postings and to promotion. She concludes that those golden years were also partly down to the BBC having more money and fewer outlets, and it was committed to more in-depth coverage than now.

When I asked her if she had experienced sexist behaviour, she replied that this mostly happened when fellow male journalists got drunk down the pub after work. Over her time as a correspondent she had been heavily persuaded to dress more like a man, preferably in suits, in order to be taken more seriously. One of the changes that particularly pleases her today is that "women are now allowed to look like women on the telly" and that women reporters don't have "to ape men".

On the other hand, the foreign correspondent's job is no longer considered as grand as it had been once. She mentioned seeing previous correspondents' memos found in the Bonn bureau when salaries and perks had been linked to those of senior civil servants. A few memos discussed whether or not a reporter's level of car should be that of a wing commander or a group captain. Another set of documents outlined the wear and tear allowances for dinner jackets for diplomatic dinners. Regarding the BBC's female pay scandal[9] she was both shocked and philosophical:

> I think at the BBC, we'd always known that were huge variations in salary, even before they were published like that. But I think it was so *in your face* when it did happen, that it was kind of gobsmacking. But at the same time, I think quite a few male colleagues have accidentally left their payslips on the photocopier over the years. And I've realized as I worked my way through the BBC, that my male colleagues were, by and large, always paid more than me. In fact I don't think I've ever met one who was paid less.

She said she hadn't taken it up with managers, usually attributing it to someone being older or more experienced or to making some people's salaries equivalent to those of commercial competitors:

> I think when Allan Little, Fergal Keane and Ben Brown and a few others were about to be poached by ITN or wherever, then their salaries went up.

She also believes the "star system" (as introduced by Director-General John Birt) had been a factor, as had starting a career at the World Service rather than at News and Current Affairs (NCA). She points out that a lot of women foreign correspondents started out in the World Service,

---

[9] BBC pay scandal is discussed at length in Chapter 6 on Carrie Gracie.

and perhaps as stringers, and therefore they were used to receiving lower salaries. Now she worries that the publication of high salary earners gives the public a very distorted view of what most people at the BBC are being paid.

> But for me, the thing that I've always loved about my job was (a) being a foreign correspondent, and (b) working for radio. And radio has always been worse paid than television and still is, unless you're Evan Davis, or, you know, presenting the *Today programme* or whatever. But people working in local radio were not being paid extraordinary salaries, they're by and large being paid minute salaries. And I think the difference is that sometimes women wanted different things out of work, that actually women sometimes prefer to bring up a family and take time out of that particular job or work part-time because of childcare.

She doesn't believe that the BBC necessarily paid women less deliberately, but unlike the Civil Service there was never "a going rate for a particular role". The BBC has always had pay bands but she argues that these were applied "very flexibly". This allowed anomalies such as World TV correspondents being paid less than correspondents working for the Ten O'clock TV bulletin. She does hold that women are not as good as men at asking for pay rises, and that it's something that "we need to teach women". She is very happy that Carrie Gracie and Samira Ahmed (among others) took the BBC to task:

> I think it's brilliant that it's out there. Yeah. I honestly think that if there are discrepancies from now on, that you cannot explain in any other way than discrimination, that shouldn't be happening now. Because there's enough openness, and also, the culture has changed so I think people do talk about money more. I'm not sure that journalists' main motivation is money, because I don't think you'd go into journalism if it were.

Caroline says that another reason women haven't pushed as much as men for better salaries is that women are just so keen to do a good job and prove themselves that they're not constantly comparing themselves to other people and scrutinising what they have.

I just think women's motivation sometimes is different, but that actually women are now wising up and getting savvier and thinking 'you know what, how you value me should be shown in my pay'. And if it's not the same as the bloke sitting next to me doing exactly the same job, then the employer needs to do something about it.

References

BBC. "BBC World Service—Heart and Soul, Faith and Healing," September 2, 2018. https://www.bbc.co.uk/programmes/w3csxfmg.

"In Conversation with Caroline Wyatt." Women in Journalism, April 6, 2021. Item no longer archived. https://www.womeninjournalism.co.uk/.

Loyd, Anthony. "Kidnapped in Syria: Anthony Loyd's Harrowing Story." *Men's Journal*, December 4, 2017. https://www.mensjournal.com/entertainment/kidnapped-in-syria-anthony-loyds-harrowing-story-20141017.

Wyatt, Caroline, and Scott Hughes. "CV: Caroline Wyatt: Bonn Correspondent, BBC." *The Independent*, February 23, 1998. https://www.independent.co.uk/news/media/cv-caroline-wyatt-bonn-correspondent-bbc-1146423.html.

Sarah Rainsford
Eastern Europe Correspondent, previously a correspondent in Moscow (twice), Istanbul, Madrid and Havana

"It was quite hardcore. And we didn't sleep very much, obviously. And most of the time the sirens are going off and it's down to the bunkers or you're in the corridor or sitting in the bathroom on the floor".

Sarah Rainsford grew up in a village in the West Midlands called Drakes Broughton, two miles from the town of Pershore and seven miles from the city of Worcester. Her father was a sales manager in a company that sold hydrovanes; her mother was a teacher, and she had two brothers. Sarah went to local state schools—the first was a Catholic primary school in Pershore and the second a Catholic high school in Worcester. She didn't grow up yearning to be a journalist but her family did watch nightly news bulletins; read the *Guardian* and listened to BBC Radio 4. She believes she wasn't focused on a particular career although she admits she found the idea of journalism "pretty glamorous". At school she loved languages and studied French, German and Latin and developed a taste for Russian from a teacher called Mr Criddle who had learned the language in the military at the Joint Services School for Linguists (JSSL). In her gap year before university Sarah spent several months in Moscow teaching English. Her college alumni magazine records her reminiscing that that period was a very exciting one for Russia.[1]

> It was the most amazing time to be there. The Soviet Union was falling apart around me. You could travel to places that were suddenly independent republics. We flew to Uzbekistan for a dollar, and then got stuck there with no flights back because nobody knew how to operate independent airlines.

Sarah studied for a degree in French and Russian at Fitzwilliam College in Cambridge. Once again the key language teachers had learned their Russian at a JSSL. One of her favourite pastimes was playing football. She describes herself as more enthusiastic than talented; in her opening game she accidentally broke a girl's collarbone and earned the nickname "Crusher". At Fitzwilliam College she met her husband to be, Kester (Kes) Aspden who would go on to work first as a lecturer before becoming a successful writer. Sarah remarked that "having a portable husband is a rare species in foreign correspondent work" (Ibid). She professed to have really enjoyed her degree, including the six months in her third year when she travelled to St Petersburg "on exchange". She was meant to be enrolled in an official institute but in reality she was working as a translator and interpreter at an Irish pub, The Shamrock. Sarah thought St Petersburg was like a mafia city back then.[2]

> There were people with guns and drugs in the back room of the pub and the mafia visiting. There was me, 19, 20 on a year abroad, serving beer and learning the best Russian I could ever have learned. I did my oral exam when I got back and I think every third word was a swear word.

Throughout her time at Cambridge Sarah hadn't been bitten by the journalism bug and she said she didn't write articles for any college papers, preferring to play football. After university, she moved to London to hunt for work, and by this time she had decided she wanted to work

---

[1] Sarah Rainsford, "Fitzwilliam 40 Years of Women," *Optima: Fitzwilliam College Newsletter*, 2019, 16.
[2] Rainsford, 17.

in the media. She applied for every journalism job she saw advertised in the *Media Guardian*. She was unlucky at first but then a friend whom she'd made in Russia, Mishal Husain, told her to apply for a job where she was working, at Bloomberg. Sarah was successful and became an assistant to the head of news, Kathy Oliver. At first this involved lots of admin, "lots of photocopying and stuff" but eventually she moved on to a role as a production assistant, "writing scripts about Hungarian pharmaceutical companies" and learning a lot about television production. In her two years there she was given many opportunities as Bloomberg was only just starting out: "It was always very high tech and had loads of money—nothing like the BBC", she laughs. By then Mishal had moved on to the BBC, and she contacted Sarah when she spotted a vacancy for a production assistant in the Russian Language Service and told her to apply. According to Sarah, "Mishal is basically my kind of guardian angel through life". So Sarah applied, got the job and she has remained with the corporation ever since.

At first she wasn't enamoured of her new position. She found that as it was a language service, as "a foreigner, there's not much you can do". But she is philosophical about what she learned there.

> It was quite a weird place. I mean there were really interesting, fascinating people. Lots of Soviet émigrés and dissidents, but they'd all kind of sit in the back room smoking and writing very long features about very little known Soviet writers or musicians. I was "producing", in inverted commas, this news programme that nobody really cared about.

Her job was "to record items onto quarter-inch tape, cut the tape and then stick it all back together again" and put the programme out. She decided her role was rather boring and uncreative and started studying for an MA in Russian Studies at London University. In the end she never finished the course. This time Sara Beck came calling from Moscow, asking her to apply for a producer vacancy there through the BBC's Newsgathering section. This meant that the job was not for the World Service, but for national radio (NCA). She reflects that this move from production assistant to producer was a "massive leg up" as she didn't have many particularly relevant skills at this point, other than her Russian. But she thinks Sara saw her "as a mini version of herself basically" and their career paths were similar. She was put onto a "local hire contract" but thought it was a decent deal as it included an apartment, even if later the contract complicated her position at the BBC because technically she was coming off a staff position to do it. Her boyfriend (later to become her husband) had a job at Leeds University at the time, but eventually he joined her in Russia. Luckily, as a writer, he was able to work remotely, only returning to the UK whenever he needed to carry out research or access archives.

In Moscow in 2000 she found a large bureau with four correspondents, four producers, a bureau chief, multiple camera crews, and the Russian language service employees, and it felt like "a complete leap into the unknown". The moment she arrived a story broke that the nuclear powered *Kursk* submarine had sunk in the Barents Sea, killing all 118 men on board. Sarah remembers wanting to hide in her flat as she was suffering from "imposter syndrome". However, the office called, she dusted herself down and set off for Murmansk, north of the Arctic Circle. She remembers it as "a baptism of fire". Sarah wrote about this story later in her book on Russia[3]:

> "The *Kursk* disaster contained all the traits of Putin's rule in an early, still evolving form: an instinctive dishonesty, wariness of the West and a chilling disregard for human life".

The crew who had survived the initial disaster and were trapped underwater would eventually suffocate as the Russian authorities at first hid the story, then in a delayed fashion sent a rescue ship, all the while refusing help from the West until it was too late to save anybody.

For the first two years Sarah was a producer "on a huge learning curve". She said she didn't land desperately yearning to be a reporter, but she just wanted to acquit herself well: "I mean I was producing Orla Guerin within a month of being there, and she is pretty demanding. And I was sort of thinking oh, oh, I've got to prove myself". After a

---

[3] Sarah Rainsford, *Goodbye to Russia: A Personal Reckoning from the Ruins of War* (London: Bloomsbury Publishing, 2024), 154.

while she realised that a foreign correspondent post was becoming her "dream job". At the time the bureau chief was Kevin Bishop and he was extremely supportive of her. Looking back she concluded that he was unusual for going out of his way to help people who had ambitions to realise them. She started to hunt for feature stories to report on at weekends, first on radio and then on TV. She laughs, "They were absolutely dreadful, those first reports". But she found there were always plenty of local stories to report on, given the empty shops and the poor state of the economy which led people to alcoholism, prostitution and even selling their hair to make money.

She worked as a producer for Caroline Wyatt for a while and reflects, "It must be awful to think that the person on the other side of the camera desperately wants your job. But I loved producing as well, I just loved the job in Moscow. And we went all over the country and all over the world with it. It was five great years". She is thankful to Kevin, Caroline, producer Chris Booth and Sara Beck for the mentoring they gave her. She got her first break in reporting covering the Dubrovka Theatre siege in October 2002. A group of Chechen rebels took hostages in a crowded theatre, "spurring a hostage standoff that ended with more than one hundred dead".[4] At this point Sarah found herself outside the scene, doing her first "live two-ways" with London on her mobile phone.[5]

After her two years producing, Sarah changed contract and became a Moscow reporter for the next three years, covering Putin's consolidation of power. One story in particular stands out for her: the September 2004 school siege in Beslan. In this siege Chechen rebels took more than 1000 hostages.[6] Eventually Russian forces stormed the building, and in the ensuing fracas 333 people were killed, 186 of them children. Sarah reported from the scene, while living with a family that had children and a grandmother inside the school. She confessed it was the most shocking

---

[4] "Moscow Theatre Siege Survivors Haunted Two Decades On," News 24, October 25, 2022, https://www.france24.com/en/live-news/20221025-moscow-theatre-siege-survivors-haunted-two-decades-on.
[5] Rainsford, "Fitzwilliam 40 Years of Women," 17.
[6] Nick Paton Walsh and Peter Beaumont, "When Hell Came Calling at Beslan's School No 1," *The Observer*, September 5, 2004, https://www.theguardian.com/world/2004/sep/05/russia.chechnya.

and distressing story of her career to that date and she returned to Beslan many times during the subsequent months and years.

Sarah also reported on the second Chechen War itself, but she insisted it was not "the dangerous kind of coverage", but more "the post obliteration coverage", as the office wasn't accredited to film behind the lines. She did occasionally get into the capital Grozny on escorted Russian army embeds but she said the problem on those trips was not getting adequate access to local people to interview. A lot of her reporting was about the humanitarian and refugee situation caused by the fighting. She remembers in particular interviewing Anna Politkovskaya, an outspoken investigative journalist for *Novaya Gazeta*, who had reported from Chechnya more than forty times and who was later shot dead in the lift of her apartment block in Moscow. She gained further opportunities working off base. Kevin Bishop was insistent that the Moscow bureau should take part in the BBC's global newsgathering operation and so two days after 9/11 she found herself in Tajikistan crossing into northern Afghanistan via a Russian military base. In 2003 she worked as a producer for correspondent Caroline Hawley in Baghdad, the day after the statue of President Saddam Hussein was toppled.

When it was time for Sarah to move on in 2005, she considered the different posts becoming available in the rotation and chose Turkey. Here she was employed as a sponsored stringer. Looking back she thinks her managers may have suggested that that destination would be a good fit. She didn't speak any Turkish but she learned it during her four years in Istanbul. At that time Turkey was considered by the BBC to be "a European job, in those wonderful days when Turkey was considered a part of the European family". The story narratives were often about Turkey's aspirations to be part of the European Union and there was also plenty of local news. "It was a massive country and a massive story and it was brilliant. I really enjoyed it, even though the language was quite a challenge". As she points out, today the Turkey job is much more about the Middle East and with Orla Guerin there as the international correspondent, the story is less about Turkey and more about the region.

Sarah explained that at the BBC, when you were on a "full overseas terms and conditions contract" (which doesn't exist anymore), then you were given two years in a posting, with an option to extend to three, "which is ridiculously short, and came from some weird idea that you would 'go native', so you could only stay for a short time, which I always found totally bonkers". She argued that defence or political correspondents didn't have to move on every three years, enabling them to build up experience over a longer period. However, when her three years in Istanbul were over, Sarah looked for other job openings and selected Italy, but the post went to somebody else. She was then advised to apply for a post in Spain. After a "pretty unpleasant disagreement" about her contract (the BBC wanted her to go as a freelance) she ended up going again as "a sponsored stringer". In a sponsored stringer contract, you get a base salary for a set number of stories, and then anything over that is yours—basically, you're assured of a regular income but you can earn extra money for what you file. She said, "It's quite a good deal when it works out" and this proved to be the case in Spain as she didn't stop working for two years. She was also able to file for non-competitors such as Australian or Irish radio. From a language point of view, Sarah found her time in Madrid much easier than in Istanbul, as her knowledge of French meant "it was simple enough" to pick up Spanish. Researching her stories from this era I found a wide range of topics from the Spanish economy, to politics, stranded Brits, World Cup football fans and earthquakes.

In 2011 Sarah went on a detour to Cuba for another sponsored reporter job where she was meant to spend only six months and then close down the bureau in Havana, following the departure of the previous correspondent. In the end she stayed for three and a half years. Cuba was one of the last communist states at the time and she found it interesting in the early days as there was a lot going on that was related to the government reforms drawn up by President Raúl Castro. She was one of only a handful of foreign correspondents who were permitted official accreditation to work there. "It's a fascinating tiny island with a massive significance beyond its size. But ultimately, as a news reporter it's death in so many ways". As she planned yet more stories on agricultural reforms, she would look at the BBC news agenda and consider "it's not going to make it. I think the number of TV stories I got onto domestic bulletins from there was minuscule". In her book on Cuba, Sarah recalls rereading her diaries from that time and finding them filled with frustration as she "struggled with the pace and peculiarities" of her new job. She missed her more constant news agenda in Madrid and being on television.

> Needing official permission to film almost anything, I wailed into my notebook that I felt "hemmed in" and wanted to scream or explode.[7]

While researching Sarah's TV stories from this period, I found her covering the visits of the Venezuelan President Hugo Chavez, who underwent several operations for cancer in Havana. She also recorded lighter features on old-style Havana taxis, an eight-year-old Fidel Castro fan who got to meet his hero, and an Australian woman who failed in her attempt to swim from Cuba to the US due to jellyfish. She was also on constant watch for the death of Fidel Castro himself. An increasingly elusive man, Cuba's former revolutionary leader was kept away from the press, but every now and then Sarah had to find proof for the foreign desk back in London that he was still alive. In the end Fidel Castro didn't die until 2016, two years after Sarah had left. She noted that sometimes going in search of major stories, you end up missing the ones for which you were waiting. In her book on Cuba she discusses her reasons for wanting to return to Moscow in 2014.

> The crunch came when I was watching colleagues reporting from Kyiv where protesters were being shot. In Havana that week I got a call from the British ambassador to announce that Tom Jones would be the guest of honour at the annual cigar festival.

Early in 2014, towards the end of her time in Cuba, she began to spend a considerable amount of time in Ukraine covering the unrest and the revolution. While there, she was introduced as the BBC's "World Affairs Correspondent". In Ukraine, President Viktor Yanukovych had been ousted following street protests in the wake of his decisions first not to sign a free trade agreement with the EU and second to create stronger ties with Russia. In the ensuing weeks, more than 3000 people were killed in the fighting and tens of thousands were forced from their

---

[7] Sarah Rainsford, *Our Woman in Havana: Reporting Castro's Cuba* (London: One World Publications, 2018).

homes. Sarah reported on the conflict in the Donetsk region, the international diplomatic moves to find a solution, and the "self-rule" referendum conducted by Russian-speakers in Eastern Ukraine. After this she applied for a job as Moscow Correspondent and she returned to her old stomping ground.

This time Sarah was a staff NCA correspondent in a bureau of two such correspondents. She was appointed at the same time as Katya Adler in Brussels, Lucy Williamson in Paris and Jenny Hill in Berlin. She laughed saying there had been quite a lot of BBC fanfare about boosting the number of women foreign correspondents, but she felt this was unhelpful as it made it look like they were appointed because they were women, rather than because they were the right people for those jobs. Sarah herself felt like she had proved herself many times over in Russia, Ukraine and elsewhere. Sarah then stayed in this job from 2014 to 2021, and during this time the BBC eased up on its "three-year rule", enabling correspondents to stay longer and to improve their expertise on the ground.

During this time her face was rarely missing from television news bulletins. The work was constant and Sarah was invariably dressed in thick jackets and scarves as she did packages, pieces to camera (PTCs) and live two-ways from all over Russia and bordering states. She covered hard and soft news; stories for major bulletins and for special programmes. Her behind-the-scenes reports peppered the radio programme *"From Our Own Correspondent"* on Radio 4 and the World Service. These stories ranged from clashes in Eastern Ukraine, to the shooting of Boris Nemtsov, floods in Tbilisi, Russia's air and missile attacks against ISIS positions in Syria, Bitcoin mining in Siberia, the metro bomb in St Petersburg and Alexei Navalny's 2020 poisoning and subsequent imprisonment. Sarah was able to provide a Russian take on Covid, from the country's use of CCTV to monitor citizens, to access to vaccines and fines for lockdown evasions. In keeping with earlier ideas that Moscow correspondents should also travel to big world events, she covered migrants on Lesbos (2016), the Biden-Putin Summit in Geneva (2021), elections in Spain (2016) and protests in Belarus (2021).[8]

Her Moscow career came to a crashing end in August 2021 when the Russian government suddenly declined her entry at Sheremetyevo Airport claiming she was a threat to national security. The BBC was later to call this a "direct assault on media freedom". It is likely that Sarah's reporting had put her under the Russian government spotlight. In preceding years Sarah had covered numerous stories on enemies of the regime, including anti-Putin politicians and dissidents such as Boris Nemtsov, Alexei Navalny and Vladimir Kara-Murza[9]. More recently she had also clashed in a press conference with the Belarus leader Alexander Lukashenko on live Belarusian state TV. In Sarah's 2024 book on Russia[10] she recounts that when she was eventually allowed into the country to pack up her belongings, she was informed at the Foreign Ministry that her expulsion was due to similar actions taken by the British government. She was forced to sign a paper which alleged she had been refused entry into Russia to "ensure the defensive capability and security of the state". Among the list of supposed British crimes were "UK sanctions against Russian officials for corruption and human rights abuses",[11] and the expulsion two years previously of a man identified as the London correspondent for the Russian state news agency TASS. Sarah argued with officials that this man hadn't been a correspondent and that sources had told her he had been a secret agent, but the ministry wasn't interested. A year earlier Moscow had moved Sarah from annual visas to ones which only lasted three months, and then two months. She had felt she was "being kept on a short leash".

Sarah and her husband then closed up their apartment and left for the UK, a place Sarah had barely visited during her twenty years abroad. She found herself suddenly without a base, and with her career, with its foundations in Moscow, upended. She has since pondered the many reasons

---

[8] All relevant stories mentioned were viewed via the Box of Broadcasts (BOB) https://learningonscreen.ac.uk/bob/

[9] Vladimir Kara-Murza was sentenced to twenty-five years imprisonment in 2022, but was released in an international prisoner exchange in August 2024.

[10] Rainsford, *Goodbye to Russia: A Personal Reckoning from the Ruins of War.*

[11] Rainsford, 138.

why she had been singled out, even asking herself if it was because she was "one of very few British journalists, otherwise almost exclusively men, who was not married to a Russian?"[12] According to Sarah the BBC worked hard via diplomatic channels to secure her return but to no avail. A senior Russian diplomat told Sarah (Ibid) that expelling her "was meant to scare the rest". The BBC broadcast her final report from Moscow on 1st September 2021. In this TV story Sarah highlighted the pressure Russian journalists were coming under for not toeing the Kremlin line and she also reflected on her early years in Moscow when free speech and freedoms "were new and precious. It feels like today's Russia is moving in reverse".[13]

After a short breathing period, Sarah readjusted to her new life outside Moscow (Fig. 1). If the Kremlin thought throwing Sarah out of the country would stop her reporting on Russia, it was wrong. Sarah began her coverage again in late 2021 when Russia attempted to close down a respected human rights group, "Memorial". She reported by following the Supreme Court hearings online and calling old contacts for interviews back in Moscow. Then, before the full-scale Russian invasion of Ukraine, Sarah was back in Kyiv providing analysis and commentary on Russia's growing war preparations. When the war broke out on 24th February 2022 she was in Kramatorsk in the Donbas. When she woke up "it was all kicking off". She wondered if the area might fall quickly, as it had a minority Russian-speaking population. She also worried that because the Russians had labelled her a threat to national security, she might be taken hostage "and end up in some kind of spy prison". In her book Sarah writes that when Putin launched the new invasion of Ukraine, "any lingering nostalgia I had for Russia, and regret at being expelled, were extinguished in an instant".

She and the team set up base first in Dnipro, from where they were able to move north to Kharkiv and south to Zaporizhzhia. They covered the east of the country, as there was a large BBC contingent operating out of Kyiv, and Mariupol on the coast was impossible to access. The BBC

---

[12] Rainsford, 138.
[13] "BBC News," *Russia "Moving in Reverse,"* September 1, 2021, BBC Box of Broadcasts, https://learningonscreen.ac.uk/bob/.

Fig. 1 Sarah Rainsford in London in 2022

also had presenters doing lives from Lviv. Once again she was reporting practically every day for the Six and the Ten TV news bulletins. This meant sometimes "half an hour news gathering, half an hour editing, and travelling like crazy through all these checkpoints". It was always tight to deadline as she was multitasking.

> I love radio editing so I always do it myself. And it's like you file for the Six O'clock TV bulletin and suddenly it's five to six. You've got to get the radio in but you haven't even written it. Then I had to write it in two minutes, edit it and if I was lucky get it in at one minute to six. It was quite hardcore. And we didn't sleep very much, obviously. And most of the time the sirens are going off and it's down to the bunkers or you're in the corridor or sitting in the bathroom on the floor.

Since the start of the war Sarah, whose home base is now Warsaw, has reported from the changing combat frontlines and the towns and cities attacked by missiles—from Kharkiv, Zaporizhzhia, Dnipro, Poltava, Bucha and Kyiv. With the title of Eastern Europe Correspondent, she has covered the plight of refugees trying to flee Ukraine, the torturing by Russia of Ukrainian civilians in Bucha, and the 19,000 Ukrainian children who were spirited across the border by Russian troops. In 2023 she reported from Poland, Germany and Armenia. She provided commentary and analysis on the Wagner Group's attempted coup in Russia and the move of its leaders to Belarus. She believes her Ukraine reporting has been the most important of her career because the ramifications are so enormous and "because it's quite personal" insofar as it's "so much part of my world that's suddenly at war with itself".

Before the war started she was part of a strong team with a producer and a camera operator—John and Tony—plus BBC safety advisers. She says they do have local producers but she doesn't need them for the same reason as she might do elsewhere, as she speaks both languages and knows the area. She has mostly worked with two local women fixer-producers—Daria, who worked in the east of the country, but then worked remotely and "was invaluable" and Mariana "who goes to all sorts of scary places". Neither of them had had much journalistic experience at the outbreak of the fighting but they have picked up plenty since. We discussed a story I'd seen early on about refugees trying to flee Dnipro and she said it reminded her of stories she'd read as a child about evacuations to the British countryside during World War II. However she now thought those earlier stories were greatly romanticised in contrast to this story, where women were leaving with children and men had to stay behind and fight, "And the men were trying be all manly and they weren't really succeeding, and they're sort of crying as well".

Another story she covered in May 2022 is being investigated by Ukrainian prosecutors as a suspected war crime. In this story two civilians, one of whom was a security guard Leonid Pliats, were working in a bicycle shop on the outskirts of Kyiv. They were executed, shot in the back by Russian soldiers, and then their premises were looted. Both men died, one slowly after calling and waiting for help. The initial CCTV pictures were given to Sarah's producer Mariana, after which they sourced other videos and spoke to Leonid Pliats' family and friends. Once again, Moscow denied that an illegal killing had taken place, despite the CCTV and the local people all telling the same story. Sarah isn't confident that the perpetrators will ever be handed over by Russia, even though there will be a war crimes tribunal at the end of the war. There have been Ukrainian, British, French and UN teams in Ukraine all cataloguing atrocities. The BBC TV item that was broadcast was handled with great care by Sarah and her team and permission was sought from the Pliats family for anything shown. Sarah was less impressed when she heard "through the fixers' network" that an American network team which was also working on the story was putting enormous pressure on the dead men's families to give interviews, and she felt their story when broadcast was unnecessarily graphic. Generally speaking she believes there have been too many gratuitously violent stories that have been shown from Ukraine.

These days news gathering is very different to how it was when Sarah started out—there is drone footage to enhance a story about the destruction of towns in Ukraine, AI-based data crunching, open-source intelligence, and there are videos from all over the country posted by eyewitnesses on social media to provide news from difficult to access places. Apart from when she is in war zones, Sarah often works with just a camera operator and without a producer or fixer. She is glad she worked as a producer at the start of her career because it means that she knows all the ways to do production skilfully, creatively and efficiently. She believes she's pretty good on the technical side of the business although she admits she never really got her head around how satellite feed frequencies worked—in particular when booking them from local TV stations in far flung places such as the Arctic. She says her husband often lugs the tripod around on shoots and he used to fend off football supporters at World Cup soccer matches.

Sarah says she's lucky her husband was able to go with her on her postings; the fact that he is a writer has made this option much easier. She reckons many things are more difficult for women correspondents who either have to juggle hard to make both careers and family work, or don't have children. Sarah doesn't have children and asks me to name any BBC women correspondents who do. I stop at four—only three of the ten women featured in this book have children. Sarah and her husband discussed IVF but in the end she wasn't in the right country at the right time when this might have been possible.

Since leaving Moscow Sarah has done a number of reasonably outspoken press interviews, commenting on her treatment but also on what she calls the "Kremlin Denial". She no longer feels the BBC should have to keep including a Russian denial when confronted with uncomfortable facts and the truth.

> Because the problem is we live in an age where there's so much disinformation and lies, by governments, and I feel like every time you repeat a lie, some idiot, somebody somewhere, will actually believe it, or it will cloud their judgement, or it will make them doubt what I'm saying. So why should I repeat something when I know it's a lie? And when I know that *this* is true. You know if I'm standing there saying this man has just been shot in the head in front of me, if you know, [Dmitry] Peskov in the Kremlin is saying, 'Actually, it was the CIA that did it or something', I'm not going to repeat that. Historically and traditionally, we have, because it's this sort of sense of balance, or allowing them to have their say. But the point is, the Kremlin gets its say all the time, the Russian government does have a say on the BBC. But I'm not saying we must never hear from the Kremlin, because they're liars. No, they need to be challenged, and they need to be represented. We certainly don't understand what they think and the way they behave and how and why they do what they do. But I just don't think that if I'm reporting on the ground about something I see before me, there's no way I'm going to input their rubbish.

She thinks the BBC Editorial Guidelines are fine, as are the references to impartiality. If anything she believes there is now an increasing emphasis on telling the truth, "I've never had any problems with any of the reports I've done, and I've certainly not included nonsense from the Kremlin in those reports". Sarah is not someone who hangs around the BBC when she's got downtime although she concedes that men say this helps their careers.

In answer to questions about the pay equity issue, I ask her if she was surprised to learn about it. She answers that she was shocked but not surprised and that it was awful once the scale of it came out. She mentions that she has had a few pay rises after that and when she asked, "Is this a pay equality thing?" the answer was "no"—it was just that they had looked at her pay and "decided to up it". The first pay rise in particular, she noted, was quite substantial. She concedes that as a public service broadcaster, she is fairly well paid, at least in comparison to nurses and teachers. She remembers a manager yelling in her face during a pay negotiation when the BBC wanted her to go as a freelancer to Madrid. She stuck to her guns because she said the contract was against employment law. She hasn't taken up the option to find out if she is paid the same as a man with a similar job, because she has had several pay rises, but admits sometimes she's curious.

We move on to discuss if there are ever any advantages to being a woman in some places. She thinks there are sometimes in the "quite sexist countries" she's worked in, such as Russia, Cuba and Turkey, because men underestimate you.

> There's a lot of challenging you need to do in Russia and there were a lot of barriers to getting near people. So, whether it's oligarchs or ministers or politicians, it's quite hard to arrange interviews with people. So often, you just need to doorstep them. And I am quite good at sort of forcing people to speak, and like persisting with it. And I think as a woman, it's easier for the security and staff not to really notice you. [They just think that's] some woman or some bird over there and then that's actually quite useful.

She suggests that she has accessed some human rights court hearings in Russia exactly because the door staff never thought she'd break the rules or be audacious enough to ask questions of the accused, who are always in a cage. She laughs, "And if you're pushy or cheeky enough, which I tend to be, then you can actually speak to the accused". She is happy with her career and says, "It's the best job in the world. I love my job. I mean, I really love it. And I couldn't see myself doing anything else". She would also recommend it to other young women even though she wonders if there will be Moscow correspondents in the future as the Russians might just close down access. Sarah has "mixed feelings" about substituting local reporters for old-school foreign correspondents as she thinks they often have language issues. She doesn't believe writing scripts back in London "full of idiomatic English" for local journalists to read back from another country is the answer. She says it can work out really well for online stories or non-voiced video stories but that very few local reporters have managed so far to cross over to providing analysis in live two-ways for mainstream bulletins. She points out that the language services have their own audiences and agendas and that this can add to the difficulties of transitioning to the domestic (national) bulletins where the audience is very different. She takes the example of Russia and says it can be very difficult to find someone who wouldn't be either an activist or a pro-Putin person who could report in the simple, impartial and direct manner needed for a BBC UK audience.

When I contacted Sarah in 2024, to catch up on her latest adventures, she asked me if she had been very gloomy when I conducted our interview following her expulsion from Russia. I said that in a way she had, as she hadn't been too sure what she would be doing next. She had found living in the UK strange after so many years but was beginning to spend more time in Poland. In 2024 she appears to have put it all behind her. She's been reporting non-stop from Ukraine and neighbouring countries and her book examining her long history with Russia was published in August. In the closing lines of the book she said she no longer feels nostalgia for Putin's Russia as "there is little left that does not seem tainted".[14] She remembers all those who have been killed along the way—Anna Politkovskaya, Boris Nemtsov and Alexei Navalny—who will never see a new Russia, should it ever come to fruition. In an interview with Jane Garvey on Times Radio on 15th August 2024, Sarah disputed that she "loved Russia".[15] Looking back over three decades of association with the country, she clarified that, "Russia today is such a different place and such a dangerous place [...] and Russia for now has been lost".

---

[14] Rainsford, *Goodbye to Russia: A Personal Reckoning from the Ruins of War*.
[15] *Putin 'Massively on the Back Foot' after Kursk Incursion | Sarah* Rainsford, 2024, https://www.youtube.com/watch?v=ikR53gLWTzE.

References

"BBC News." *Russia "Moving in Reverse,"* September 1, 2021. BBC Box of Broadcasts. https://learningonscreen.ac.uk/bob/.

News 24. "Moscow Theatre Siege Survivors Haunted Two Decades On," October 25, 2022. https://www.france24.com/en/live-news/20221025-moscow-theatre-siege-survivors-haunted-two-decades-on.

Putin 'Massively on the Back Foot' after Kursk Incursion | Sarah Rainsford, 2024. https://www.youtube.com/watch?v=ikR53gLWTzE.

Rainsford, S. "Fitzwilliam 40 Years of Women." *Optima: Fitzwilliam College Newsletter*, 2019.

Rainsford, S. (2021) "Expelled: Russia, repression and me". BBC online video story, 11 October 2021. Accessed 29 September 2023. https://www.bbc.co.uk/news/av/world-europe-58849004.

Rainsford, S. *Goodbye to Russia: A Personal Reckoning from the Ruins of War*. London: Bloomsbury Publishing, 2024.

Rainsford, S. *Our Woman in Havana: Reporting Castro's Cuba*. London: One World Publications, 2018.

Walsh, Nick Paton, and Peter Beaumont. "When Hell Came Calling at Beslan's School No 1." *The Observer*, September 5, 2004. https://www.theguardian.com/world/2004/sep/05/russia.chechnya.

Shaimaa Khalil
Tokyo Correspondent (Previously Islamabad and Sydney Correspondent)

"That thing that you're not ready for? Do it, just do it!".

Shaimaa invites me into her inner Sydney apartment wearing a singlet and shorts. It is a glorious summer day in January 2022 and her apartment is airy, bright and extraordinarily close to the harbour bridge. Walking into the living room I glimpse a makeshift gym containing a punch ball, a skateboard and a bicycle. It turns out that these have particular significance for her, but we'll come to that. There was a lull in the Covid-19 pandemic at the time of this interview when Australians living abroad were finally allowed to return home, but not so Shaimaa's non-Australian husband, fellow journalist Ahmed Zaky who works for the BBC World Service in London. Shaimaa seemed happy to have somebody visit her in her des res, in that way that we were all a bit stunned by free association when lockdown measures started to loosen up.

Shaimaa Khalil spent her formative years in the Egyptian city of Alexandria. Her father was a lieutenant colonel in the army, the son of another army officer, and her mother was an academic. Along with her sister Shaza, she spent many weekend afternoons in the swimming pool of the officers' beach club, playing with other children whose fathers were also in the military.[1] She thinks she had a relatively easy-going childhood with few limitations posed by being a girl. "I was told that I can do anything and be anything and you know I was a tomboy, and that was okay. And I loved swimming, and that was okay. And I loved singing and performing in school assemblies". But she noted that everything changed when she hit puberty and girls were no longer given the same freedom as boys. "I think one of the seeds of wanting to become a foreign correspondent, even before I knew I wanted to become a correspondent, or to be in different places, was from my childhood. I was told I couldn't go anywhere on my own. And I wanted to go places on my own".

She remembers her hometown with fondness, but also as a place from which she wanted to escape.[2] She spent a couple of years in the United States, because her mother was studying for a PhD. This is where Shaimaa gained her strong command of the English language. "It was almost between my childhood and puberty. And when I came back home to Egypt, it was to a completely different life. It was 'you have to live by the rules'. You had to behave in a certain way, because you were a young woman. And so all those freedoms that young men or boys get hitting puberty, you, on the other hand lose as a young woman".

Shaimaa didn't really read newspapers, remembering that that was something her father and grandfather did. Instead, she was captivated by Egyptian radio which was always switched on in her house. She emphasised that Egypt had a very strong radio history, and she would listen to "The Arabs' Voice", Egyptian official radio "and BBC Arabic of course". She would often play with her sister pretending to be a presenter. She added that she fell in love with broadcasting before she fell in love with journalism, but eventually one led to the other.

Her mother was always a fierce proponent of education, and even today will ask her daughter, "So have you thought about your PhD yet? Do you have a proposal? Have you wasted another year?" According to Shaimaa her mother still thinks journalism is "a phase" and that

---

[1] Shaimaa Khalil, "Growing up in an Egyptian Military Household," *BBC News*, June 28, 2012, https://www.bbc.com/news/world-middle-east-18633877.
[2] Shelley Davidow and Shaimaa Khalil, *Runaways* (London: Ultimo Press, 2022), 8.

sooner or later she will switch to a more suitable career of teacher or university professor. She reminds me that Egypt is the Hollywood of the Middle East and there are famous Egyptian singers and there is a great art scene, "And yet, the average Egyptian family would really frown on their daughter doing that".

At the end of high school she moved to Doha, where her mother had secured a job at Qatar University. Shaimaa also attended the university studying English Literature. She enjoyed her student years, but it was also a carefully controlled environment for women. She made close friends with a young South African lecturer Shelley Davidow with whom she would go on to write "Runaways" in 2022. In this book they both explore their friendship which began in Doha, and they examine what it is to be a woman in the Middle East and beyond.

While still at university Shaimaa began to do fill-in work for the local English-speaking Qatar radio station QBS. First she worked as a continuity presenter and stayed as a radio DJ for seven years. She relished the independence and the fact she could get paid for playing music. In her book she describes how she became hooked by radio: "Those padded, soundproof walls. The radio desk and the faders! I know it's a major cliché, but this was the only 'love at first sight' moment I had".[3] Shaimaa became adept at leading a secret double life—for example, by taking up smoking as a "small act of rebellion" and by keeping some friendships secret. At one point she almost married an American-Egyptian man chosen by her family, but then decided she needed to take hold of her own life and decisions. In 2006, her old friend and colleague Ahmed was about to leave Qatar to take up his new post at the BBC World Service; they reconnected and decided to tie the knot and Shaimaa left, quick as a flash for London.

Newly arrived in the UK, she decided to study for a master's degree in journalism at the University of Westminster, eschewing the international stream and instead selecting the UK stream so that she could understand how the UK media worked. This was more of a challenge than she'd appreciated: "I didn't know what the history of *The Sun* was. I didn't know what the history of *The Times* was. I mean, these were big names.

---

[3] Davidow and Khalil, 35.

And I didn't know what they represented. And so I had a lot of ground to cover". Through the university programme she found a work experience placement with the BBC World Service "and that was that". She worked on the English-language programme, "World Update", and at the end of the internship she went up to Erica Brown, who worked on the programme and was in charge of placements and informed her she'd do anything. She was told to leave her contacts and when the summer came around, she applied for the "casual round" which led to a job for a couple of years and then she moved on to a more permanent position as a producer.

Over the following few years she worked across several World Service programmes and then applied for a scheme called "the Career Path Framework", where they send you to a department or programme where you've never worked before. This landed her outside her comfort zone in the World TV newsroom, as a producer on the news desk. Her workload increased inexorably when the Arab Spring started and she was called on-even at home-to do translating, often in the middle of the night. In 2011 the BBC needed an extra Cairo producer, and she applied successfully and found herself back where her story began, in Egypt. On one night, she was asked to review an update about crowds refusing to leave Tahrir Square. She decided to go herself and with only a phone, rather than accompanied by a camera operator. But she later realised that she could be taken for a journalist as well as a protester. When she began to take pictures, she was picked up instantly by the army.

> I thank God that I had the presence of mind to make two very frantic phone calls, one to the actual desk, the Foreign Desk [in London], and one to the office manager [in Cairo]. Because then they took everything [phones] away. And you're like, in a black hole, literally. And once they'd separated the boys from the girls, you knew something was up; you knew that they were going to do something. And a lot of it is psychological. A lot of it is about uncertainty. A lot of it is about mind games.

She was happy to have been trained on the BBC's Hostile Environment (HEFAT) course, in particular relating to how to stay calm in dangerous surroundings. In the end, she was stuck in a cell for a day and a half and then, suddenly, she was set free. The BBC said she could leave Cairo or take leave, but Shaimaa decided to stay.

She repeated several times that one of the joys of working for the BBC was the size of the corporation and the opportunities there were to move around. In her mind her career trajectory had more to do with her identity as coming from elsewhere:

> The gender thing for me was never an issue. I think for me, it was always 'Is there a place for me with my name and my background? And my lack of BBC-ness?' I had come from an entirely different place, you know, entirely different country, entirely different experience. And, you know, the big question that I asked myself, as always, was 'Do I have something to contribute?'

She thought the World Service was a great landing spot, and that for people from the Middle East, the World Service was the entire BBC. But after she'd become accustomed to working at the World Service, she realised the BBC had a whole other world: "Then you realise that being in 'Newsgathering' [NCA] is a completely different ballgame and the needs are completely different".

She also discovered that being "on the road" for the BBC was also useful, "It was a really good way of getting to know the relevant people in Newsgathering and getting noticed by Newsgathering". She thought that she had to be entrepreneurial to get noticed by people as she believed you could work somewhere for 20 years in the corporation and not get noticed by "the people on the Six O'clock bulletin". She added:

> But it's how you place yourself in the different situations on the different stories that gets you noticed. And I think the Arab Spring really helped in that way. It wasn't necessarily that I made the jump to Newsgathering right away. But it was that some producers and editors noticed my presence, I guess.

She believed the Arab Spring helped her career as she was wary of being pigeonholed as "the girl from the Middle East. I realised that it's not what I wanted to be, I wanted to be a BBC correspondent. I didn't want to be a BBC Arabic-speaking correspondent, doing Arabic-speaking things. There's nothing wrong with that and it helped a lot. But there's a certain profile that I wanted to be".

At the end of 2012 two job postings came up—one was to be a BBC bilingual reporter in Cairo with a Middle East roving brief, and the other was for a presenter for the World Service's programme "*Newsday*". Contrary to all expectations she chose the latter, even though she had never been a programme presenter before. But this was exactly the point she wanted to make. After discussing it with her husband, they both decided she should go for the role she'd never had as it was something new with a different profile and "you then become a BBC presenter". There were times when she questioned her decision, especially when big stories broke in the Middle East. But she felt it helped her down the line:

> Everybody then sees you in a different light, where you're reporting on the Middle East, but you're also reporting on Ukraine, and Crimea. And I think, long term, that was really valuable. Because then, when a job in Pakistan came up, Newsgathering knew me, and they knew I could report from a conflict zone. But they also knew that the World Service trusted me enough with their programmes. So it just puts you in a different light.

She admitted being terrified when heading for Pakistan, because it was a very large bureau and "a legacy job" that had had big names attached to it such as Lyse Doucet, Aleem Maqbool and Owen Bennett-Jones. Shaimaa says she finds "boards" (BBC job interviews) terrifying but approaches them like having a vaccine: "The plan was just to go in and get 20 minutes with Newsgathering bosses" and say, "This is what I look like—pay attention to me! Yeah, and then I ended up getting it!" This approach to boards, where "there is so much build up" has helped her be philosophical when she hasn't succeeded in some of her job bids.

Shaimaa loved her time in Pakistan, a place she'd never visited beforehand. She found Islamabad really beautiful, but she had a lot to absorb, and she hadn't learnt Urdu before arriving, "But you have to push yourself and just jump in at the deep end". Luckily there was a strong infrastructure in the bureau, including some 20 people working for BBC Urdu. Shaimaa had her own local producer and access to two camera operators and there was always somebody who spoke the language. Not long after she arrived there were some big stories, including in 2014 the "Peshawar School Massacre" "in which more than 140 people—mostly children—were killed by the Pakistani Taliban.[4] When you watch her TV pieces from this story, even the people who lost children appear at ease when they talk to her, patiently, in English. In her piece to camera (PTC) she is wearing a scarf, even though she had recently come to a decision to not wear one anymore."

According to Shaimaa, the Peshawar School Massacre was the biggest and most shocking story of her time in Pakistan. She also remembers interviewing Asia Bibi's family when they were still in hiding. Asia Bibi was a Christian woman on death row for several years, who was accused of blasphemy in 2010.[5] Shaimaa also travelled to Afghanistan and covered bombings and fighting in Helmand Province. She managed to cover a number of stories about the treatment of women in Pakistan—including a harrowing one about victims of acid attacks[6] plus stories about women in public teahouses,[7] honour killings[8] and body-shaming.[9] She said such stories continue to haunt her. Regarding the so-called "honour killing" of British-Pakistani woman Samia Shahid, a murder allegedly committed by the victim's father and first husband,[10] she said:

> We also found out that she'd been raped before she died. And then it was one of those stories where you hung around the court the whole day. And then there were a couple of times where we saw the dad and the husband coming in. And that was really confronting. So, I think for me, yes, the bombing stories were horrible, horrible, and the aftermath

---

[4] "Shock and Disbelief in Peshawar over Taliban School Massacre," *BBC News* (BBC, December 18, 2014), YouTube, https://www.youtube.com/watch?v=7mShS_I4g3U.
[5] Shaimaa Khalil, "Family of Asia Bibi Appeal for Help over Blasphemy Charge," *BBC News*, February 4, 2015, https://www.bbc.com/news/world-asia-31092447.
[6] Shaimaa Khalil, "100 Women: The Salon Helping Acid Attack Victims," *BBC News*, October 28, 2014, https://www.bbc.com/news/world-asia-29727876.
[7] "Pakistan: The Women Hanging out in All-Male Teahouses," *BBC News* (BBC, April 2, 2016), https://www.bbc.com/news/av/world-asia-35942068.
[8] Shaimaa Khalil, "Four Sentenced to Death for Pakistan 'Honour Killing,'" *BBC News*, November 19, 2014, https://www.bbc.com/news/world-asia-30113128.
[9] "Countering Body Shaming in Pakistan," *BBC News* (BBC, May 15, 2016), https://www.bbc.com/news/av/world-asia-36291748.
[10] The case against the father and the first husband of Samia Shahid was never concluded.

was horrible. And that school story will obviously stay with me for the rest of my life. But I think the stories about violence against women, in particular, I found really confronting.

As a woman from Egypt, Shaimaa discovered that in Pakistan she occupied a place where she could melt in with the local crowd but was not a member of the crowd. This is similar to the state other women correspondents have mentioned, about being taken for the "third sex"—a professional working foreign woman in an otherwise male-dominated society.

I think I occupied a weird, a strange space, because I looked like everybody else, and I could pass for a Pakistani. But I was also foreign. And so being with a cameraman and a producer kind of allowed you that eccentric existence, if you will. Because you know, you're not *of* there. But also, if you needed to knock on a door and go into a household, the men of the household would feel okay for you to be there. So you're kind of like the eccentric, female category but you know, you're not a tall white dude, trying to speak to their wives because that wouldn't happen.

She is absolutely convinced in the power of role models and mentors and says most of hers have been women. She was assigned Caroline Wyatt (See Chapter 9) as her official mentor and mentioned Lyse Doucet as an unofficial one. Caroline she described as being "beautiful and a force of nature" (although she says she has never told her this). She thought she had "a delicious voice, like the equivalent of chocolate". But before anybody else, she had been a long-term fan of Lyse Doucet and she'd taken note of her before she'd even set foot in the BBC.

And I remember very distinctly a picture of her dressed like a man in Afghanistan, I don't know if she was interviewing a Haqqani official or a Taliban official. But she was told that she had to dress like a man if she were to make it to that area. And I just, I think it was that specific moment where I didn't know what she was doing. And I didn't know what a foreign correspondent was. Because I was still too young and just wanting to go to nightclubs. But I just, I just felt like this is what I want to do, whatever she's doing.

Once she landed in the BBC Shaimaa remembers occasionally dallying at desks near where Lyse was working so that she could hear her news assignment conversations. When she heard her discussing trips to Afghanistan and other countries in the Middle East, her goals crystallised. When people asked her what job she wanted to do in the future she simply stated that she wanted to be like Lyse.

> She just represented everything about what you want to be, in that she was really nice, and really alert and so entrenched in these stories, and also, it felt like eventually, when I had the privilege of working with her, everywhere she lands is home. Everywhere she lands, she owns the story. And she knows—from the driver to the President, and all in between, she just knows everyone. And so she's definitely, I mean, she's still my role model, even though I know I can't be like her.

She remembers in particular Lyse's generosity towards her during the Arab Spring. Knowing that she really wanted to be a correspondent one day, Lyse would say to the news editors:

> Oh, I can't do this "Live" [interview]. Shaimaa, do you want to give it a go? And I'd be like, "Oh, my God". And only a person who's so secure would do that and would help people, and she's just so magnanimous in the way that she handles herself around people who know what a star she is. Right. But she she's never like that. She's not a diva.

She mentioned she'd had many female bosses in her time: Imelda Flattery in Australia and Kate Peters in Pakistan. She'd also had two female bosses in Newsgathering and more in the World Service. She has never sought out any diversity schemes at work and said her fight was against people thinking her only past job had been with the Arabic Language Service. As she spoke perfect English and had successfully ticked off a variety of different roles, she thought these schemes weren't suited for her as she wanted "to be able to function in the mainstream".

One of the biggest gripes for bureau-based reporters is when they are "big-footed" [swept aside] by bigger names in Newsgathering, when a major story breaks. She had been big-footed by John Simpson "for the Ten" in Afghanistan and had duly handed over all her footage. But in a sign that these days women have achieved more prominence, she has also been big-footed by other women:

> So for example, when Malala won the Nobel Peace Prize, I was not part of that coverage. It was Orla Guerin who did the main coverage because, well, Orla Guerin is Orla Guerin. And also she was the Pakistan correspondent when the Malala story exploded, and when Malala was shot, and so Orla was sent to cover that story. But also, when the Peshawar Massacre happened, Mishal Husain was flown in to present the 10 O'clock News and to do the main package.

Shaimaa is philosophical and doesn't hold a grudge:

> I think you kind of have to find your way around it mentally, right? If the story is big enough that you're big footed, that means there's a lot of story out there. Right? And so, yes, you're not going to be the first piece on the Ten. But that particular day, for example, the Ten, you know, was consumed with that story and was interested in that story, so that they took two pieces. So I was the second piece. There was enough interest that you were on World TV all the time and on the radio all the time. So you're kind of de-graded to another cog, as opposed to the main correspondent.

After Pakistan she returned to London to present "Newsday" for a while. She believes that presenting stints are a really good discipline; and that they taught her there were many ways to tell a story and many ways to shed light on a story through interviews. Again, she loved it, but she still had itchy feet. She did a fair amount of travel—to Mosul (post-ISIS), and to Washington for election coverage for the World Service. What she found interesting about this juxtaposition was that it led her to ask a lot more questions in the US about future policies and plans concerning Iraq.

Shaimaa remembers hearing about the Sydney correspondent vacancy while travelling; there had been a very short window in which to apply. She ended up being interviewed over Skype, with panel members repeating, "Shaimaa, Shaimaa, we can't hear you!" She got the job and once again got thrown in the deep end. No sooner had she landed in

November 2019 then she was sent off to cover the extraordinary bushfires that were sweeping Australia.

> I remember it being the third day in the country, I remember being on a plane in the middle of smoke landing in Coffs Harbour. And it was just blanketed in this haze of smoke. And my earliest memory of Australia is the smell of smoke. And every time I smell smoke, it kind of triggers me and takes me back. But it was also just so awesome to start on a story like that, because you almost just landed into the biggest debate that this country has ever had, you know about climate change, about politics, and you're just landing in the middle of this chatter.

She believes that after covering bombings and conflict, Australia allowed her to exercise different journalistic muscles, for example, regarding the coverage of natural disasters. She also mentions the acquittal of Cardinal George Pell, after his conviction for child abuse was overturned. She noted that it was a huge story with difficult legal issues which trained her to finesse her legal knowledge and language. She also moved into sports while covering the Women's Football World Cup, and the court appearances in 2022 of Serbian tennis player Novak Djokovic (who lost his bid to play in the Australian Open as a non-vaccinated person during Covid-19). A story she mentions from New Zealand that was particularly poignant was the murder of British backpacker Grace Millane. When I interviewed her, she said that the onset of the pandemic in 2020 had curtailed her travelling for reporting. She had wanted to visit a lot more of Australia, including Western Australia, and she had also hoped to deepen her coverage of New Zealand. She had found the pandemic hard because she couldn't see her family due to Australia shutting down to non-Australians.

In 2022 Shaimaa had no idea where she would head next. She wanted to remain as a foreign correspondent and thought that eventually she would like to return to the Middle East, adding "but there's so much more I want to explore before". Over the years she has reported from Libya, Iraq, Kuwait, Saudi Arabia, Lebanon and Jordan. In January 2023 Shaimaa moved to Tokyo to take up a new correspondent role; however, she sometimes returns to help out with Australian coverage, due to the

Fig. 1 Shaimaa Khalil reporting from the Tokyo streets (2024)

relative proximity of Japan. In June 2024 she flew to the US territory of the Northern Mariana Islands in the Pacific to cover Julian Assange's court bid for freedom from jail. In Japan, Shaimaa has continued to cover environment stories, with one in particular resonating with her. It concerned the stricken Fukushima nuclear plant and plans to release treated radioactive water into the ocean.[11] Shaimaa donned protective clothing and toured the plant (Fig. 1).

---

[11] "Fukushima: Can These Fish Tanks Prove Radioactive Water Is Safe?" (BBC News, July 13, 2023), https://www.bbc.com/news/av/world-asia-66191784.

Shaimaa has thought long and hard about her identity as a citizen of the world. She constantly re-examines what it is to be an Arab and a woman in the journalism public sphere. A dual Egyptian-British citizen, she has now lived abroad for half her life. She is still very committed to her marriage, even while she and Ahmed live in different countries due to their respective careers. In "Runaways" (2022) she discussed at some length her decision to stop fertility treatment and has been open about not wanting children enough to go on with the difficult quest.[12] She has also been transparent about deciding to no longer wear a hijab. In the Middle East, Shaimaa had at first ignored her family's requests that she wear a hijab, but in 2002 she decided it was finally time "to do the right thing". For the next ten years, during which time she started working at the BBC, she wore one. In a *BBC online* article in 2014 she said, "My motto was 'I'm a BBC journalist, not a headscarf-wearing BBC journalist'".[13] Over the years she asked herself if she was wearing it out of conviction or out of habit: "How much of my faith did I want to exhibit? Would I, I asked finally and crucially, be any less Muslim if I took off the headscarf? The final answer was no". As she notes, there was an irony in her taking off her hijab just as she was about to go to Pakistan as a correspondent. However she did, using it only where necessary in coverage, such as on religious occasions or attending mourning.

When I interviewed her in 2022 she was just like most Aussie women, greeting me in shorts and a tee shirt. She was introducing challenges to her life—like learning to box, which she thought was a good job for a foreign correspondent. She had also taken up skateboarding, even though her husband had joked after she fell over that unlike kids who would need just a cast, she would need a hip replacement. And finally she had borrowed a bicycle from her camera operator as he'd been appalled that she couldn't ride one. When I met her she was still unsure how to begin.

She loves her new freedoms and has definitely fulfilled her childhood desire to escape and to travel. In her book she recounts a trip to visit her

---

[12] Davidow and Khalil, *Runaways*, 152–59.
[13] Shaimaa Khalil, "Why I Took off My Headscarf… Only to Put It Back on Again," *BBC News*, August 30, 2014, https://www.bbc.com/news/magazine-28967146.

old friend Shelley Davidow on the Sunshine Coast. She noted that in the whole week of her stay she hadn't once considered her appearance:

> "I was in my shorts, my tank top and my bathing suit most of the time and I didn't really give that a second thought. [...] I haven't felt that free and unburdened about what I wore since I was ten or eleven".[14]

I asked her if she'd ever checked that she earned as much as her male colleagues. She referred to when she left Pakistan and returned to the UK just after there had been a big review and a change in the pay grades. She said she felt those tweaks had resolved any issues at her level. She admitted she didn't like talking about money but was unsure if that was "a female thing" or her "Middle Eastern culture" talking. She thinks she's at a point where "the job is much more important than the money for me. It's just it's more important to establish myself as a person that they can rely on as a foreign correspondent". She believes it will still take some time for her to feel confident enough to talk about her salary. She does remember disputing a pay grade once and arguing that she had "this and that experience" which meant she should be paid more. She didn't get the pay rise, but she felt glad she had raised it: "It was more about negotiating with myself and not comparing myself to male colleagues".

With regards to the value of promoting local reporters to carry out more of the journalism, she thought there was a lot of benefit in that, "because of their knowledge and being in the region". However she could also see the value that the BBC correspondent brings from outside the region. She said she'd been the equivalent of a local reporter immersed in the story in the Middle East and now she also had the benefit of being a BBC correspondent. She thought this gave her:

> The understanding of the demands, the understanding of the expectations, the understanding of the BBC style of doing things which is crucial, it's crucial. And it's definitely a skill that not everybody that hasn't done it, would naturally have, you know? Because there is a thought process that happens when a story happens, about demands—where you know that there's a despatch that you're going to write, you know that you're

---

[14] Davidow and Khalil, *Runaways*, 288.

going to write it long and short for World Service and for Radio Four. And then you look at your time zones, and in your head, you know which programmes you need to hit. And then you need to calculate how far you are from the Six and Ten [TV] and the 1800 [radio]. And that doesn't come naturally to someone who's just immersed only in that story. Because I think there are two skills, there's the knowing of the story, and then being able to relay that story to the different BBC audiences. And I think these two things are very important. And so I think there's definitely a place for local journalists and local knowledge, which is hugely important. But I also think that the foreign correspondent who comes in—if they do their job right (and know the value that local journalists bring)—they also bring with them a way of operation in the way that they tell that story.

And finally, what would she tell a young woman journalist who wants to be a foreign correspondent and is just starting out? She replies quickly, "That thing that you're not ready for? Do it, just do it!" She thinks women too often imagine that they have to wait until they're the perfect fit. She believes she's been brave so far in jumping into challenges—for example, the first time she went to work for World TV. But she also knows that there are some jobs you might want to wait for, and it can pay to be flexible. She has a role in mind that she thinks she won't be ready to undertake for another ten years or so. She won't reveal what it is but it's there as a secret goal. She also repeats that it is invaluable to find mentors and to reach out and to be honest about things with your closest colleagues. Her go-to colleagues over the years have been Laura Bicker and Karishma Vaswani.[15] She says she feels free to run things past them, especially when things haven't gone as well as they might. She admires Lyse Doucet's epithet of "find your tribe".

Friendships are very important to her, and she stays in touch with Shelley Davidow from her student days in Qatar. She says, "finding Shelley was like finding my Tardis because she represented this other world where women could go places, and do things, and be on their own and wear shorts. And she said I was like her Rosetta Stone because I decoded the Middle East for her". She argues that the fact that Shelley

---

[15] Karishma Vaswani is now working at Bloomberg.

is Jewish and she is Muslim doesn't get in their way. They joke that they really shouldn't be friends, but they are, "And then we do the kosher/halal situation, because technically, we're both not allowed to have bacon. And so we say to each other, what if we both have bacon? What happens? What's gonna happen? I don't know. I've never had bacon".

References

"Countering Body Shaming in Pakistan." *BBC News*. BBC, May 15, 2016. https://www.bbc.com/news/av/world-asia-36291748.

Davidow, Shelley, and Shaimaa Khalil. *Runaways*. London: Ultimo Press, 2022.

"Fukushima: Can These Fish Tanks Prove Radioactive Water Is Safe?" BBC News, July 13, 2023. https://www.bbc.com/news/av/world-asia-66191784.

Khalil, Shaimaa. "Growing up in an Egyptian Military Household." *BBC News*, June 28, 2012. https://www.bbc.com/news/world-middle-east-18633877.

Khalil, Shaimaa. "100 Women: The Salon Helping Acid Attack Victims." *BBC News*, October 28, 2014. https://www.bbc.com/news/world-asia-29727876.

Khalil, Shaimaa. "Four Sentenced to Death for Pakistan 'Honour Killing.'" *BBC News*, November 19, 2014. https://www.bbc.com/news/world-asia-30113128.

Khalil, Shaimaa. "Why I Took off My Headscarf… Only to Put It Back on Again." *BBC News*, August 30, 2014. https://www.bbc.com/news/magazine-28967146.

Khalil, Shaimaa. "Family of Asia Bibi Appeal for Help over Blasphemy Charge." *BBC News*, February 4, 2015. https://www.bbc.com/news/world-asia-31092447.

"Pakistan: The Women Hanging out in All-Male Teahouses." *BBC News*. BBC, April 2, 2016. https://www.bbc.com/news/av/world-asia-35942068.

"Shock and Disbelief in Peshawar over Taliban School Massacre." *BBC News*. BBC, December 18, 2014. YouTube. https://www.youtube.com/watch?v=7mShS_I4g3U.

Appendix

Initial interviews with BBC (and former BBC) journalists were conducted during the Covid-19 pandemic on the dates below, and emailed updates and follow up interviews were done subsequently until December 2024:

Kate Adie, 22 February 2022 in Dorset, UK.

Diana Goodman, emailed correspondence from New Zealand 2021–24.

Elizabeth Blunt, 11 August 2021, London, UK.

Lyse Doucet, 22 April 2022, London, UK.

Orla Guerin, 13 July 2022, via Zoom from Istanbul.

Carrie Gracie, 12 August 2021, London, UK.

Sara Beck, 24 July 2022, Oxford, UK.

Sarah Rainsford, 23 June 2022, London, UK.

Caroline Wyatt, 16 August 2021, London, UK.

Shaimaa Khalil, 3 January 2022, Sydney, Australia.

Ian Richardson, 11 August 2021, London, UK.

Glossary

Autocue/Teleprompter Used in television to show a script that a presenter reads while fronting a camera.

Back fill Working in a bureau while a correspondent is away, on holiday or ill.

Big foot When a bureau-based correspondent is replaced on a major bulletin by a "big name journalist" who is sent in to front the programme on a major event, or conduct the main story.

Boards The BBC name for a job panel.

Dateline The name of the place from where a story is sent.

Domestic/National News These are the main news services that broadcast on radio stations and TV channels such as Radio 4 or BBC 1. National output is paid for via the Licence Fee and the BBC World Service is paid for by the Licence Fee, advertising from BBC Studios, and the Foreign, Commonwealth and Development Office.

Embedded An embedded correspondent travels with military units in conflict zones and may be subject to censorship regarding operational information.

Fixers These are local people whom foreign correspondents often hire on an ad-hoc basis to assist with reporting and logistics when abroad. These people are sometimes called producers and they are often local journalists.

Freelance A journalist who sells stories to the media without being on staff or on a contract.

HEFAT This stands for Hostile Environment and First Aid Training. This tuition is given to journalists operating in difficult conflict zones and is often given by military or ex-military operatives. Similar courses are called "security training" or "environment awareness training".

Local Hire Contract A BBC work contract where the person abroad is paid as per hiring rates in the country concerned. This means there is no payment to cover accommodation or expat extras such as schooling for children.

Mic A common shortened version of the word microphone.

Millennium bug Also known as the Y2K Bug was a worldwide computer scare that software would fail when technology ticked over to the new millennium—2000. This ended up not taking place.

MoD Ministry of Defence

NCA News and Current Affairs at the BBC (NCA) largely deals with radio, television and online programming/stories that go out via domestic channels, as opposed to the World Service radio, television and online news services. Both streams employ different foreign correspondents to focus on particular strands of programming but some correspondents work across all programming.

Newsgathering This is the BBC's central area for planning and gathering news. These days it is also referred to as "News Content" or "BBC Content". It deals more with the gathering side of news rather than the output of news, but is obviously linked.

On the road/in the field These terms describe travelling individuals or teams (reporters, producers, camera operators) who are working away from base for the purposes of gathering news.

Packages/packaging A radio or TV package is a broadcast story narrated by a journalist and incorporating soundbites from interviewees.

Piece to camera/PTC This shows the reporter speaking straight to the camera from wherever they are—partly to show that they are on location at a particular spot.

Producers These people work with reporters in radio and particularly in television to prepare all the parts of the stories or programmes. They arrange filming, secure interviews, research background and generally do everything except voice the story.

Quarter inch tape This was the high quality audio tape used on reel-to-reel recorders before the arrival of digital technologies.

Rip and Read A simple radio presenting job in which short news headlines are read.

Stringer In BBC terms this means somebody abroad who is paid per story sold to the corporation.

Sponsored Stringer This is a BBC employment role for a person who has come off staff to go abroad and is being paid a flat rate per year with any additional newsgathering commissioned being paid on top of the base rate.

Talks Writer This person wrote foreign analyses stories that could be voiced by a reporter or presenter in one of the language services of the BBC World Service.

Tandy An early type of laptop computer sold by the Tandy Corporation from the 1970s onwards.

Taxi rank Reporters on the "taxi rank" are those who are in a queue to be assigned the next breaking news story.

Telex A communications system popular from the middle of the twentieth century for short typed messages between locations. It was a precursor to the fax machine or email.

Track and rushes A track is a pre-recorded voice track. The filmed camera rushes are edited with the track to make a television package.

Two-ways This is when a radio or television correspondent speaks directly to a presenter in the studio back in London.

UHER A brand of portable reel-to-reel tape recorder used in recording on the road from the 1960s to the 1980s.

Unilaterals These are reporting teams working on their own during wars and conflicts, rather than being embedded with a military unit.

Voice tracks See Track and Rushes above

World Service This service is separate (but increasingly linked) to the national/domestic news services. Journalists tend to work for programming that is largely broadcast abroad. The service is mainly funded by the UK Licence Fee with additional funding from the Foreign, Commonwealth and Development Office.

BBC Journalists & Presenters

A
Adams, Paul 95, 156
Adie, Kate 11, 17, 20, 24, 27, 31, 33–36, 104, 122, 134, 146, 170, 223
Adler, Katya 1, 97, 123, 124, 139, 144, 197
Ahmed, Samira 146, 186, 207, 209, 219

B
Bamford, David 79
Barron, Brian 32
Beck, Sara 13, 60, 151, 157, 165, 191, 193, 223
Bennett-Jones, Owen 98, 212
Blunt, Liz vii, 11, 12, 50, 67, 70, 76, 77, 82–84, 90, 133, 184, 223

Booth, Chris 176, 193
Brown, Ben 185
Buerk, Michael 31

C
Coomarasamy, Jamie 153, 155
Croxall, Martine 38, 147

D
Davies, Wyre 105
Doucet, Lyse 1, 12, 69, 71, 87, 93, 103, 106, 123, 127, 212, 214, 221, 223
Doyle, Mark 79, 83

F
Foster, Anna 105, 123

G

Gibbons, Liz 99
Golestan, Kaveh 157
Goodman, Diana vii, 11, 43, 48, 50, 52, 58, 60, 61, 70, 100, 113, 153, 155, 157, 170–172, 176, 184
Gracie, Carrie 12, 80, 104, 105, 139, 141, 144–147, 153, 160, 185, 186
Guerin, Orla vii, 1, 12, 13, 97, 100, 103, 104, 126, 192, 194, 216

H

Harding, Andrew 155
Hill, Jenny 197
Horsley, William 171, 173, 176
Hughes, Stuart 157
Husain, Mishal 191, 216

J

Jalil, Mirwais 94

K

Keane, Fergal 103, 104, 138, 185
Kearney, Martha 5, 6
Kendall, Bridget 170, 184
Kermani, Secunder 100
Khalil, Shaimaa vii, 14, 100, 207–209, 213, 219, 220
Kuenssberg, Laura 1, 97

L

Little, Allan 104, 105, 185
Lloyd-Roberts, Sue 135

Loyn, David 94

M

MacGregor, Sue 9, 49
Muhamed, Kamaran Abdurazaq 157
Myrie, Clive 1, 97, 156

O

O'Connell, Paddy 87
O'Reilly, Miriam 138, 146

P

Parsons, Rob 155
Paxman, Jeremy 98
Peters, Kate 102, 116, 153, 215

Q

Quist-Arcton, Ofeibea vi, 184

R

Rainsford, Sarah 1, 13, 97, 103, 117, 176, 189, 190, 192, 193, 196, 198, 205
Richardson, Ian 10
Rippon, Angela 9, 170
Russell, Audrey 5–7

S

Simpson, John 31, 62, 157, 215
Singleton, Valerie 170
Sixsmith, Martin 155
Smith, Sarah 1, 97
Sopel, Jon 144, 145, 147, 160

T
Tully, Mark 79

W
Williamson, Lucy 197
Wyatt, Caroline 13, 103, 170, 171, 181, 193, 214

Index

A

Afghanistan 12, 34, 88, 91–97, 103, 122, 175, 179–181, 194, 213–215
Afghanistan reporting 88
Afghan War 91
Africa reporting 12
Africa Service 68
Amanpour, Christiane 106, 123
Arab Spring 14, 97, 140, 210, 211, 215
Australia reporting 11, 48, 217

B

Bamber, Hylda 9
BBC Equal Pay 159, 226
BBC High Risk Department 115
BBC management
   Abramsky, Jenny 49
   Angus, Jamie 163
   Baxter, Jenny 57, 60, 156, 159
   Birt, John 37, 186
   Cramer, Chris 25, 26
   Downing, Malcolm 157
   Hall, Tony 144, 145, 147
   Harding, James 138, 139, 144, 182
   Mitchell, Steve 160, 161
   Munro, Jonathan 139, 144
   Ray, Vin 159
   Sambrook, Richard 15, 36
   Van Klaveren 157
BBC Monitoring 126, 161–163
BBC News and Current Affairs (NCA) 171, 185, 226
BBC Newsgathering 15, 60, 126
BBC radio news 49, 50
BBC reporting guidelines 203
BBC Star System 185

BBC Television News v, 23, 26, 202
Benzie, Isa 2
Bhutto, Benazir 91
Birt, John 37, 38, 185
Blair, Tony 35, 179
Bloomberg 191, 221
Bourdieu, Pierre 14
Boys' club 38, 123
Briggs, Asa 5
Bush House 10, 68, 69, 90, 91

C

Canada 11, 12, 89, 93, 96, 105, 169
Canadian accent 88
Channel 4 News reporters 35, 98, 100
  Frei, Matt 156
  Hilsum, Lindsey 35, 98, 99, 123
  Kermani, Secunder 100
Chechen war 153, 194
Children vii, 44, 52, 55, 57–59, 61, 68, 69, 73, 88, 97, 105, 106, 121, 123, 124, 135, 141, 148, 164, 167, 182, 184, 193, 201–203, 208, 213, 219, 226
China reporting 13, 30, 136, 140–142
City, University of London vii, 170
Colvin, Marie 123, 127, 181
Covid-19 pandemic 207
Cuba reporting 14, 195, 196
Curran, Charles 8

D

Danziger, Nick 101, 102
Davidow, Shelley 209, 220, 221
Defence reporting 13

Dimbleby, Richard 7
Doe, Samuel 74–77, 82
Donovan, Paul 9

E

East Germany 19, 51, 54, 56, 112, 172, 184
Egypt 12, 97, 122, 208–210, 214
Embedding 176, 177
Equal Pay Act, 1970 7
Ethiopia 12, 80, 81
Europe reporting 11, 122, 171, 173, 178, 185

F

Falklands War 28, 152
Fielden, Lionel 5
First woman foreign correspondent 11, 49
Fixers viii, 15, 102, 136, 154, 155, 202, 225
Fogarty, Michael 8
Former Nazis 52, 58
Franks, Suzanne 7, 9
Frontline reporting 88

G

Gellhorn, Martha 49
German reunification 56
Gillard, Frank 6, 7
Glossary 225
Gorbachev, Mikhail 57, 58
Grade, Michael 29
Greer, Germaine 46, 64
Gulf War 1991 33, 176
Gulf War 2003 13, 157

H

Havel, Václav 56
HEFAT training 114, 181, 226
Hekmatyar, Gulbuddin 94
Helmand Province, Afghanistan 180, 213
Hendy, David 2
Heywood, Neil 142
Higgins, Charlotte 5
Hodgson, Larry 49, 50
Hollingworth, Clare 49
Howe, Geoffrey 92

I

Independent Television News (ITN) v, vii, 11, 25, 48, 92, 95, 109, 113, 114, 170, 177, 185
  Barnes, Carol 25
  Thirkettle, Joan 25
India 49, 79, 97, 119, 157, 174, 176
Iranian Embassy siege 17
Iran-Iraq war 48
Iraq reporting 35, 36, 157, 174
ISIS 119, 122, 182, 183, 197, 216
Israel-Palestine and Gaza 95
Ivory Coast 11, 12, 71, 72, 78, 81, 83, 89, 90

J

Joint Services School for Linguists (JSSL) 189, 190

K

Kabul 91, 92, 94, 97, 98, 100, 101, 122, 180
Karpf, Anna 4, 5
Karzai, Hamid 91, 95
Kohl, Chancellor Helmut 54, 55, 172
Kramarae, Chris 4

L

Lamb, Christina 123
Languages and language services 13, 126, 153, 155, 158, 191, 192, 205, 227
Lebanon War & Beirut 175
Leslie, Ann 49
Liberian Civil War 78
Limitations to the Recruitment and Advancement of Women in the BBC 8, 9
Lukashenko, Alexander 198

M

Madsen, Virginia 3, 4
Marshall, Howard 6
Matheson, Hilda 2, 5
McKay, Anne 4
Media production 202
Merkel, Angela 55
Middle East reporting 8, 119, 129, 212
Misogyny 22, 23, 28
Multiple Sclerosis (MS) 183
Murphy, Kate 2–4

N

New Zealand vii, 11, 43, 45–48, 60, 64, 171, 217, 223
Nicholas, Sir David 48
9/11 World Trade Center bombing 194

Index

Northern Ireland and Belfast 23

O

O'Halloran, Julian 31
O'Keefe, Meryl 9
Ouedrago, Salifou 73

P

Pakistan reporting 12, 79, 122, 212
Peshawar school massacre 213
Pick, Hella 49
Poland Democracy 51
Producers 12–15, 21, 22, 24, 30, 31, 38, 46, 48, 49, 51, 56, 68, 79, 95, 99, 102, 111, 115–117, 125, 134, 136, 139, 141, 153, 155, 157, 170, 173, 176, 182, 183, 191–194, 201, 202, 210–212, 214, 225, 226
Putin, Vladimir 128, 155, 174, 192, 193, 199, 205

R

Reith, Lord John 2, 3
Religious Affairs reporting 13
Romania coup 33
RTÉ & Journalists
    Cassin, Anna 111
    Hanley, David 113
    MacAnna, Ferdia 110
    Mulholland, Joe 113
    O'Connor, Rory 113
    Powell, Bob 111
    Ronayne, Eoin 111
Russia 13, 58, 152, 175, 192–194, 205

Russia dissidents 194, 197, 198, 205
Russian orphanages 58
Russo-Ukrainian War 109

S

Sambrook, Richard 15, 35, 105, 157
Savile, jimmy 161
Seater, Robert 2
Seaton, Jean 8
Sex Discrimination Act, 1975 7
Simons, Susannah 49
Sims Report, 1984 9
Smeeton, David 51
Snow, Dan 144
Somerville, Julia 46, 49
Somerville, Mary 2, 3
South Africa reporting 121
Stasi files 55
Stringer and super stringer 10
Syria reporting 97

T

Taylor, Charles 73, 77, 83
Tebbit, Norman 18, 28
Thatcher, Margaret 29, 152
Tiananmen Square protests 17
Tomforde, Anna 51
Tripoli bombing 17, 18, 28
Turkey reporting 12, 14, 109

U

Ukraine reporting 115, 201
    Kyiv 201
    war crimes 202
USSR 57

V
Vaughan Thomas, Wynford 6
Velvet Revolution 56

W
Walesa, Lech 56
WhatsApp reporting 116
Wiesbaden Air Force Base 51
Wilmot, Chester 6
Women and Top Jobs Report, 1970 8
Women and war reporting 103
World Service radio 10, 12, 14, 68, 71, 99, 226
World TV News 210
Wyndham Goldie, Grace 8

Y
Yeltsin, Boris 57, 153
Yugoslavia break up 12, 33, 35, 57, 112–114, 153, 174

GPSR Compliance

The European Union's (EU) General Product Safety Regulation (GPSR) is a set of rules that requires consumer products to be safe and our obligations to ensure this.

If you have any concerns about our products, you can contact us on

ProductSafety@springernature.com

In case Publisher is established outside the EU, the EU authorized representative is:

Springer Nature Customer Service Center GmbH
Europaplatz 3
69115 Heidelberg, Germany

www.ingramcontent.com/pod-product-compliance
Lightning Source LLC
LaVergne TN
LVHW050427250825
819359LV00040B/726